EAST·WEST

TEACHER'S GUIDE 1

by Kathleen Graves and David P. Rein

Oxford University Press
1988

Oxford University Press

200 Madison Avenue
New York, NY 10016 USA

Walton Street
Oxford OX2 6DP England

Oxford is a trademark of Oxford University Press.

Library of Congress Cataloging-in-Publication Data

Graves, Kathleen.
  East–West / Kathleen Graves, David P. Rein.
    p. cm.
  ISBN 0-19-434242-5 : $7.50
  1. English language—Textbooks for foreign speakers.
I. Rein, David P.   II. Title.
PE1128.G654 1988
428.2′4—dc19   88-17821
                                                      CIP

Developmental Editor: Susan Lanzano
Consulting Editor: Joan Saslow
Production Editor: Gail Cooper
Associate Editor: Jeanne Rabenda
Editorial Assistant: Mary Sutherland
Art Director: Shireen Nathoo
Art Researcher: Paula Radding
Designer: Terry Helms

Illustrations by:
Lisa Adams, Rowan Barnes-Murphey (represented by Evelyne
Johnson), Bryan Haynes, Marie-Heléne Jeeves, Maggie Ling,
Barbara Maslen, Robbie Marantz, Jacqui Morgan, Anna Rich,
Mark Rowney, Joseph Shea, Debra Solomon, and Anna Veltfort.

Studio and location photography by:
Richard Haynes, Paul Chakmakjian

*The publishers would like to thank the following for permission
to reproduce photographs:*
E. Adams/Gamma-Liaison; Stan Barouh/JVC Jazz Festival New
York; The Bettmann Archive; M. Biggins/Gamma-Liaison;
Brazilian Tourism Foundation; British Tourist Authority; Larry
Chiger/Four By Five; Ginger Chih/Peter Arnold, Inc.; Ray Ellis/
Photo Researchers, Inc.; Eunice Harris/Photo Researchers,Inc.;
Harry Hartman/Bruce Coleman, Inc.; Dan Helms/Duomo;
Italian Government Travel Office; Japan National Tourist
Organization; Mark Keller/Four By Five; A. Knudsen/Sygma;
Kodansha International; B. Lacombe/Gamma-Liaison; J.J.
Lapeyronnie/Gamma-Liaison; Robert Llewellyn/Four By Five;
David J. Maenza/Image Bank; Benn Mitchell/Image Bank;
Hanae Mori USA, Inc.; Jeffry Myers/Four By Five; Bradley
Olman/Bruce Coleman, Inc.; Phototeque; J. Rozsa/Gamma-
Liaison; P.A. Savoie/Bruce Coleman, Inc.; S. Schapiro/Gamma-
Liaison; S. Schapiro/Sygma; Secretaria de Turismo de Mexico;
Martha Swope; Norman Owen Tomalin/Bruce Coleman, Inc.;
J. Travert/Gamma-Liaison; Turner Entertainment Co.; Universal
Pictures; UPI/Bettmann Newsphotos; Alvis Upitis/Image Bank;
Warner Brothers

Graphics by:
Maj Britt-Hagsted, Oxford University Press Technical Graphics
Department

Additional thanks for providing printed pieces for reproduction:
Amtrak; Capital Sports; Carnegie Hall Archives; James F. O'Leary,
General Manager, MBTA; Mike Quon

Cover illustration by Barbara Maslen, photograph by Karl
Steinbrenner.

Special thanks to Nancy Haffner, Stylist; Sally Foord-Kelcey, Art
Editor, OUP Britain; Denise Johnson, Photo Researcher; April
Okano, Designer

Printing (last digit): 10 9 8 7 6 5 4 3 2 1

Printed in Hong Kong

Contents

Student Book 1 Scope and Sequence

UNIT	GRAMMAR	FUNCTIONS/NOTIONS	TOPICS	PRONUNCIATION

1	subject pronouns
	present tense of *be*
	yes-no questions and short
	   answers
	Where questions
	a/an
		informal introductions
		asking to borrow something
		thanking
		apologizing
			countries
			nationalities
			occupations
			
			Culture Capsule:
			  shaking hands
				yes-no and
				*Wh-*question
				intonation

2	*there is/are*
	one/some/any
	a/an/the
	noun plurals
	prepositions of place
	ordinal numbers
		asking for and giving names
		  and addresses
		describing a room
			colors
			furniture
			rooms of a house
			indoor locations
			addresses
			letters
			
			Culture Capsule:
			  a typical apartment
				-s as /s/, /z/ or /əz/

3	simple present tense possessive adjectives possessive forms of nouns *What* and *Who* questions	formal introductions greeting someone new greeting someone informally leaving a conversation politely saying good-bye formally and informally	family members jobs names addresses	intonation of *or* questions

4	simple present tense
	frequency expressions
	time expressions
	can for ability
	How often questions
		giving telephone numbers
		beginning a telephone
		  conversation formally and
		  informally
		making an appointment
		checking your understanding
		talking about ability
			telephone numbers
			time
			business hours
			habits and routines
			breakfast
			dates
			
			Culture Capsule: a
			  typical breakfast
				can/can't

UNIT	GRAMMAR	FUNCTIONS/NOTIONS	TOPICS	PRONUNCIATION
13	*will* vs. *going to* *will* for promising, offering and deciding	inviting someone accepting and declining invitations welcoming someone offering, accepting and declining food offering help	holidays dinner at someone's house restaurants Culture Capsule: Thanksgiving	word stress
14	*might* for possibility *can't* for impossibility *must* for probability *Whose* questions tag questions with *be, will* and *can*	inviting someone to do something, formally and informally offering something informally expressing uncertainty	games future plans Culture Capsule: games	sentence stress

INTRODUCTION

OVERVIEW

EAST WEST is a three-level course in English as a Foreign or Second Language (ESL/EFL) for adults and young adults. It develops the four skills of speaking, listening, reading and writing, with an emphasis on speaking and listening. It is based on a carefully organized syllabus that integrates grammatical, functional, topical and situational content with its use in discourse. The course is useful for all teaching situations that stress communication. EAST WEST has been shown to be particularly helpful in encouraging the participation of students who are reluctant to speak, and is very effective in large classes.

EAST WEST follows a gradual progression. Level 1 is designed for false beginners—that is, students who have studied English previously but who have not had much chance to actively use what they have learned. Level 2 is for low intermediates, and Level 3 is for intermediate to high-intermediate students.

COMPONENTS

Each level of EAST WEST consists of these components:

Student Book

The Student Book is a communicative text that engages students' interest, draws on their life experience and encourages them to take initiative. At the same time, it provides the support that students need through careful build-up and recycling of language content and the presentation of manageable tasks. Pair and small-group work is used extensively.

Each unit follows a consistent format. It begins with the **Opening Conversation,** which introduces the teaching points of the unit. Next comes the **Speaking** section, with conversational activities that develop students' accuracy as well as their fluency. This is followed by the language **Checklist,** which summarizes all the grammatical points, situational language, functions, notions and idiomatic expressions that were introduced in the unit. The last part of the unit, **Listening** and **Reading,** is devoted to the receptive skills.

An expanded explanation of all unit parts is presented below under the heading *Student Book 1.*

Cassettes

The Conversation and Listening sections of the Student Book are available on two cassettes. A dramatic reading of *The Moon of India* is available on a separate cassette. The conversations are spoken at natural speed. We strongly encourage the use of the cassettes. They help students improve their listening comprehension, and are highly motivating. They also provide students with opportunities to hear many different speakers of English, which is especially important for students in foreign settings where it is difficult or impossible to hear English spoken by natives. Suggestions for using the cassettes in the language laboratory are presented below under the heading *Using EAST WEST in the Language Laboratory.*

The tapescript of the listening exercises is included at the back of this Teacher's Book.

Workbook

Designed for independent use by students as a supplement to the Student Book, the Workbook provides written reinforcement of the oral skills practiced in the Student Book and controlled writing exercises that expand these skills. Each unit of the Workbook parallels the corresponding unit of the Student Book in language content (grammar, communicative areas and vocabulary). Answers to all exercises are at the back of the Teacher's Book.

Teacher's Book

The Teacher's Book is interleaved with the Student Book for ease of use. In addition to this Introduction, it contains complete teaching suggestions for each exercise in the Student Book, answer keys for the Student Book and Workbook, the tapescript of the Listening exercises in the Student Book, and the Contents page and appendices from the Student Book: Word List, Irregular Verbs and a U.S. map. More detailed information is presented below under the heading *Teacher's Book.*

SKILLS BALANCE

EAST WEST has been designed to offer flexibility. The course emphasizes speaking and listening, and also provides a solid means to develop reading and writing skills.

	speaking	listening	reading	writing
Student Book	✓	✓	✓	
Cassette		✓		
Teacher's Book	✓	✓	✓	✓
Workbook			✓	✓

COURSE LENGTH

The Student Book can be completed in class for a 60–90 hour course. However, if class time is limited, the story on the last page of each unit can be read at home, and the Speaking and Listening sections completed in a shorter period of 45–60 hours. The Listening sections can also be done in the language lab. (See *Using EAST WEST in the Language Lab* below.) Conversely, if more time is available, the additional activities suggested in the **If You Have Time** sections of the Teacher's Book can be used. The Workbook provides an additional 10–20 hours of practice and can be used either at home or in class. Thus, depending on how its components are used, EAST WEST can fit into a variety of time frames, ranging from 45–60 hours to 90–120 hours, and can be used for one or two courses.

GUIDING PRINCIPLES

EAST WEST has been designed to provide the following:

Extensive Speaking and Listening Practice

The language introduced and used is conversational American English. The numerous speaking activities in each unit generally flow from more controlled use of the language to freer use of the language. They enable the students to speak both accurately and fluently. They are never mechanical drills; rather, they actually provide students with an opportunity to speak with each other. As a result, these activities have a strong listening comprehension component as well. Many of the pronunciation exercises, a feature of Level 1, emphasize stress and intonation, since improper stress and intonation interfere with intelligibility more than incorrect pronunciation of individual sounds. Each unit's listening activities are tightly linked to the unit's content. As in real life, listening activities are purposeful. Students listen in order to complete certain tasks, sometimes listening for general meaning and sometimes for specific information.

An Integrated Syllabus

EAST WEST is a communicative, grammar-based course. In designing it, we began with a carefully graded grammatical syllabus and an analysis of the situations in which students would need to use English, both with native speakers and in the international community. We asked: *What would a student need to understand and convey to an English-speaking visitor to his/her country? as a visitor himself/ herself to an English-speaking country? in an international situation with another non-native speaker of English?* From questions, we identified a full range of essential language functions (such as introducing someone, asking for directions, agreeing and disagreeing) and notions (such as words for locations, and time periods) that would, together with the grammatical structures, form the core of our syllabus.

The integration of grammatical, functional, notional and topical elements and their use in realistic contexts in the text is designed to enable students to use English effectively in situations they are likely to encounter outside of the classroom.

For each situation, we provide the student with the language necessary to interact effectively. This sometimes calls for the formulaic use of certain structures when appropriate to a given situation. For example, in Unit 1, when the student is asked to use *Could I borrow your . . . ?*

we are not introducing the modal *could,* as such, but enabling the student to ask to borrow something.

Motivating Activities

Students become motivated when they are interested and engaged in what they're learning, when they can learn successfully, and when they can integrate what they've learned into their own experience. We have asked ourselves the questions: *What can students best talk about? What do they know best?* The answers obviously are: themselves, their experiences, feelings, opinions and surroundings. For this reason, EAST WEST personalizes activities extensively. Whenever possible, students are asked to talk about themselves, and thus not only to see, but to experience the language as something useful and meaningful for them. The activities are designed to draw the student in. They call for some form of student initiative, and yet, since they draw on conceptually and linguistically known material, they can always be accomplished successfully.

Language Support

Each unit is carefully designed to build on the previous one and to recycle what the students have learned. Each unit follows a consistent pattern, building from controlled activities to ones in which students can express themselves more freely. Each task is manageable and provides the necessary support for students to accomplish it successfully.

Adaptability to Multi-Cultural and Same-Culture Classes

Each activity has been designed so that it can be successfully accomplished in both multicultural and same-culture classes. For example, an exercise about nationalities allows for role-play in a class of students of the same nationality, and provides the conjunction *too,* so that students can also practice what they would say in a real-life situation.

STUDENT BOOK 1

UNIT ORGANIZATION
Opening Conversation and Speaking

The consistent format of each eight-page unit gives students the security of knowing what to expect and what is expected of them. It also aids the teacher in planning. The Opening Conversation, the first one or two pages of each unit, introduces and provides a context for the grammar, functions and some of the major themes of the unit. The conversation is followed by Speaking, four pages of speaking or speaking-listening exercises, which develop the material introduced in the Opening Conversation. These exercises are generally done in pairs or small groups and take the form of role-play, questions and answers, games or information gaps (explained below in *Using the Student Book*). They flow from more controlled to freer use of the language. In most units this section includes a **Pronunciation** exercise as well as a **Culture Capsule.** The Culture Capsule describes some aspect of American culture and asks students to discuss that aspect in terms of their own culture.

Most exercises emphasize accuracy while some emphasize fluency, or communicative effectiveness. By accuracy we mean correctness in terms of grammar, pronunciation, vocabulary usage and so on. Fluency, on the other hand, is largely a matter of getting one's meaning across, whether or not "mistakes" are made. Exercises that stress accuracy target a structure or communicative area and control the vocabulary tightly so the students can be expected to use the language with few errors. Other exercises emphasize fluency. These target a task (such as "giving directions") so students are encouraged to use a range of language and variety of resources. The culminating speaking activity, called **Put It Together,** always emphasizes fluency. Many activities emphasize both, because ultimately we want our students to speak accurately and fluently. To this end, all exercises emphasize facility with the language, providing the students with practice in speaking in a connected, non-disjointed way. Active listening practice is also a part of all speaking exercises, since a correct and appropriate response is facilitated by accurate listening.

Throughout the unit, activities are personalized so that the students can use the language in a way meaningful to them. Put It Together calls for the students to integrate the major language points of the unit in a personal or imaginative context. This is the freest conversational activity in the unit, and it has been placed on the page facing the unit language summary, or Checklist, so that students can refer to it for language support if needed.

Checklist

The Checklist, on the sixth page of each unit, serves as a convenient summary of the grammar, functions, topics and idiomatic expressions introduced in the unit. It is there for students to refer to as needed when doing the activities in the Speaking section and to review after completing that section. The Checklist also serves as a useful reference for the teacher, as it shows at a glance the various threads of the unit.

Listening

The seventh page, Listening, provides practice both in getting the gist of a spoken text and in capturing specific information contained in it. These exercises involve the students in accomplishing a task, such as listening for and writing down phone numbers or answering questions about someone's schedule.

In the final exercise of each Listening page, students listen to questions and respond with answers that are personally true for them.

Reading

The eighth (and last) page of the unit is the Reading. In Level 1, this is an episode of a continuing adventure story called *The Moon of India*. Research has shown what common sense tells us: students will be more likely to make the effort to read a relatively difficult passage of intrinsic interest than a relatively easy one that does not hold their attention. *The Moon of India* has been written with this in mind. It is a fast-paced adventure story that maintains interest and builds from episode to episode. The story is also available on cassette.

USING THE STUDENT BOOK
Getting Started

Before beginning Unit 1 of the Student Book, it is a good idea to provide your students with some basic tools for classroom communication. The following expressions, from the *To the Student* page of the Student Book, will be helpful.

Please say that again.
I'm sorry. I don't understand.
Please speak more slowly.
What does .... mean?
How do you say .... in English?
How do you spell that?
How do you say this word?
I don't know.
May I ask a question?

Provide appropriate contexts for the above and have various students use the expressions. For example, say something very quickly. Have the students say, *Please say that again.* OR *I'm sorry. I don't understand.* OR *Please speak more slowly.*

Encourage the students to use these expressions in asking questions or asking for repetition or clarification. This use of English will enable students to become more active in the learning process as well as prepare them for situations they will encounter outside the classroom.

Spend a few minutes leafing through the Student Book with the students. Show them its general format. Point out the appendices. These consist of a word list, an irregular verb list, and a map of the United States. Tell the students that the Word List contains all the words that occur in the Student Book, with the exception of the words that appear only in *The Moon of India.* The list is presented alphabetically with an indication of the page on which each word first appears. Tell the students that the irregular verb list includes all the verbs introduced in the text that have an irregular past form (including verbs used only in

The Moon of India). Point out the map of the United States and encourage students to refer to it as places in the U. S. are mentioned during the course.

Teaching Vocabulary

The words and expressions used in EAST WEST include both active and receptive vocabulary. The active vocabulary in Student Book 1 has been chosen for its usefulness in basic communication. The language used in most of the speaking activities is intended as active vocabulary, and words that students don't know should be learned, both for comprehension and productive use. They are practiced in the Student Book and in the Workbook.

The sections of the Student Book that involve longer texts—the Opening Conversations, Culture Capsules, Listening tapescripts and *The Moon of India*—include some additional, receptive vocabulary that reflects authentic language usage. As long as students are able to understand these texts and can do the exercises connected with them, it is not necessary that they understand every word.

Which words need to be taught?

As you come to each New Words and Expressions section, you will need to determine which words students actually need to understand in order to do each activity. A word that may be receptive in one exercise may be key in another. For example, in the third conversation that opens Unit 5, the speaker says, "I was in the movie *Giant* too, but you probably don't remember me." *Movie* and *remember* are key words, whereas *probably* is not. However, in Unit 12, *probably* is a key vocabulary word because students need to understand and use it in various exercises.

The next step is to determine which key words you need to teach. Asking students whether they understand all the words in a passage is not usually a reliable way of finding out. You will often know, intuitively or from experience, which words are likely to cause trouble. List these on the board and ask students to identify which words they are unsure of. To confirm those that they "know," check to see if they can provide an explanation or example. For example, in Unit 6, the terms *formal* (clothes) and *dress casually* are introduced. Ask for examples of formal and casual clothes.

How to teach new vocabulary

In deciding how to teach a vocabulary item, consider how you can get the meaning across most clearly and most quickly. Many new words can be understood through the context in which they appear or through the accompanying illustrations. Draw students' attention to these aids wherever they exist. Concrete, visual examples are usually best. If the Student Book does not provide relevant illustrations, use classroom realia, the clothes students are wearing that day, mime, stick-figure drawings on the board, or pictures from a magazine or a picture dictionary such as the *New Oxford Picture Dictionary*. Where illustration is not possible, use synonyms or paraphrased verbal explanations, provided you can keep your language simple. As you speak, write on the board to ensure that students follow your explanation. Certain vocabulary items are best understood in a larger context and may require that you act out a situation to convey meaning. Later on in the course (Student Books 2 and 3), we recommend the use of a good learner's English dictionary, such as the *Oxford Student's Dictionary of American English*.

After teaching a vocabulary item, it's always desirable to check students' understanding. This can frequently be done by asking them to provide examples, as described above with the words *formal* and *casual*. In other cases, you can ask appropriate questions.

Bilingual dictionaries and translations

Where there is no other efficient way to teach a vocabulary item, have students use a bilingual dictionary, or you or a student can offer a translation; but consider the use of native language a last resort. Dependence on bilingual dictionaries encourages students to see English in terms of their native language and to translate word for word. More seriously, it prevents them from relying on context and other clues essential to effective language learning. This said, it is also important for students to know how to make proper use of a bilingual dictionary. As a class exercise, have students look up a few example words from EAST WEST that have more than one definition, and teach them how to determine which definition works by trying out each one in context.

For further reading on the teaching of vocabulary, we recommend two books from Oxford University Press: *Techniques in Teaching Vocabulary* by Virginia French Allen (1983), and *Vocabulary* by John Morgan and Mario Rinvolucri (1986).

Facilitating Practice

Almost all exercises begin with a model so that students can see what they will be doing. It is very important to go over the model provided in the book. Demonstrate with a student, and then have one or two students practice the model. It is often useful to do this more than once. Once the exercise is under way, circulate around the room and listen to hear whether students are performing the exercise correctly.

Most of the activities in the Student Book are pair conversations. Students should always take turns being Student A and B, so each student gets practice using all the language in that activity. Asking students to practice the conversations more than once will help develop fluency. When students are speaking, be sure they are looking at each other, and not at their books.

Some exercises for pair work have a special format called *Information gap*. Information gaps are used extensively throughout EAST WEST, as they provide a means for controlled, but communicative, practice. They are highlighted in Student Book 1 by a blue tint and pages vertically divided into two parts, an **A** side and a **B** side. Using a mask provided in the Student Book, students cover their partner's side. Thus, Student A looks only at the A side and Student B looks only at the B side. Then, following the instructions in the book, partners have to ask each other for information they are missing but that their partners have. This information may include times, dates, or locations.

Information gaps are more than manipulations of grammatical structures; they encourage the development of students' confidence in their ability to share information in a meaningful, yet controlled and systematic manner. However, as your students may not be familiar with information gaps, you will need to demonstrate how they should be done. For example, in Unit 2, Exercise 8, Students A and B have the same picture of a room, but A's room has pieces of furniture B's doesn't, and vice versa. They must find out from each other where the missing pieces are, to complete their pictures. Demonstrate how they are to cover their partner's information. Continue with a few more items of furniture. If necessary, model the entire exercise. Then have the students do the exercise. While the students are doing the exercise, circulate to make sure they are doing it correctly.

Providing Feedback and Correction

Accuracy and fluency

It is important for teachers to provide feedback on their students' use of language, on both their accuracy and their fluency. Accuracy, as mentioned earlier, involves the correctness of their language in terms of grammar, pronunciation, intonation, vocabulary usage, and so on. Fluency, or communicative effectiveness, encompasses larger issues, such as whether they have been able to make their meaning clear, use language appropriate to the situation and their role in it, and listen carefully and respond appropriately to another speaker.

Teachers commonly pay attention to developing accuracy, but if students are to acquire the skills they need for effective communication, it is important that they also have opportunities to develop fluency, without worrying about accuracy unless their errors interfere with communication.

Effective communication entails more than facility with verbal language. It involves the appropriate use of nonverbal elements such as eye contact, body position, facial expression, gestures and tone of voice. Except for some very obvious examples, like hand-shaking, these are often very difficult to isolate and teach because of their complexity and subtlety. However, when students are having conversations or doing role-plays, you can be very helpful to them by observing whether they are using appropriate nonverbal behavior and, where necessary, modeling it for them. No matter how perfect the word choice, how accurate the grammar, intonation and pronunciation, if your students deliver their lines woodenly, without looking up from their books, they are not communicating effectively.

When and how to correct

Giving feedback when the students are using language correctly is usually easy—and it is important to let students know they are doing the right thing. It is much harder to know when and how to intervene when students are making mistakes. In other words, when and how should you correct? There is no prescription for correction, but they are guidelines.

Mistakes are a natural part of learning, but if students are not aware of their mistakes, they won't learn to correct them. If your students are generally reluctant to speak, then it is important to let them feel comfortable with what they need to say in an activity before correcting them, otherwise you risk inhibiting them rather than encouraging them. Providing clear instructions, a clear model, and giving them time to practice the model are very important. Always try to let the student say the complete utterance before correcting. Don't stop a student in the middle of an utterance.

When should you correct? When the student asks for correction, when the student cannot be understood, or, depending on the instructional focus, when the student is not doing something correctly—in the area of either accuracy or fluency. Thus, in an activity that focuses on accuracy, it is appropriate to ask students to get the grammar right. In an activity that focuses on fluency (a communicative task), it is appropriate to ask the students to use a range of language—to not stick to one fixed pattern—and to help their partners express themselves, just as they would in their native language. For example, during the Put It Together activity, it is counterproductive to correct students' grammar, and preferable to let the students accomplish the task as much as possible on their own. However, it is necessary to intervene if the students are not able to convey their meaning effectively and thus carry out the activity.

There are two important factors in effective correction: working towards having students correct their own mistakes, and letting students know that the corrections you make are offered as help, not criticism. Simply telling students what is wrong or giving the correct answer yourself does not teach students to correct themselves. Students have to have the opportunity to do their own correcting, so that they will remember and be able to use that particular language in other contexts.

Promoting self-correction

When focusing on accuracy, get the students to figure out as much as possible, so they learn to rely upon themselves.

If a student clearly does not know what is wrong, then you or another student can correct it. You can clue students that an error has been made by raising your eyebrows or looking quizzical. These can become your signals to let your students know that something isn't right. If a correction is not offered by a student, then you can indicate where the error is. On the board, draw a dash for each word in the utterance and point to the place where the error occurred. With this technique you can also point out words that are missing or superfluous.

Another technique for eliciting student correction is to repeat the incorrect part or parts. For example, if a student says "She like it," repeat "like" with a rising intonation, to indicate there is some question about the correctness of that word.

One very nonjudgmental way to correct (when it is unlikely that a student will make the correction) is to rephrase what a student has said. When the student has completed an utterance with mistakes in it, rephrase the utterance correctly by saying something like "So you mean. . . " or "Uh huh. So. . . ." You are giving the message that the student has been understood, while giving him or her an opportunity to hear the correction. A good follow-up is to ask the student to restate the response correctly.

If you find that students consistently make a certain error, then you may wish to take some time out for explanation. It is helpful to use numerous examples contrasting correct and incorrect language as a support for your explanation.

Asking other students to help can be an effective and non-threatening technique if you are careful not to give the message that the student supplying the correction is better or smarter than the one who made the mistake.

Establishing criteria

When focusing on fluency, it is helpful to establish criteria with your students. For example, before doing an activity, decide on one or two areas on which you will give feedback. You can have the students choose these areas in the form of questions: *Am I using all the language I know to get my message across? Am I speaking in a lively way? Am I listening carefully? Am I using eye contact? Am I encouraging my partner?* At the end of an activity, you can give feedback to your students just in those areas chosen. When students are having difficulty, ask them to supply the "correction." For example, if students are not using a wide enough range of language (various grammatical forms, numerous vocabulary words), then elicit a wider range of language from them and list this on the board. For example, in the Put it Together in Unit 3, students are asked to talk about their extended families. If students are sticking to only one or two questions about their families, have them generate as many questions as possible, put these on the board and ask students to use each question at least twice. If, in any activity, the students are speaking

listlessly or in a monotone, have them do the activity again in a lively manner.

Checking answers

At the end of each activity, when applicable, review the answers with the class, preferably by eliciting them from the students. In the Teacher's Book, specific suggestions are given for ways to review the answers for each activity. The answers to the Speaking exercises are given in an answer key at the back of the Teacher's Book, while answers to the Listening exercises and to the comprehension questions for the Reading are on the corresponding page of the Teacher's Book.

Grouping Students for Exercise Effectiveness

The activities throughout the units are done in a variety of ways in order to vary the pace and motivate the students. Most activities are done in pairs because EAST WEST's emphasis is on spoken discourse, and this requires at least two speakers. Pair activities are easiest for classroom management purposes, and they intensify student participation. At times, we have also suggested the mixer format (see below) as an alternative to pairs. We encourage this alternative as a lively way to have different students make contact with each other.

Throughout the Teacher's Book, you will find the following terms used as descriptions of the activities they refer to.

whole class—activities in which the attention and participation of the class as a whole are required. Activities in which material is introduced or reviewed use this format.

individuals—activities in which students are required to write or to read alone.

pairs—activities in which pairs of students have a conversation or complete a task together.

threes or fours—activities in which the conversation must take place among three or four people, as when one student is introducing other students, or where a wider range of experience and ideas is desired.

two pairs—activities in which two pairs get together to exchange information acquired in a pair activity, or activities in which two pairs have a conversation, as when one pair invites another pair to do something.

mixers—activities in which the students circulate around the classroom to obtain and share information. These give students the opportunity to practice the same language with many different people, thus building their confidence and skill while still giving them a fresh opportunity for communication each time.

Using EAST WEST in the Language Laboratory

If you have access to a language laboratory, you may wish to have students practice the Opening Conversation and do the Listening and Reading sections of the Student Book there.

Opening Conversation

After you introduce the Conversation in class, students can go to the lab to listen to it and do the listen-and-repeat step as many times as they need to in order to gain fluency with the lines. For this purpose, the Conversation has been recorded twice, the second time with pauses after each line.

Listening

When assigning the Listening exercises to the language laboratory, it is best to preview each unit in class. The suggestions below are based on an in-class preview. Where time does not permit this, familiarize students with the procedure below and allow them to take a bilingual dictionary to the lab for Steps 1 and 2.

1. Have students read the directions and questions in their books and become familiar with word lists or illustrations used in the exercises. Allow them to ask questions, and go over anything they don't understand.

2. Go over any key vocabulary words identified in the Teacher's Book.

3. In the language lab, have students open their books to the appropriate Listening page and follow this procedure for each exercise: Listen to the exercise once or twice without writing.

4. Play the cassette again. This time, students answer the questions. If they have difficulty, play the cassette again, as many times as needed.

5. Answers should be checked as soon after listening as possible. They can be checked in the language lab, either by a lab attendant or by the students themselves if you give them the answers in advance. Allow students to hear the passage again while checking answers.

The Moon of India

The Moon of India has been recorded on a separate cassette so that it can be used independently of the rest of the Student Book. If you are assigning it for lab use, you may wish to wait until students have completed Unit 6 in the Student Book so they are familiar with the simple present, present continuous and past tenses.

If you can introduce each episode in class, follow the teaching suggestions given in the unit-by-unit **Notes** of this Teacher's Guide, and go over key words with students yourself. If this is not possible, recommend this procedure to your students:

1. Follow the words in the book as you listen to the tape.

2. Turn off the tape and read the passage silently to yourself.

3. Look up any words you need in a dictionary.

4. Answer the comprehension questions, looking back at the text as necessary.

5. (Optional) Listen to the episode again, this time following the words in the book. (This allows students to see the correspondence between the spoken and the written language.)

6. (Optional) Close the book and listen to the tape several times without reading.

7. Answers can either be checked in class or you can give students the answers and let them check their own work.

THE TEACHER'S BOOK

Throughout the Teacher's Book you will find clearly defined goals and specific teaching suggestions for each activity in the Student Book. In addition, there are frequent extension suggestions and optional writing activities.

CONVERSATIONS, SPEAKING AND LISTENING EXERCISES

Language Focus, Culture Focus

Each unit and each Speaking and Listening exercise begins with a Language Focus section, which identifies its instructional content in terms of GRAMMAR and COMMUNICATIVE AREA. Culture Capsules are, similarly, preceded by a Culture Focus section, which defines the aim of the Capsule.

New Words and Expressions

All words and expressions that occur for the first time in each Opening Conversation and exercise are listed in this section. Much of the new vocabulary can be understood from the context or the accompanying illustrations. Only some of the words listed need to be actively used by the students for the purpose of the Student Book activities.

Names

The phonetic transcription of the names of people and places that occur in each activity is given after the New Words and Expressions. This list does not include common geographic names or nationalities, as transcriptions of these are easily available in dictionaries. A key to the phonetic alphabet is given at the end of this Introduction. Only primary stress is marked. The transcriptions are for your reference and were included to help you pronounce names you might not be familiar with. We recommend pronouncing these names for the students before they begin the exercise, so that pronunciation difficulties do not interfere with their performance.

Teaching Suggestions

The Teacher's Notes provide detailed suggestions for doing

each activity. For the Opening Conversations, a basic procedure is recommended. This is explained below.

Opening Conversation

1. *Warm up: Ask questions based on the picture.* This will prepare students for what they're going to hear and encourage them to use the context to figure out meaning.

2. *Personalize: Ask personalized questions.* This is designed to draw on students' life experience, activate their prior knowledge, and thereby both engage their interest and help them understand what they are about to hear.

3. *Play/read the conversation. Students look only at pictures:* Have students listen to the conversation without looking at the text. This can be done with books closed, by covering the text and/or looking only at the picture. It is important to allow students to hear and try to understand the conversations before reading them. This approximates what happens when listening to real conversations, and will encourage the development of their listening skills. This skill is of particular important for EFL students, who often have little opportunity to hear native speakers.

4. *Play/read it again. Students listen and read silently, with books open this time:* This allows students to see the correspondence between the spoken and written language and to confirm or correct what they have understood aurally.

5. *Teach new words and expressions as needed:* This step is delayed, so that students have the opportunity to figure out as much from context as possible, a skill that will help them as they learn and use English both inside and outside the classroom. After students have listened to and read the text, have them tell you which words they still don't understand. See Teaching Vocabulary on page xi for general suggestions on teaching vocabulary.

6. *Let students ask questions about the conversation:* This is an opportunity for them to ask for clarification when they don't understand a grammatical pattern, the meaning of something, a cultural point, or how to pronounce something. A section called **Additional Information** follows the Teaching Suggestions, and provides background information about the grammar, vocabulary and usage, pronunciation and culture points in the conversation.

7. *Students read/repeat the conversation:* Students read the conversation aloud together or repeat line for line after you or the cassette. Choral repetition gives students oral practice without "exposing" individuals who may feel uncomfortable with the new material. It is important here to emphasize accurate stress, rhythm and intonation, and feeling. Add gestures and appropriate facial expressions as you say the lines. Where lines are very long, they can be broken up into smaller pieces at first. Do this step as many times as necessary.

8. (Optional) *Divide the class into two or three groups,* depending on the number of speakers. Have each group read one character's lines.

9. *Students practice the conversation in pairs or groups of three,* depending on the number of speakers in the conversation. During this stage, you should circulate, listening to students and checking for accuracy.

10. (Optional) *Have one or more groups role-play the conversation for the rest of the class.*

Speaking

In doing the speaking exercises, it is important to 1) ensure that students know what they are supposed to do, and then 2) get them to do as much of the speaking as possible. We suggest that you begin by modeling each activity with another student and then have two students model it for the class, more than once if necessary, so that you can assess whether the students have understood what to do. As soon as students are clear about the exercise, turn the activity over to them.

Listening

In working with the Listening exercises, encourage the students not to listen word for word, but to grasp the overall meaning, or to listen for the specific information required by the activity. The conversations in the Listening exercises are based on the language introduced in the unit. Any new vocabulary that is introduced in the recorded material is not essential to completing the exercise, and this point should be conveyed to the students so that they learn not to depend on word-for-word understanding.

We recommend these steps in doing the Listening exercises:

1. Have students read the directions and questions in their book and become familiar with word lists or illustrations used in the exercise. Allow them to ask questions and go over anything they don't understand.

2. Go over any key vocabulary words identified in the Teacher's Book.

3. Play or read the first item as an example. Go over the correct answer.

4. Play the entire exercise on the cassette or read the tapescript and have students listen once without writing.

5. Play the cassette again. This time students answer the questions. If they have difficulty, play the cassette again, as many times as needed.

6. Have students listen again to review their answers.

7. Check answers, and, if time permits, allow the students to hear the passage again while doing this.

Pauses have been built into the cassette. Where an

activity requires students to listen to a longer passage and then answer several questions, you may sometimes wish to allow more time by stopping the tape.

Optional, Alternative, and If You Have Time

Teaching suggestions that are marked Optional provide ideas for additional teaching steps. Suggestions that are marked Alternative can replace the previous step. Suggestions marked If You Have Time are additional activities that expand on the themes of the unit.

Workbook Management

The Teacher's Book indicates at which points in each unit appropriate Workbook follow-up exercises can be assigned.

CHECKLIST

The Checklist page serves as a summary of the material presented in each unit. It can be assigned as a whole, after the Speaking exercises, or sections of it can be used as particular language points are taught.

Teaching Suggestions

Optional teaching suggestions are given for ways to work with the various components of the Checklist. For example, students can practice saying the example sentences in order to work with stress, rhythm and intonation. Or students can ask questions or make statements about themselves and their classmates using the grammatical patterns in the Checklist. Or you can review the communicative points in the unit by having students supply examples that illustrate those points.

Optional Writing Practice

An optional controlled writing task based on the points covered in the unit appears at the bottom of each Checklist page.

THE MOON OF INDIA

Language Level

The language in *The Moon of India* is controlled; however, it is not limited to what has been used in the preceding pages of the unit. Assuming that students are false beginners and will be able to understand more English than they can actively produce, we have used all of the

basic tenses covered in Book 1 from the beginning. In addition, the story introduces a new tense usage—that of narration—for the simple present tense. You may want to point out to your students that this tense is frequently used in story telling.

Key Vocabulary

The Moon of India introduces vocabulary not encountered in the rest of the book. Much of this can be understood in context. Certain words can be "passed over," as they are not essential to comprehension. Other words are important to understanding the story, and these appear under *Key Vocabulary*. We suggest you teach these as necessary. At the same time, explain to your students that they do not need to understand all of the vocabulary in each episode in order to understand the plot of the story. Encourage them to read for the gist and not to translate every word.

Teaching Suggestions

The Moon of India can be used in class or assigned for homework or language lab work. The unit by unit notes provide suggestions for in-class use. For at-home reading, see *Teaching Suggestions for Reading at Home,* below. For language lab use, see page xiii.

Teaching suggestions for reading at home

1. Explain to your students that there will be words in the story they don't know, but that they should not worry about every single word, only the key vocabulary. If possible, give them the list of key vocabulary from this Teacher's Book for each episode they read at home, and present any words you feel will be of particular difficulty.

2. Teach students this basic procedure:
   a. Look at the illustrations to get a sense of what will happen in the episode.
   b. Read the story once for a general idea. (If they have access to the story on cassette, they should read along as they listen.) Look up in a dictionary any key vocabulary words they did not understand.
   c. Read the story again.
   d. Answer the comprehension questions. These can be checked at the next class meeting or self-checked by students if you want to give them the answers in advance.

3. (Optional) Follow one or more of the Teaching Suggestions 8–10 on page 8 in class.

Key to Phonetic Transcriptions in Teacher's Book

The phonetic transcriptions are based on the International Phonetic Alphabet. For the sake of simplicity, the pure vowel sounds /o/, /i/ and /u/ are used to represent the more diphthongal sounds found in *coke, eat* and *boot*. /ɑ/ is used to represent the American English sound that is actually between an /ɑ/ and an /ɔ/ as in the word *top*.

Vowels		**Consonants**	
ɑ	father	b	boy
ɛ	let	d	dog
i	heat	f	fit
o	low	g	go
u	loot	h	hot
ɪ	lip	j	yellow
ɔ	caught	k	cat
ʊ	book	l	long
ʌ	love	m	man
ə	lover, nation	n	nap
æ	cat	p	pen
ei	cape	r	ran, arm
ɑi	ice	s	say
ɔi	point	t	top
ɑʊ	out	w	walk
ɑr	arm	z	eggs
ər	hurt	ʃ	short
iər	here	tʃ	chalk
ɛər	hair	ʒ	leisure, pleasure
ur	poor, *sure*	dʒ	joke
ɔr	or	θ	thing
ær	Harry	ð	this
ɛr	Terry		
uər	tour		

UNIT 1

Andrew: Excuse me, do you speak English?
Kenichi: Yes, I do, a little.
Andrew: Great! Could we borrow your map?
Kenichi: Sure. Here it is.
Andrew: Thank you.

Andrew: Where are you from?
Kenichi: I'm Japanese, from Osaka. What about you? Are you from the States?
Laura: Yes, we are. Are you in Paris on vacation?
Kenichi: No, I'm studying French.
Andrew: Really? What do you do?
Kenichi: I'm a fashion designer.
Laura: Well, it's a small world! I'm a fashion designer, too!
Andrew: By the way, I'm Andrew Scott, and this is my wife, Laura.
Kenichi: My name's Kenichi Nakano. How do you do?

UNIT 1

Unit Language Focus

GRAMMAR: present tense of *be,* subject pronouns, contractions, *a/an, yes/no* questions and short answers, *where* questions

COMMUNICATIVE AREAS: introducing oneself—name, occupation, nationality, country; introducing another person; asking to borrow something; thanking

OPENING CONVERSATION

Each "New Words and Expressions" section includes all words and phrases that occur for the first time in the corresponding section of the Student Book. Please note that only some of the words listed need to be understood or used by the students for the Student Book activities. Your students may already know many of them. Frequently this "active" vocabulary is illustrated in the Student Book or easily understandable from context. Additional suggestions for teaching vocabulary are given on page xi.

New Words and Expressions

a little, am, and, are, borrow, by the way, could, English, Excuse me, fashion designer, French, from, great, Here it is, How do you do?, I, in, It's a small world, Japanese, map, my, name, no, on vacation, Osaka, Paris, really, speak, study (*v.*), sure, Thank you, the States, this, too, we, well, What about you?, where, wife, yes, your

Names

Andrew Scott /ǝndru skɑt/
Kenichi Nakano /kɛnitʃi nɑkɑno/
Laura /lɔ́rǝ/

Teaching Suggestions

1. Ask warm-up questions based on the picture: *Where is this? Who are the people? (tourists?) What are they doing?* Describe the picture: *The conversation takes place in a cafe in Paris. The Eiffel/áifǝl/Tower is in the background. . . .*

2. Personalize the questions: *Do you know Paris? Is Paris beautiful? Have you been there?*

3. Play the cassette or read the conversation aloud once or twice: students listen with their books closed or looking only at the picture.

4. Play/read it again. Students listen and read along silently.

5. Teach new words and expressions, as needed. Explain that *the States* means *the United States.*

6. Let students ask questions about the vocabulary, grammar, pronunciation, or other elements of the conversation.

7. Students read the conversation aloud together or repeat the conversation line for line after you or after the cassette. Pay careful attention to pronunciation and intonation.

8. (Optional) Three students come to the front of the class to mime the roles of Kenichi, Andrew and Laura. They sit at two "café tables." The class speaks their lines. Andrew gets Kenichi's attention. Kenichi gives Andrew a map when saying *Here it is.* All three stand and shake hands when Andrew introduces himself and his wife.

9. (Optional) Divide the class into groups of three to practice the conversation. Before they begin, give an example of the difference between a stiff, wooden delivery of the lines and an animated delivery of the lines. Use the following example: *Well, it's a small world! I'm a fashion designer, too.* Repeat it twice, and ask: *Which is better?* Remind them to use gestures.

Additional Information

General Notes

Kenichi is being polite when he answers that he speaks English *a little.* Actually he speaks English well.

Grammar

1. Contractions: In spoken English, *am, is* and *are* are usually contracted with sentence subjects and question words, in both formal and informal situations. (A common exception to this rule is when *am, is,* or *are* is the first or last word in a sentence, or when the sentence ends in a pronoun.)

contraction	no contraction
Where're you from?	*Are you from the United States?*
I'm a fashion designer.	*Yes, I am.*
	Where are you?

2. *Am* is never contracted with *not.* However, *are* and *is* are contracted with *not* unless special emphasis is intended.

normal	emphatic
No, she isn't.	*No, she is not.*

3. *Do* and *does* can be contracted with *not.* They are never contracted with sentence subjects or question words.

Vocabulary and Usage

Where're you from? and *Where do you come from?* have similar meanings and elicit similar answers: *I'm Japanese, I'm from Japan,* or one possible answer not given in this unit, *I come from Japan.*

SPEAKING

EXERCISE 1 (individuals, whole class)

Language Focus

present tense of verb *be* in *yes/no* and *wh-* (information) questions and answers in third person, singular and plural; contractions with *be*

New Words and Expressions

actress, American, an, fill in, he, not, or, she, they, use (*v.*), verb

Teaching Suggestions

1. Ask individual students to read the questions and answers, filling in the verbs orally. Do not give them time to write. Point out the use of contractions where there is an apostrophe. Make sure they use contractions.

2. Go over the questions and answers as a chain drill with the class.

    T: *Where are Laura and Andrew Scott from?*
    S1: *They're from the United States.*
    T: *S2, ask the second question.*
    S2: *Is Kenichi Nakano in Paris on vacation?*
    S3: *No, he isn't.*
Continue to the end.

EXERCISE 2 (pairs)

Language Focus

same as Exercise 1

New Words and Expressions

ask, answer, carefully, in any order, listen, questions, them, to

Teaching Suggestions

1. Teach new words and expressions, if needed.

2. B listens to A's question and then answers.

OR **2.** B answers without looking at the book.

3. Repeat the exercise with students who played A now playing B, and vice versa.

EXERCISE 3 (pairs, role-play)

Language Focus

wh- and *yes/no* questions

Teaching Suggestions

1. Use the example to show students how to do the exercise. Students work in pairs, each student getting the chance to be A and B. Circulate around the room to check that students are doing the exercise correctly.

2. (Optional) You and a student or one or two pairs of students role-play the conversation for the class.

Speaking

1

Fill in the verbs. Use *are/'re* or *is/'s*. Then match questions with answers.

1. Where .... Laura and Andrew Scott from?

2. .... Kenichi Nakano in Paris on vacation?

3. .... Andrew and Laura American?

4. Where .... *are* .... Laura, Andrew and Kenichi?

5. .... Laura an actress?

6. Where'........... Kenichi from?

7. .... Andrew and Laura from France?

8. .... Kenichi a fashion designer?

a. No, she ....n't.

b. Yes, they ....

c. He'........... Japanese.

d. Yes, he ....

e. No, he ....n't.

f. No, they ....n't.

g. They'.*re*................ in Paris.

h. They'........... from the United States.

2

A, ask B the questions in Exercise 1 in any order. **B**, listen carefully to A's questions. Answer them.

A: Where are Laura, Andrew and Kenichi?
B: They're in Paris.

3

A, ask B questions. **B**, you're Kenichi Nakano. Answer A's questions.

. . . *English?*

A: Do you speak English?
B: Yes, I do, a little.

1. . . . English?   4. . . . on vacation?
2. . . . map?   5. . . . do?
3. . . . from?

4

A, ask B for a pen and a dictionary.
B, ask A for a pencil and an English book. Have conversations like these:

A: Excuse me, could I borrow your
....................?
B: Sure. Here it is.
A: Thank you.
B: You're welcome.

OR

A: Excuse me, could I borrow your
....................?
B: I need it right now. I'm sorry.
A: That's OK.

5

Pronunciation

At the end of a *yes/no* question, your voice goes up: Do you speak French?

At the end of an information question, your voice goes down: Where's Brasilia?

Practice asking and answering questions like these:

A: Do you speak French?   A: Where's Brasilia?
B: Yes, I do.   B: It's in Brazil.
   OR   No, I don't.   OR   I don't know.

Languages	**Capital cities**	**Countries**
Arabic	Brasilia	The United States
English	Cairo	Canada
French	Moscow	Egypt
Italian	Ottawa	France
Japanese	Paris	Italy
Portuguese	Rome	Japan
Russian	Tokyo	The Soviet Union
Korean	Washington, D.C.	Brazil
....	....	....
	....	....

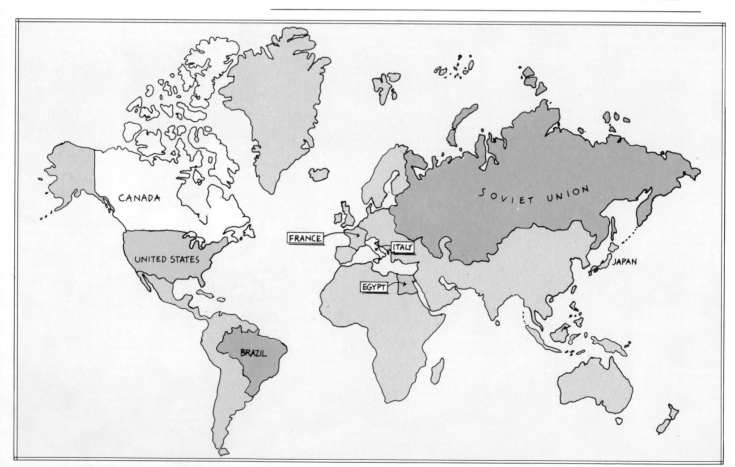

EXERCISE 4 (individuals, pairs)

Language Focus

asking to borrow something

New Words and Expressions

ask for, book, conversation, dictionary, have, I'm sorry, need, pen, pencil, right now, That's OK, You're welcome

Teaching Suggestions

1. Teach new words and expressions, as needed.

2. T: *We will ask to borrow a pen.* Write .... *pen?* on the board. Under that write: *Sure, here it is.* Demonstrate with a student.

    T: *Excuse me. Could I borrow your pen?*
    S1: *Sure. Here it is.*

Make sure S1 hands you the pen. Write: .... *I need it right now.* Demonstrate with another student.

    T: *Excuse me. Could I borrow your pen?*
    S2: *I'm sorry. I need it right now.*

3. The students do the exercise in pairs, each student getting the chance to be A and B.

4. Ask the class what other things they might want to borrow. Tell them to use those items in similar questions. (Remind them to borrow items they know their partners have!)

Workbook

You can now assign Exercises A–D.

EXERCISE 5 (individuals)

Language Focus

intonation of *yes/no* and *wh-* questions

New Words and Expressions

Arabic, at, Brasilia, Cairo, capital, city, country, end, go up/down, I don't know, information, Italian, know, languages, like (similarly), Moscow, of, Ottawa, Portuguese, practice, pronunciation, Rome, Russian, Tokyo, voice, Washington, D.C.

Teaching Suggestions

1. Teach new words and expressions, if needed.

2. On the board write: *Is Kenichi Nakano Japanese? Is Andrew Scott Japanese?* (or use your students' names).

    T: *These are called* yes/no *questions. Why are they called* yes/no *questions?*
    S: *Because the answer is* yes *or* no.

Ask for other examples of *yes/no* questions. List the examples on the board.

    T: *At the end of a* yes/no *question your voice goes up. For example: Is Kenichi Nakano Japanese?*

Have students say the other examples from the board.

3. On the board write: *Where is Kenichi Nakano from? What do you do?* Say: *These are called information questions. Why?*

    S: *Because the answer gives information.*
    T: *Yes. In the first question the information is a place; in the second, an occupation.*

Ask for other examples of information questions. List the examples on the board.

    T: *At the end of an information question, your voice goes down. Where is Kenichi Nakano from? What do you do?*

Have students say other examples from the board.

4. T: *Look in your books. Let's practice the examples.* Practice saying the names of the countries, languages and capital cities. Have students add any that would be useful for them to know.

5. Have students practice the questions, using the information in the lists.

If You Have Time

Students think of famous places in the cities listed above. For example: *I'm at the Louvre. Where am I?* or *I'm in the Ginza. Where am I?* and so on.

EXERCISE 6 (whole class, individuals)

Language Focus

third person of verb *be;* affirmative and negative statements about country/nationality and occupation

New Words and Expressions

businesswoman, false, famous, make, people, picture, remember, singer, statement, That's right, true, writer

Names

Harold Robbins /hǽrəld rábɪnz/
Brooke Shields /bruk ʃildz/
Catherine Deneuve /kǽθrən dənʌ́v/
Hanae Mori /hɑnɑé móri/
Pierre Cardin /piéər kardǽn/
Diana Ross /dɑɪjǽnə rɔ́ss/
Gloria Vanderbilt /glóriə vǽndərbɪlt/
Yasushi Inoue /yɑsuʃi ɪnoweɪ/

Teaching Suggestions

1. Teach new words and expressions, if needed.

2. Go over the pronunciation of the names and occupations with the class.

3. Ask students to tell you which occupations are preceded by *a* and which by *an.*

4. Go over the example with the class. If necessary, explain *true* and *false,* using examples from the exercise.

5. Have students do the exercise, making statements as quickly as possible so that interest is maintained.

EXERCISE 7 (pairs)

Language Focus

third person *wh-* questions about country/nationality and occupation

New Words and Expressions

close, these

Teaching Suggestions

1. After all students have had a chance to be A and B, ask review questions: *Where's he/she from?* and *What does he/she do?* Point out that the answer to the first question can be either the country, *He's/she's from ....,* or the nationality, *He's/she's ....*

2. A and B both close their books and ask questions and give answers again.

EXERCISE 8 Guess Who? (fours)

Language Focus

first- and second-person verb *be* in *yes/no* questions and answers

New Words and Expressions

guess, person, who

Teaching Suggestions

1. To prepare for the exercise, ask students the names of other famous people, including their nationalities, countries and occupations. List this information on the board.

2. Students do the exercise in groups of four.

EXERCISE 9 (pairs)

Language Focus

first- and second-person *wh-* questions about name, country/nationality and occupation

New Words and Expressions

each other

Teaching Suggestions

1. Tell students to use *too* if they are from the same country or have the same occupation. For example:
  S1: *What do you do?*
  S2: *I'm a student. What about you?*
  S1: *I'm a student, too.*

2. Tell each student to choose a famous person from the book or from the board and do the exercise.

OR **2.** (mixer) Everyone in the class circulates for five minutes and tries to find out the name, nationality and (when appropriate) occupation of as many people as possible. At the end of three minutes, the teacher points to various students and says *Who is she/he?* The other students must give the information.

If You Have Time (teams)

Students and/or teacher bring in pictures of at least five famous people from each of three or four different countries. List the names of the people on the board. Play one of the following variants of Guess Who:

The pictures are placed in two piles. The class is divided into two teams. Individuals come up one at a time to look at one picture. Their teammates ask them *yes/no* questions until they guess the correct person. The team that guesses all the people in its pile first wins. Students ask, *Are you ....?* Or teammates can begin by asking, *Is it a man?* or, *Is it a woman?* and continuing with third-person questions. Or, instead of asking about nationality, teammates can ask about languages. For example: *Do you speak French?* instead of *Are you French?*

Workbook

You can now assign exercises E, F and G.

6

Make true and false statements about the famous people in the pictures. Use *a* or *an*. For example, *a politician, an actress.*

A: Brooke Shields is American.
B: That's right.
C: She's a businesswoman.
D: That isn't right. She's an actress.

Names	Countries	Professions
Harold Robbins	The United States	writer
Catherine Deneuve	France	businesswoman/actress
Brooke Shields	The United States	actress
Hanae Mori	Japan	fashion designer
Diana Ross	The United States	actress/singer
Pierre Cardin	France	fashion designer
Gloria Vanderbilt	The United States	businesswoman
Yasushi Inoue	Japan	writer

Gloria Vanderbilt

Yasushi Inoue

Brooke Shields

Hanae Mori

Catherine Deneuve

Hanae Mori photograph by MORT KAYE STUDIOS INC.

Harold Robbins

Diana Ross

Pierre Cardin

7

A, ask questions about these famous people. **B**, close your book and answer the questions.

A: Where's Harold Robbins from?
B: The United States.
   OR   He's American.

A: What does Pierre Cardin do?
B: He's a fashion designer.

8

Guess Who !

Work in groups of four. **A**, you're a famous person. **B**, **C**, **D**, guess A's name.

B: Are you American?
A: No, I'm not.
C: Are you from France?
A: Yes, I am.
D: Are you a businesswoman?
A: No, I'm not.
C: You're Pierre Cardin.
A: That's right!

9

A and **B**, you're famous people. Ask each other questions.

A: Where .... from?
B: .... What about you?
A: .... (too!)
B: What do you do?
A: I'm .... What about you?
B: .... (too!) By the way, I'm ....
A: My name's .... How do you do?

10
Culture Capsule

These people are meeting for the first time.

They're shaking hands.

They're bowing.

What do people do in your country?

11

Repeat the conversation in Exercise 9. This time give true information about yourself.

Nationalities	Occupations
Brazilian	teacher
Italian	student
Russian	writer
Egyptian	photographer
Spanish	actor
Chinese	doctor
Mexican	....
....	....

12

Two pairs get together. Introduce yourself and your partner.

I'm ____(name)____ I'm a/an ____(occupation)____ I'm from ____(place)____ This is ____(name)____ He's/She's a/an ____(occupation)____ (too). He's/She's from ____(place)____ (too).

13
Put It Together

● Choose two new nationalities, occupations and names for yourself.

Country/nationality	Occupation	Name
1.	....	....
2.	....	....

● You're in Toronto, Canada. You're waiting for a bus to Ottawa. Start a conversation with your partner. Ask to borrow something. Then introduce yourself and find out about your partner.

In Conversation 1, **A**, you want to borrow B's bus schedule.
In Conversation 2, **B**, you want to borrow A's newspaper.

EXERCISE 10 Culture Capsule (whole class)

Culture Focus

body language in greetings

New Words and Expressions

bow (*v.*), Culture Capsule, first, shake hands, meet (*v.*), time

Teaching Suggestions

Note: When Americans and other native English-speaking people are introduced, the men usually shake hands, especially in formal situations. Traditionally women don't shake hands with each other, and men and women shake hands only if the woman offers her hand first, but these distinctions are becoming less evident. A handshake should be firm, not limp. In all introductions, both men and women should make eye contact.

1. Teach new words and expressions, as needed.

2. Ask: *What do people in your country do when they meet? Do they shake hands? Do both men and women shake hands? When? How? Do people in your country make eye contact? When?* (Mime eye contact or illustrate with stick figures and dotted lines on the board.) Ask: *Is it polite or impolite to make eye contact?*

3. Write on the board: A: *My name's* .... *How do you do?*
B: *I'm* .... *It's nice to meet you.*
Ask various students to fill their names into the blank, and to introduce themselves to you while maintaining eye contact. Be sure the handshake is firm.

EXERCISE 11 (pairs)

Language Focus

asking and answering questions about oneself: name, nationality, occupation; introducing oneself

New Words and Expressions

actor, doctor, give, nationality, occupation, photographer, repeat, student, teacher

Teaching Suggestions

1. Teach new words and expressions, as needed.

2. On the board, write out any nationalities and occupations of your students not listed in the book. If your students are not working, they can invent an occupation or they can say, *I'm a student.*

3. Practice this exercise with one or two students before having them do it themselves. First you play A and then you play B, giving true information about yourself. Finally, shake hands with the student at the end. Remind students to use *too* when they have the same nationality or occupation.

Workbook

You can now assign Exercises H and I.

EXERCISE 12 (two pairs)

Language Focus

introducing oneself and another person; giving information about one's nationality and one's occupation, and another person's nationality and occupation

New Words and Expressions

get together (*v.*), introduce, pair, place, two

Teaching Suggestions

Students should be able to do this exercise without using the book. After A and B have done the exercise with C and D, tell them to join another pair of students, and B to give the information this time.

EXERCISE 13 Put It Together (pairs)

Language Focus

getting someone's attention, asking to borrow something, introducing oneself, asking and answering questions about country and occupation

New Words and Expressions

begin, blanks, bus, bus schedule, new, newspaper, put, Toronto, wait (*v.*), with, choose

Teaching Suggestions

1. Teach new words and expressions, as needed.

2. Tell students that this is a chance to use everything they have learned in the unit, as well as anything else they know, in a free conversation. You will not correct them.

First have them look at the picture and make sure they understand the situation. Help them to choose a new name, country and occupation for each conversation. Ask: *How will the As begin the conversation?* S1: *Excuse me. Could I borrow your bus schedule?*

Ask them what kinds of questions they might ask. Let them look at the Checklist page (opposite) for more ideas. List questions on the board. For example: *What do you think of Toronto? Where do you live? Where are you going?*

(continued)

3. Students practice Conversations 1 and 2 with their partners. Remind them to refer to the Checklist if necessary.

4. (Optional) Students choose a new name and nationality. This time B wants to borrow A's bus schedule.

5. After the students have had a chance to practice the Conversations, ask: *Were the conversations difficult or easy? Why? Did you think of other questions to ask? What were they?* Thinking up and adding questions is an important first step toward building conversation skills.

CHECKLIST

Teaching Suggestions

1. The Checklist page serves as a summary of the material presented in the unit. It can be assigned either all at once, when you get this far, or little by little during your work in other parts of the unit. At the start of the next unit, you may wish to ask students if they have any questions about the summary.

2. (Optional) For greater fluency with the conversational language in the unit, have students practice saying the example sentences in the second and third sections of the Checklist. Work with them on natural stress, rhythm and intonation.

3. (Optional) For additional grammar practice, have the students make statements or ask questions about the people in the class, using the verb *be*. Have students use the patterns on the Checklist page as guides.

4. (Optional) From time to time, you may wish to have students review the Checklist part by part and then quiz them orally in class, with books open or closed. For example:

T: *How do you ask to borrow someone's pen?*
S1: *Could I borrow your pen?*
T: *How do you introduce yourself?*
S2: *I'm* .... And so on.

OPTIONAL WRITING PRACTICE

Write the information below on the chalkboard. Then explain this situation to the students.

You are going on a tour to Paris with 100 people. It is very expensive. You need to find a roommate. You leave information about yourself at the travel agency.

For the "Paris in the Sky" Tour
April 12, 1989

I'm *(name)*. I'm *(nationality)* from *(country)*. I speak *(language)*. I also speak a little .... I'm a (an) *(occupation)*. Do you speak ....? Could we share a room?

I know how to . . .

USE THESE FORMS

☐ **Subject Pronouns**

I, he, she, it, you, we, they

☐ **Present Tense of Be**

I am ('m)		I'm not	

he	is ('s)	he	is not (isn't)
she		she	
it		it	

you	are ('re)	you	are not (aren't)
we		we	
they		they	

questions
Is he American?   Where's he from?

short answers
Yes, he is.   No, he isn't.

statements
This is Billy Joel. He's a singer.
He isn't a fashion designer.

☐ **A/An**

He's	a	teacher
		doctor
	an	eye doctor
		actor

USE ENGLISH TO

☐ **get someone's attention**
Excuse me.

☐ **ask to borrow something**
Could I/we borrow your map?
Sure.

☐ **show interest**
Really?

☐ **introduce myself**
I'm Andrew Scott./My name's Kenichi Nakano.

☐ **introduce someone else**
This is my wife, Laura.

☐ **greet someone new**
How do you do?

☐ **give and accept thanks**
Thanks.
You're welcome.

☐ **ask and answer these questions**
Do you speak English?
Where are you from?
What do you do?

☐ **talk about these subjects**
names   countries   nationalities   occupations

☐ **UNDERSTAND THESE EXPRESSIONS**

Great!	be on vacation
By the way, . . .	shake hands
That's right/wrong.	
What about you?	
It's a small world.	

CHECKLIST

Listening

1

Complete these conversations.
(Circle *a* or *b*).

1. a. No, I'm not.
   b. Yes, I do, a little.

2. a. Thank you.
   b. Sure. Here it is.

3. a. That's OK.
   b. Thank you.

4. a. I'm a writer.
   b. I'm Mexican, from Cuernavaca.

5. a. No, I'm studying English.
   b. No, I'm here on vacation.

6. a. Really? What do you do?
   b. Yes, we are.

7. a. I'm a teacher.
   b. I'm studying Italian.

8. a. What about you?
   b. How do you do? I'm Koji Asaba.

2

Listen to each question and answer
about the famous people in this unit.
Mark the answers *T* (true) or *F*
(false).

1. ___   4. ___   7. ___
2. ___   5. ___   8. ___
3. ___   6. ___

3

Margaret Winters is an English teacher. She and a friend are looking at this
picture of Margaret's class. Fill in the countries and the occupations, using
the information below.

Brazil	Italy	actor	singer
Canada	Japan	designer	teacher
Egypt	The Soviet Union	photographer	writer
France	The United States		

1. Akiko   2. Christophe   3. Sami   4. Maria

-------------------   -------------------   -------------------   -------------------

-------------------   -------------------   -------------------   -------------------

4

Give true answers.

1. ....
2. ....
3. ....
4. ....
5. ....
6. ....

LISTENING

EXERCISE 1
Language Focus

asking to borrow something, verb *be* in *yes/no* and *wh-* questions, asking and answering questions about nationality and occupation, introducing oneself

New Words and Expressions

complete

Names

José Montoya /hozéi mantója/

Teaching Suggestions

For Listening exercises, follow the basic procedure on page xv. Specific suggestions are given below.

1. In this exercise, students will hear parts of conversations they have studied and practiced in the unit. For example, in number 1, the students hear *Do you speak English?* The correct answer is *Yes, I do, a little.*

2. Play the cassette or read the tapescript, and have the students figure out the answers.

3. Listen again, pausing after each one. Have students supply the answers orally.

Answers: 1. b 2. b 3. b 4. b 5. a 6. a 7. a 8. b

EXERCISE 2
Language Focus

yes/no and *wh-* questions about country/nationality and occupation

Teaching Suggestions

1. You may wish to give the first one as an example: *Is Brooke Shields American? No, she isn't. Is that true or false?*

2. Play the cassette or read the tapescript and have students give the answers.

3. Listen to the tape again and have the students supply the answers orally.

Answers: 1. F 2. T 3. F 4. T 5. T 6. F 7. T 8. F

EXERCISE 3
Language Focus

questions and answers about countries/nationalities, occupations

New Words and Expressions

class, friend, looking at, uh-huh (on cassette), using

Names

Margaret Winters /márgrət wínterz/
Akiko /akiko/
Christophe /krístóf/
Sami /sami/
Maria /məría/

Teaching Suggestions

1. Ask students to look at the picture. Ask them to try to guess the nationality of each person from the names. On the board write, *I think she's .... I think he's ....*

2. For fun, ask students to try to guess the occupation of each person.

3. Explain that *uh-huh* is an informal way of saying *yes.*

4. Play the cassette or read the tapescript, and have students figure out the answers.

5. Ask students to provide the answers orally.

Answers: 1. Japan, writer 2. Canada, teacher 3. Brazil, actor 4. Italy, singer

EXERCISE 4 (individuals)
Language Focus

personal and *wh-* questions based on the language taught in the unit

Teaching Suggestions

1. Read the tapescript or listen to the cassette and have students write their answers.

2. Ask the students what the questions were, and have them supply their answers orally.

Answers: Since answers are personal, they will vary with each student.

EPISODE 1 The Moon of India

Please see introductory notes on page xvi.

The Moon of India is for your students' enjoyment. You can work with it in class, or assign it for homework or language lab. We have made suggestions below for in-class use. See page xvi for at-home use and xiv for language lab use.

Key Vocabulary

be missing, be worth, director, four million, gunshot, kill, museum, necklace, newspaper reporters, partner, phone booth, police, *Princess,* ship, suspect (*n.*), Venice

Names

Alexander Gray /ǽlɛgzǽndər gréɪ/
Casey /keísi/
Paul Richardson /pɔl rítʃərdsən/
Venice /vénɪs/
Lieutenant Vance /luténənt vǽnts/

Teaching Suggestions

1. Talk about the pictures with the students as a way to introduce the episodes. Introduce key vocabulary depicted in the illustrations. Write key vocabulary on the board.

2. (Optional) Have students listen to the reading of the story on cassette (or read by you), books open. Repeat this step as many times as desirable.

3. Have students read the episode and note the words they need to understand.

4. Explain the key vocabulary as needed, using the illustrations, concrete examples and examples drawn from your students' own experience.

5. Go over the pronunciation of the names with the students.

6. Have students read the episode again.

7. Ask the comprehension questions. If your students need help answering the questions, show them where they can find the answers in the story. Accept complete sentences, long and short answers, and/or one-word answers where appropriate.

Answers: 1) The Moon of India is a necklace. It's important because it was taken from the City Museum. It's worth $4,000,000. 2) No, he doesn't. 3) Alexander Gray is the director of the City Museum. Paul Richardson is one of the men who stole the necklace. (He calls the police station to tell them about it.) Officer Casey is a police officer. (Paul Richardson talks to Officer Casey.) Lt. Washington is Officer Casey's boss. (He is responsible for finding the thief.) 4) He called the police to tell them about the necklace and about his partner. 5) Paul Richardson's partner probably shot him. 6) Venice is a city in Italy, and *Princess* is the name of a ship. The *Princess* leaves Venice on April 21.

8. (Optional) Other possible questions. What are the police going to get from the ship? Who are they going to put on the ship?

9. Have students close their books and relate the important points of the episode. For example: "Someone took a necklace from the City Museum in New York. The necklace is famous. It's worth $4,000,000. The police are trying to find the thief. A man, Paul Richardson, calls the police. He stole the necklace with another man, his partner. But someone kills him, maybe his partner. He tells the police, 'Princess, Venice.' There is a ship called the *Princess.* It leaves Venice on April 21. A police officer is going to go on the ship in Venice." Check their understanding of the story as they tell it. Correct any misunderstandings.

10. (Optional) Role-play. Students can role-play the dialogues between Alexander Gray and the reporters; Casey and Richardson; Casey and Vance. Put the dialogues on separate cards. (Students may try to imitate the actors on the cassette.) For example:

Paul Richardson

I know about the Moon of India.

The necklace from the museum. Please, I don't have much time.

Richardson, Paul Richardson.

My partner and I took it. But now he's gone.

Venice . . . *Princess*

Officer Casey

The Moon of India? Really?

OK. What's your name?

OK, what do you know about the necklace?

Where is he?

Venice? *Princess?* What about them? Richardson. Richardson, are you there?

MOON OF INDIA

"MOON OF INDIA" IS MISSING

New York: The famous "Moon of India" necklace is missing from the City Museum. According to Alexander Gray, museum director, the necklace...

Episode One

It is April 17. Alexander Gray, the director of the City Museum, is talking to newspaper reporters. "This is a terrible loss for the museum. The Moon of India is a very important necklace."

"How much is it worth?"

"More than four million dollars."

"Mr. Gray, are there any suspects?"

"Not yet. But the police are working on it day and night."

"Do you think the thief is somebody from the museum?"

"The police are looking at all the information we have. That's all. Thank you."

A man is walking along a street at night. He is worried and looks behind him. He goes into a phone booth and calls the police. Officer Casey answers the phone and hears something very strange: "I know about the Moon of India."

Casey says, "The Moon of India? Really?"

"The necklace from the museum. Please, I don't have much time."

"Okay. What's your name?"

"Richardson, Paul Richardson."

"Okay, what do you know about the necklace?"

"My partner and I took it. But now he's gone."

"Where is he?"

There is a gun shot. Richardson tries to talk, "Venice ... the Princess ...."

Casey repeats, "Venice? Princess? What about them?"

Richardson is silent.

"Richardson. Richardson, are you there?"

Officer Casey is reporting to Police Lieutenant Washington; "One suspect, Paul Richardson, 48, is dead. His partner is gone."

"Maybe his partner took the necklace and then killed Richardson."

"Maybe. What about Richardson's last words—"Venice ... Princess ... What do they mean?"

"The partner is going to Venice with a princess? Or a princess is in Venice? Is there a Princess Hotel in Venice?"

"Maybe it's a ship." Lieutenant Washington looks in the newspaper at ships' schedules and sees that a ship called 'The Princess' leaves Venice on April 21.

"Okay, get a list of people on the Princess. We're going to put a police officer on that ship."

Comprehension Check

1. What is the Moon of India and why is it important?
2. Does Alexander Gray know who took the Moon of India?
3. Who are Alexander Gray, Paul Richardson, Officer Casey and Lt. Washington?
4. Why did Paul Richardson call the police?
5. Who probably shot Paul Richardson?
6. What is the meaning of "Venice ... Princess"?

UNIT 2

Announcer: Ladies and gentlemen, the Incredible Zarkov, mind reader!

Zarkov: Thank you. . . . I see some letters. The first letter is a *C*. There's an *L*, too, and an *E*. No, that's wrong. There isn't an *E*. I see an *O*, an *R* and an *A*. *C-L-O-R-A*?

Woman: Is it my name?

Zarkov: What's your name, please?

Woman: Carol.

Zarkov: And you spell it *C-A-R-O-L*, right?

Woman: That's right!

Zarkov: Now I see some numbers. There's a *7*. There are two *9*s, and there's an *11*. Tell me, Carol, what's your address?

Woman: 799 11th Street! That's incredible!

Zarkov: Are there apartments in that building, Carol? Is there one on the second floor? Is that your apartment?

Woman: Yes! Yes! How many rooms are there?

Zarkov: Three. I see the living room. There're two windows. There's a brown sofa in front of the windows. There's a chair across from the sofa. It's an easy chair. There's a door to the right, and there's a bookcase next to it. There're some plants in the bookcase, but there aren't any books.

Woman: That's right!

Zarkov: This is very strange. There's a bed in the living room, and there isn't any furniture in the bedroom. Hmm. Are you painting your bedroom, Carol?

Woman: Yes! Zarkov, you're incredible!

UNIT 2

Unit Language Focus

GRAMMAR: *there is/are, one/some/any, a/an/the, how many,* noun plurals, prepositions of place, cardinal and ordinal numbers, alphabet
COMMUNICATIVE AREAS: asking someone's name and address, asking how to spell something, describing a room

OPENING CONVERSATION

New Words and Expressions

across from, address, announcer, apartment, bed, bedroom, bookcase, brown, building, chair, door, easy chair, floor, furniture, incredible, in front of, ladies and gentlemen, letter, living room, mind reader, next to, number, on the right, plant, please, paint (*v.*), room, second, see, sofa, spell, strange, street, tell, three, window, woman

Names

Zarkov /zárkov/
Carol /kǽrəl/

Teaching Suggestions

1. Warm-up. Ask: *What is a mind reader? Look at the picture: What does the man see?* (some letters, some numbers, a room). Describe the picture: *Zarkov, the mind reader, is on stage in an auditorium or large room somewhere.*

2. Personalize: *Are you a mind reader? What am I thinking? About vacation? About class?*

3. Play/read the conversation. Students look only at the picture. Ask them to point to the letters, numbers and pieces of furniture as they hear them mentioned.

4. Play/read it again. Students listen while reading silently.

5. Teach new words and expressions, as needed.

6. Let students ask questions about grammar, vocabulary and pronunciation.

7. Students repeat the conversation aloud line for line.

8. Divide the class into two groups. One group reads Zarkov's part and the other reads Carol's part. You read the first line.

9. Quiz students about objects mentioned in the conversation, using *Is there a/Are there any . . . ?*
   T: *Is there a bookcase in the living room?*
   S1: *Yes, there is.*
   T: *Are there any plants in the living room?*
   S2: *Yes, there are.*
   T: *Is there a bed in the bedroom?*
   S3: *No, there isn't.*

OR **9.** Have students do this with books closed.

10. Position yourself in relation to a desk in the classroom or use objects in the classroom to demonstrate the meaning of *across from, in, in front of, next to, on the right/left.* Ask: *Where am I? Where's the book?*

   List the objects on the board: *sofa, easy chair, door, bookcase, plants, bed.* Write: *Is there* .... *sofa in the living room? Where's* .... *sofa?* Point to the first blank and ask: *What goes here?* Elicit *a* and say: *It's the first time we've talked about it.* Point to the second blank and ask: *What goes here?* Elicit *the* and say: *This is not the first time we're talking about the sofa.* To be sure students understand the point, put two or three similar examples on the board and ask them to fill in *a* and *the.*
   T: *Where's the sofa?*
   S1: *In front of the windows*
   T: *Where're the plants?*
   S2: *In the bookcase.*
Continue with the other objects.

11. Ask students if they can describe the location another way. T: *Where's the door?* S1: *Next to the bookcase.*

Additional Information

Grammar

1. *a/an* The indefinite article can be reviewed with occupations from Unit 1 and the occupations of people in the class. Here it is practiced with letters of the alphabet and with numbers.

2. Ordinal numbers: *the first letter, the first floor.*

3. *There is a* + a noun and *are some* + nouns are used with location either explicit or understood; for example: *There's an* E *in your name. There's a* 1 *in your address. There're some books on the table.* Note that contractions are usually used when speaking. Also, it is becoming increasingly common—although it is not correct—to hear *there's* + a plural noun phrase. E.g., *There's some magazines on the table.*

4. *A/the* In English, all singular, countable, common nouns must be preceded by a determiner, usually a possessive determiner (my, her, etc. . . .), a demonstrative determiner (this, that) or an article (a/the). If the noun is preceded by an article, the indefinite article a/an is used when the noun—
a) has no specific referent for, or is unfamiliar to, the speaker: *You're wearing a new dress!*
b) has no specific referent for or is unfamiliar to the listener: *This is a new dress. Do you like it?*
c) has no specific referent for or is unfamiliar to both: *I need a new dress.*
On the other hand, the definite article *the* is used only when the noun has a specific referent for the speaker and the listener. In this unit, *the* is used because the noun is made specific through—
a) prior mention: *There's a sofa. Next to the sofa is a table.*

b) being part of a given setting: *In the living room there are two windows.*

c) place in a series: *the first one, the second letter,* and so on.

Vocabulary and Usage

1. *Ladies and gentlemen* is the most usual form of address in any kind of large gathering, banquet or public meeting.

2. *Please* in *What's your name, please?* indicates an impersonal situation. *Please* would not be used in a social setting.

3. *Tell me, Carol. . . .* It is not unusual for a stranger to use a person's first name in such a situation in the United States.

SPEAKING

EXERCISE 1 (individuals)
Language Focus

a/an, cardinal numbers, furniture vocabulary

New Words and Expressions

coffee table, curtain, dresser, end table, floor lamp, mirror, table lamp, telephone

Teaching Suggestions

1. Go over the furniture items with the class, using the pictures in the Student Book.

2. Have students look at the picture. Do the example with them. Then you begin and let students take over:

T: *What's number one?*
S1: *A mirror.*
S2: *What's number two?*
S3: *Curtains.*

3. Point out that *a* is used with singular nouns, and no article is used with plural nouns.

EXERCISE 2 (pairs)
Language Focus

prepositions of location, *is there a/there's one, are there any/there are some*

New Words and Expressions

between, in back of, location, on the left of, one

Teaching Suggestions

1. Once again, teach the prepositions of location as needed. Position yourself in relation to a desk in the classroom, or use objects in the classroom, to demonstrate the meaning of *between, in back of, on the left of.* If necessary, review the meaning of: *across from, in, in front of, next to, on the right.*

2. Put the following questions and answers on the board:
A: *Is there a sofa in the room?*
B: *Yes, there's one in front of the windows.*
A: *Are there any plants?*
B: *Yes, there are some in the bookcase.*

3. Point out the use of contractions here.

4. (Optional) Write on the board: *end table* and *table lamp.* Can they think of other adjective + noun compounds? *(mind reader, fashion designer, coffee table).* Practice saying these with the stress on the first word.

5. Go through the example with the students. Then have them do the exercise in pairs.

6. (Optional) Ask students to look for other things in the room that were not mentioned.
S1: *Is there a rug in the room?*
S2: *Yes, there is.*
OR *Yes, there's one on the floor.*

If You Have Time

1. Students can play mind reader with their classmates' names; for example: *I see an S, and there are two As and one N. No, that's wrong. There isn't an N. There's an M. (Masa)*

2. Working in pairs, S1 closes the book and tries to describe the living room, while S2 checks the accuracy.

Workbook
You can now assign Exercises A–C.

Speaking

1

Identify these objects by their numbers:

floor lamp	dresser	curtains
telephone	books	mirror
coffee table	easy chair	end table
table lamp	pictures	bed

A: What's number one?
B: A mirror.
A: What's number four?
B: An end table.
A: What's number two?
B: Curtains.

2

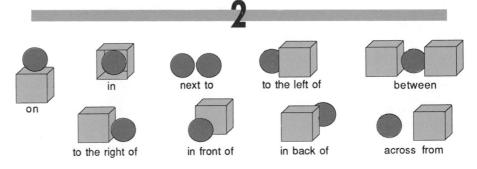

on   in   next to   to the left of   between

to the right of   in front of   in back of   across from

Talk about the locations of the objects in Carol's living room. Use these phrases:

on the window/end table/coffee table
between the windows
to the right/left of the sofa
in front of/across from the sofa

A: Is there a floor lamp in the living room?
B: Yes, there's one to the left of the sofa. Are there any books?
A: Yes, there are some on the coffee table.

3

- Fill in the missing ordinal numbers. Then practice saying them.

1 first (1st)   9 ninth (9th)
2 ....   10 ....
3 third (3rd)   11 ....
4 fourth (4th)   12 twelfth (12th)
5 fifth (5th)   13 thirteenth (13th)
6 ....   14 ....
7 ....   15 fifteenth (15th)
8 ....   last

- Review the alphabet in English. Then ask and answer questions about the letters in REMEMBERED.

A: What's the eighth letter?
B: The eighth letter is an *R*.

4

What's My Word?

A, think of a word. **B**, give letters to guess the word.

(A's word is *please*.)

B: How many letters are there in your word?
A: Six.

—— —— —— —— —— ——

B: Are there any Es?
A: Yes, there are two. The third letter and the sixth letter are Es.

—— —— e —— —— e

B: Are there any Ts?
A: No, there aren't.

—— —— e —— —— e

B: Is there a P?
A: Yes, there's one. It's the first letter.

p —— e —— —— e

B: Is the word "please"?
A: Yes, that's right.

p l e a s e

5

Pronunciation

Practice saying these addresses:

200 Woodland Street (St.)   Two hundred Woodland Street

409 Fuller Avenue (Ave.)   Four oh nine Fuller Avenue

799 11th St.   Seven ninety nine Eleventh Street

1712 Park Road (Rd.)   Seventeen twelve Park Road

555 Highland Ave.
1987 East Rd.
206 Green St.

6

- Choose a first name, last name and address.

Carol McMann
100 East Main St.

Anne	Cline, Klein	19 Amherst Rd.
Carol	Conn, Kahn	100 East Main St.
Larry	Haines, Haynes	315 Elm St.
Mark	McMahan, McMann	802 Lake Rd.
Roy	Reilly, Riley	6876 University Ave.

- Practice this conversation:

A: What's your name, please?
B: Carol McMann.
A: How do you spell your last name?

B: M-C, capital M-A-N-N.
A: And what's your address?
B: 100 East Main Street.

- Practice the conversation again. Give true answers.

7

Pronunciation

Some nouns add an **s** or a **z** sound for the plural. Others add an **ǝz** sound for the plural. Practice saying these words.

/**s**/	/**z**/	/**ǝz**/
lamps	chairs	bookcases
plants	doors	boxes of books
desks	pictures	paintbrushes
....	*windows*	pieces of chalk
....	....	....

Ask and answer questions about your classroom.

A: Are there any pictures in the classroom?
B: Yes, there's one.   OR   No, there aren't.

EXERCISE 3 (pairs)

Language Focus

a/an, letters of the alphabet, *the* + ordinal numbers

New Words and Expressions

alphabet ordinal numbers, say (*v.*), word

Teaching Suggestions

1. Write the numbers 1–15 and repeat them with students. Then write your name, point and say: *The first letter is* ...., *the second* .... Have students fill in the missing numbers in the chart. Provide help as needed.

2. Go over the pronunciation of the numbers with them.

3. Write the alphabet on the board. Ask students to say the alphabet a new way, using *a* or *an* for each letter: *an A, a B, a C,* and so on. (*a:* BCDGJKPQTUVWZ, *an:* AEFHILM NORSX)

4. Students do the exercise in the book.

5. (Optional) Students can do other words.

EXERCISE 4 (pairs)

Language Focus

alphabet, *are there any/is there a*, cardinal numbers, *how many, it's,* ordinal numbers

New Words and Expressions

correct, think of

Teaching Suggestions

1. Do the example with the class.

2. Tell them to each think of a word and then do the exercise in pairs.

If You Have Time

Students give key letters in a word and the other students must guess what the word is.

EXERCISE 5 (whole class)

Language Focus

intonation of addresses

New Words and Expressions

avenue, road

Names

Woodland /wúdlənd/
Fuller /fúlər/
Highland /háɪlənd/

Teaching Suggestions

1. Say the addresses. Highlight the use of *oh* for *0* in *409 Fuller Ave.*

2. On the board write other examples of numbers: *300, 313, 602, 1602,* and have students say them out loud.

3. Have students read the addresses aloud.

4. Point out that *street, road* and *avenue* mean practically the same thing.

EXERCISE 6 (pairs)

Language Focus

asking for and giving names and addresses; asking how to spell, and spelling, last names

New Words and Expressions

again, capital (letter), first name, last name

Names

Anne /æn/   Mark /mɑrk/
Cline, Klein /klaɪn/   McMann /məkmǽn/
Amherst /ǽmərst/   Nancy /nǽnsi/
Conn, Kahn /kɑn/   Olsen, Olson /ólsən/
Larry /lǽri/   Roy /rɔɪ/
Haines, Haynes /heɪnz/   Reilly, Riley /ráɪli/

Teaching Suggestions

1. Go over the pronunciation of the names and addresses.

2. As in the opening dialogue, explain that *please* is used here in an impersonal situation. In a social situation (at a party or in class), students should not use *please* when asking people their names.

3. Practice the conversation in the book with the class. Point out that in the conversation, B says *M-C capital M,* only because the second M is capitalized.

4. Have the students practice the conversation in pairs.

5. Before doing the last part of this exercise, in which students give their own addresses, write a few sample addresses on the board. Explain: *4-40* is *four dash forty.*

6. Have students practice the conversation in pairs, giving true answers.

Workbook

You can now assign Exercises F–H. Exercise F introduces *dentist, supermarket, post office.*

EXERCISE 7 (whole class, individuals)

Language Focus

pronunciation and spelling of regular plural endings; *are there any* ....?

(*continued*)

New Words and Expressions

add, chalk, classroom, desk, noun, paintbrush, piece, plural, sound

Note on plural endings:
/s/ follows /f/, /k/, /p/, /t/
/z/ follows /b/, /d/, /g/, /l/, /m/, /n/, /r/, /v/, /j/, /ŋ/
and all vowel sounds
/əz/ follows /əz/, /dʒ/, /ks/, /s/, /ʃ/, /tʒ/, /z/
See key to phonetic symbols on page xvii.

Teaching Suggestions

1. Ask students to repeat the first few words in each group after you.

2. Ask students if they can add any words to the columns. Some words from Unit 1: /s/ *maps, States;* /z/ *Americans, answers, beds, designers, pencils, questions, rooms, sofas, vacations;* /əz/ *actresses, buses.*

Have students ask and answer questions about the classroom, using the words given in the book (and any appropriate words they've added). You begin and students take over:

> T: *Are there any pictures in the classroom?*
> S1: *Yes, there's one.*
> S2: *Are there any paintbrushes in the classroom?*
> S3: *No, there aren't.*

Workbook

You can now assign Exercise D.

EXERCISE 8 (pairs)

Language Focus

colors, furniture, *is there a/an, it's,* prepositions of location, *where's the*

New Words and Expressions

black, blue, brown, check, cover, different, draw, gray, green, hers, his, orange, pink, purple, red, same, thing, white, yellow

Teaching Suggestions

First and Second Parts

1. Go over the colors with the class, using the color swatches in the book or items in class.

2. This is the first information gap exercise in the book, and students will probably need more careful modeling than usual. Demonstrate how A should cover B's side of the page and vice versa. See page xi for an explanation of information gap exercises.

3. With a student, demonstrate the example in the book for the class. Continue with a few more items of furniture. If necessary, model the entire exercise.

4. Have students do Parts 1 and 2 of the exercise. Circulate to make sure they are doing it correctly. Let students switch roles and do the exercise again.

Third Part

1. If necessary, review the prepositions from the conversation: *on, in, between, to the left of, next to, to the right of, in front of, across from, in back of.*

2. Have one pair, or you and one student, do the example from the book for the class.

3. Have students do Part 3 of the exercise. Circulate to make sure they are doing it correctly.

4. When they have finished, ask them where the items are: *Where's the white end table?/ green lamp?* and so on; or have them describe the complete room.

Workbook

You can now assign Exercises I and J.

8

| red | orange | yellow | green | blue | purple | pink | black | white | gray | brown |

You and your partner have different pictures of the same room.
Cover your partner's side of the page. Ask about the furniture in his/her room.

bookcase   floor lamp   end table   table lamp   coffee table   sofa   easy chair   telephone

A

1. Ask about your list of furniture. Check the correct ones.

   A: Is there an orange bookcase in the room?
   B: No, there isn't.
   A: Is there a gray bookcase in the room?
   B: Yes, there is.

2. Answer your partner's questions about your picture.

3. Ask your partner where things are. Draw them in your picture.

   A: Where's the gray bookcase?
   B: It's next to the floor lamp.

B

1. Answer your partner's questions about your picture.

   A: Is there an orange bookcase in the room?
   B: No, there isn't.
   A: Is there a gray bookcase in the room?
   B: Yes, there is.

2. Ask about your list. Check the correct ones.

3. Ask your partner where things are. Draw them in your picture.

   A: Where's the gray bookcase?
   B: It's next to the floor lamp.

9
Culture Capsule

Some Americans live in houses. Some Americans live in apartments. In an apartment, there are usually one or two bedrooms, a kitchen, a bathroom and a living room. Sometimes there's a dining room.

Think of an apartment in your country. How many rooms are there? What are they? Is there usually a lot of furniture in the living room?

Do you live in an apartment? Do you live in a house?
Describe your living room.

10
Put It Together

This is an empty living room. There are three windows.

Draw this room on a piece of paper. Add furniture. Describe the living room to your partner. For example: *There's a sofa. It's brown. It's in front of the first and second window. . . .*

Your partner draws the living room. Is his/her picture right or wrong?

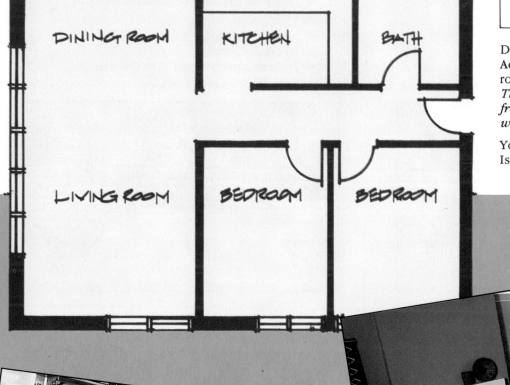

DINING ROOM   KITCHEN   BATH

LIVING ROOM   BEDROOM   BEDROOM

EXERCISE 9 Culture Capsule (whole class, pairs)
Culture Focus

typical houses and apartments

New Words and Expressions

a lot, bathroom, describe, dining room, house, kitchen, live, some, usually

Teaching Suggestions

1. Teach new words and expressions as needed.

2. Read the information about the picture aloud to your students.

3. Ask them to show you where the bedrooms, kitchen, bathroom and living room are in the picture in the book.

4. Read the questions and ask them of various students. If your students are from the same country, discuss any differences of opinion. If they are from different countries, discuss the differences and similarities.

Ask: *Is there usually a lot of furniture in the living room?* Have students list the kind of furniture found in a living room.

5. Ask: *Do you live in an apartment? Do you live in a house?* Poll your students and see how many live in an apartment and how many live in a house.

6. Say: *Describe your living room.* This can be done in pairs.

If You Have Time

If Cuisenaire rods are available, have students use them as pieces of furniture in describing a room in their home.

EXERCISE 10 Put It Together (pairs)
Language Focus

colors, furniture, *it's*, prepositions of location, *there is/are*

New Words and Expressions

empty

Teaching Suggestions

1. Have students read the instructions. Copy the picture twice on the board. Ask: *What kind of furniture goes in a living room?* and list the furniture from the previous exercise.

2. Sketch in some of the furniture listed on the board. (In case you draw well, draw something very simple and rudimentary so as not to overwhelm your less artistic students.)

3. Ask students to describe the locations of what you have drawn. Help them, if necessary.

4. (Optional) Erase what you have drawn. Draw two squares and ask one student to come to the board and draw three pieces of furniture in one of the squares. Don't look at what the student has drawn. Have the class describe the furniture and its location to you. You draw in the blank square. Then you check yours against the other square.

5. Tell the students to draw their pictures, but not to let their partners see. Have them describe their pictures to each other and then compare. Remind them to refer to the Checklist if necessary.

6. Ask them how the exercise went. Did they enjoy it? Did they draw their partner's room correctly? Did they have problems? What were they? The group may want to show their pairs of pictures around, for laughs.

OR **6.** If you have duplicate sets of miniature furniture, you can use them to do an activity similar to Put It Together. With one set of miniature furniture, students can tell other students where to put different pieces in an imaginary house.

CHECKLIST

Teaching Suggestions

1. Follow the general suggestions for the Checklist page detailed in Unit 1.

2. (Optional) For additional grammar practice, make statements or ask questions about the people in the class, using *there is/are, one/some/any,* prepositions of place and ordinal numbers. Have students use the patterns on the Checklist page as guides.

3. (Optional) From time to time, you may wish to have students review the Checklist part by part and then quiz them orally in class, with books open or closed. For example:

T: *How do you ask for someone's name?*
S1: *What's your name?*
T: *How do you ask how to spell something?*
S2: *How do you spell that?* and so on.

OPTIONAL WRITING PRACTICE

Look at the illustration on page 13. Pretend that this is the living room of your new apartment. You want to tell your parents about it in a letter.

Dear Mom and Dad,
   I'm so happy about my new apartment. I am still painting the bedroom, but the living room is finished. Let me tell you about it.

_____

_____

_____

_____

_____

_____

I hope you'll come to visit soon!

Love,

I know how to . . .

C H E C K L I S T

USE THESE FORMS

☐ **There is/are**

questions

Is	there	a lamp	in the room?
Are		any lamps	

short answers

Yes, there	is.	No, there	isn't.
	are.		aren't.

statements

There	's a	lamp	on the table.
	are	lamps	
		two	
		some	
	aren't any	lamps	

☐ **One/Some/Any**

questions

Are there any books in the room?

statements

There	's one	in the bookcase.
	are some (books)	
	aren't any (books)	

☐ **A/An - The**

There's *an end table* and *a lamp* next to the sofa.
The end table is green and *the lamp* is white.

☐ **Noun Plurals**

/s/	/z/	/əz/
lamps	chairs	bookcases
desk	windows	boxes

☐ **Prepositions of Place**

in	on	between	to the right/left of
in front of	across from	next to	

☐ **Ordinal Numbers**

1st first	5th fifth	9th ninth	13th thirteenth	21st twenty-first
2nd second	6th sixth	10th tenth	14th fourteenth	22nd twenty-second
3rd third	7th seventh	11th eleventh	15th fifteenth	23rd twenty-third
4th fourth	8th eighth	12th twelfth	20th twentieth	25th twenty-fifth

USE ENGLISH TO

☐ **ask for someone's name and address**
What's your name (please)?
Carol McMann.
What's your address?
100 East Main Street.

☐ **ask how to spell something**
How do you spell your last name?
M-C, capital M-A-N-N.

☐ **describe a room**
The living room has two windows.
There's a sofa in front of the windows. . . .

☐ **talk about these subjects**

colors	rooms of a house
furniture	addresses
	numbers

☐ UNDERSTAND THESE EXPRESSIONS

Ladies and gentlemen   Thank you.   That's incredible.

Listening

1

Anne is taking people's names and addresses.

Part 1: Listen for the spelling of each person's name. Circle the correct letter.

1. Frank's last name is
   a. Gillmore.
   b. Gilmore.
   c. Gilmour.

2. Ray's last name is
   a. Braun.
   b. Brown.
   c. Browne.

3. Ingrid's last name is
   a. Andersen.
   b. Anderson.
   c. Andresen.

4. Rich's last name is
   a. Reade.
   b. Read.
   c. Reid.

5. Pat's last name is
   a. MacLeod.
   b. McCloud.
   c. McLeod.

6. Doris's last name is
   a. Wait.
   b. Waite.
   c. Waitt.

Part 2: Listen again to the conversations and fill in the street number in each person's address.

1. (Frank) .... Harris Ave.

2. (Ray) .... Green Street

3. (Ingrid) .... Hill Road

4. (Rich) .... Belmont Avenue

5. (Pat) .... Williams Road

6. (Doris) .... High Street

2

Gail and Manuel are playing *What's My Word?* Fill in the correct letters as you hear them.

$\overline{}$ $\overline{}$ $\overline{}$ $\overline{}$ $\overline{}$ $\overline{}$ $\overline{}$ $\overline{}$ $\overline{}$ $\overline{}$
1   2   3   4   5   6   7   8   9   10

3

Sandy wants to take a picture of some people in her office. Find the people in the picture. Write their numbers below their names.

Janice	Allen	Howard	Doug	Diane	Rosa	Kristin	Sandy
....	....	....	....	....	....	....	....

4

Give true answers.

1. ....

2. ....

3. ....

4. ....

LISTENING

EXERCISE 1
Language Focus
names, addresses, spelling of last names

New Words and Expressions
take

Names
Frank Gilmore /fræŋk gílmɔr/
Harris /hǽrɪs/
Ray Braun /reɪ brɑun/
Ingrid Andersen /íŋgrɪd ǽndərsən/
Rich Reid /rɪtʃ ríd/
Belmont /bélmɑnt/
Pat McCloud /pæt məklául/
Williams /wíljəmz/
Doris Waitt /dɔ́rɪs wéɪt/

Teaching Suggestions
1. For each part of this exercise, play the cassette or read the tapescript. Then stop to let the students answer.

2. When the students have done the exercise, go over the answers with them.

Answers: Part 1 1. b 2. a 3. a 4. c 5. b 6. c
Part 2 1. 50 2. 80 3. 1276 4. 500 5. 905
6. 50

EXERCISE 2
Language Focus
alphabet, ordinal and cardinal numbers, questions with *is there/are there*

New Words and Expressions
hear, play (*v.*); on cassette: long, easy, nope

Names
Gail /geɪl/
Manuel /mænuél/

Teaching Suggestions
1. Teach new words and expressions as needed.

2. Play the cassette or read the tapescript. You may want to refer students to Exercise 4, as it's the same exercise.

3. After students have had a chance to do the exercise, ask them what the word is.

Answer: *incredible.*

EXERCISE 3 (individuals)
Language Focus
prepositions of location

New Words and Expressions
line, office, take a picture

Names
Allen /ǽlən/
Janice /dʒǽnís/
Howard /hɑ́uwərd/
Doug /dʌg/
Diane /dɑɪjǽn/
Rosa /rózə/
Kristin /krístən/
Sandy /sǽndi/

Teaching Suggestions
1. Go over the pronunciation of the names of the people first, so that students will know what to listen for. (*Allen, Howard,* and *Doug* are men's names; they should figure this out from the tape. Do not tell them which are men's names.)

You may want to review some of the prepositions with your students. Ask them which prepositions they expect to hear; for example: *the left, right, next to, in front of, in back of* and *between.*

2. Play the cassette or read the tapescript.

3. After they have done the exercise, ask the class, *Where are the men? Where are the women?*

Answers: front row, left to right: Janice, Howard, Diane, Rosa, Allen; back row, left to right: Doug, Sandy, Kristin.

EXERCISE 4
Language Focus
personal questions based on the language taught in this unit

Teaching Suggestions
1. Play the cassette or read the tapescript.

2. After they have answered the questions, ask them what the questions were.

Answers: Since answers are personal, they will vary with each student.

EPISODE 2 The Moon of India

Key Vocabulary

aunt, bell, boarding, Egyptian art, film, forgetful, glasses, handsome, hobby, husband, jewelry, luggage, passengers, purser, ring (v.), specialty, wear, white uniform

Names

Christina Jordan /krɪstínə dʒɔ́rdən/
Agatha /ǽgəθə/
Egyptian//idʒípʃən/
Frank Adams /frǽŋk ǽdəmz/
Robert Grant /rɑ́bərt grǽnt/
Lucy Cardozo /lúsi kɑrdózo/

Teaching Suggestions

1. Have students tell what happened in the first episode. (See Step 9 of the Teaching Suggestions for Episode 1 for a summary.)

2. Follow steps 1–6 from Episode 1.

3. Ask the comprehension questions.

Answers: 1) Christina Jordan works for a museum in New York. Her specialty is Egyptian art. Her hobby is photography. She's staying in Cabin 30 on B deck with her aunt. 2) Frank Adams is a passenger on the ship. He walks in front of Christina's camera. He's sitting at the same table with Christina. 3) Agatha Jordan is Christina's aunt. She didn't go to lunch. She's forgetful. 4) Christina Jordan, Frank Adams, Lucy Cardozo and Robert Grant.

4. Have students relate the main points of the episode. For example, "The *Princess* is a ship. It's leaving Venice, in Italy. Christina Jordan and her aunt, Agatha Jordan, are passengers on the ship. Christina's hobby is photography. She takes pictures on the ship. She meets Frank Adams. They talk. She works for a museum in New York. She and Frank are sitting at the same table. They have lunch. After lunch, Christina goes to her cabin. Her aunt is there. Her aunt is forgetful. Christina tells her about the people at their table. Lucy Cardozo comes from New York. Robert Grant is very handsome." Check their understanding of the story as they tell it. Correct any misunderstandings.

5. (Optional) Expansion questions. Ask students if they have ever been on a ship. Students who have can describe their cabin location, how many people ate dinner at their table, where the ship was going, etc. . . .

6. (Optional) Role-play. Students can role-play the dialogues between Christina and Frank and Christina and Agatha. See Step 10 of Episode 1.

MOON OF INDIA

Episode Two

It is April 21. In Venice passengers are boarding the *Princess*. People are carrying flowers and luggage. A man in a white uniform, the purser, is giving directions and information.

"I'm Christina Jordan and this is my aunt, Agatha Jordan," says one of the passengers to the purser.

The Purser looks at a list: "Welcome aboard. Jordan. . . . Yes, here you are. Cabin 30, that's on B deck. There's an elevator over there."

"Thank you."

The *Princess* is leaving Venice. People are calling out, "Goodbye! Bon voyage! Have a good trip!" and taking photographs. Christina is taking a photograph of Venice and a man walks in front of her camera. She photographs him by mistake.

"I'm very sorry, excuse me. I didn't see you," the man says.

"Don't worry, please. I have lots of film."

"Are you a photographer?"

"Oh no. It's only a hobby. I work for a museum in New York. My specialty is Egyptian art."

"Really? I like Egyptian art very much, especially the jewelry."

"And you?" asks Christina. "What do you do?"

"Me? A little of this and a little of that. I'm Frank Adams. Glad to meet you."

"My name's Christina Jordan. How do you do?"

A bell rings.

"It's time for lunch. I'm hungry. Where's your table?" Frank asks.

"We're at Table 5."

"Oh, you and your husband?"

"No, I'm with my aunt."

"Really? I'm at Table 5, too. After you, Miss Jordan."

"Please call me Christina."

After lunch, Christina returns to her cabin where her aunt is resting.

"How are you feeling, Aunt Agatha?"

"Just fine, dear. Now where are my glasses?"

"You're wearing them, Aunt Agatha!"

"Why yes, I am. I'm so forgetful!"

"Did you have lunch?"

"Yes. It's two thirty."

"Are there any interesting people at our table, Christina dear?"

"Well, yes, there are. There's Frank Adams. He's the one who walked in front of my camera today. He's really very nice. There's Robert Grant . . . He's very handsome. And there's Lucy Cardozo. She's from New York."

"Well, dear," says Aunt Agatha. "I think dinner at Table 5 is going to be very interesting."

Comprehension Check

1. What do you know about Christina Jordan?
2. Who is Frank Adams? How does he meet Christina?
3. What do you know about Agatha Jordan?
4. Who ate lunch at Table 5?

U N I T 3

At the Miami Health Institute, Miami, Florida

Nan: Hi, Jon. How's it going?

Jon: OK. Thanks, Nan.

Nan: Dr. Hummel, I'd like you to meet Jonathan Wilkins. Jon, this is Dr. Paul Hummel. He's from Switzerland.

Dr. Hummel: How do you do, Mr. Wilkins?

Jon: Hello, Dr. Hummel. It's nice to meet you.

Nan: Jon writes our newsletter, Dr. Hummel. He'd like to interview you.

Dr. Hummel: Certainly.

Nan: Well, I'd better get back to work. Goodbye for now, Dr. Hummel. See you later, Jon.

Jon: Where do you work, Dr. Hummel?

Dr. Hummel: At the Eisen Company, in Basel. We make medical supplies.

Jon: Oh, and what exactly do you do there?

Dr. Hummel: I'm in charge of the research department.

Jon: Do you live in Basel, too?

Dr. Hummel: No, I don't. I live in a small town near the city.

Jon: Do you have a family?

Dr. Hummel: Yes, I do. My wife's also a chemist. She works at the same company. We have two sons. They're both in school.

Jon: How old are they?

Dr. Hummel: Twelve and seventeen.

Jon: Do they want to be chemists, too?

Dr. Hummel: Well, the older one does, but the younger one doesn't. Right now he wants to be a rock singer. Who knows? He changes his mind every day.

UNIT 3

Unit Language Focus

GRAMMAR: simple present tense for general information, possessive adjectives, possessive form of nouns, *what* and *who* questions

COMMUNICATIVE AREAS: introducing another person, formally; formal and informal greetings and good-byes; asking about work, family, where someone lives

OPENING CONVERSATION

New Words and Expressions

also, be in charge of, both, certainly, change one's mind, chemist, company, day, department, does, every, exactly, family, get back to, good-bye, had better, hello, hi, How's it going?, institute, interview (*v.*), medical, meet, near, newsletter, old, research, rock singer, school, See you later, son, supply, thanks, town, Who knows?, work (*n.*), would like to, write, young

Names

Nan /næn/
Jonathan Wilkins /dʒánəθɪn wílkənz/
Paul Hummel /pɔl hʌ́məl/
Eisen /aízən/

Teaching Suggestions

First Conversation

1. Warm-up. Ask: *Where is this? Who are the people? Two are co-workers and one is a visitor from Switzerland. Who's the visitor?*

2. Personalize: *Miami is in Florida. Where's Florida? What do you know about Florida?*

3. Play/read the conversation aloud once or twice. Students look only at the picture.

4. Play/read it again. Students listen while reading silently.

5. Teach new words and expressions, as needed.

6. Students can ask questions about vocabulary, grammar or pronunciation.

7. Have students repeat the conversation line by line after you or the cassette.

8. Ask students: *Are Jon and Nan friends?* Lead them to answer, or explain: *Yes, they are.*
  T: *How do you know?*
  S: *Because she calls him Jon, not Mr. Wilkins,* or, *They use informal language.*

9. On one board make two columns, one labeled FORMAL and the other INFORMAL. Write *Hi, Jon* under INFORMAL and *Hello, Mr. Wilkins* under FORMAL. Elicit from students where you should put these sentences and write them on the board. FORMAL: *How are you? Fine, thank you. Good-bye for now.* INFORMAL: *How's it going? OK, thanks. See you later.*

10. In Unit 1, students practiced introducing themselves and each other informally. For example, *I'm Andrew Scott and this is my wife, Laura.* In this unit, they will practice formal introductions. Point out that full names are used. Because of Dr. Hummel's status, Nan addresses him first. (Note: As a rule, men are introduced to women, regardless of status.)

11. Divide the class into groups of three and have each group practice the conversation together.

12. (Optional) Have one or more of the groups role-play the conversation for the rest of the class.

Second Conversation

1. Follow suggestions 1–6 above.

2. Divide the class into pairs to practice the conversation.

3. Lead the class in a discussion of salutations. In your students' country or countries, do co-workers greet each other by their first names? How would Jon and Nan greet each other in front of Dr. Hummel?

Additional Information

Grammar

1. The simple present tense is used mainly for general information and for habits or routines. This unit focuses on the general information usage. For example: *I work, I live, She has, She wants, Do you live? Where does he work?*

2. Note that the plural of *supply* is *supplies*. Nouns ending in *y* change the *y* to *i* and add *es* for the plural.

Vocabulary and Usage

1. In the introduction, Nan calls Jon by his short name, *Jon,* but introduces him with his full name, *Jonathan Wilkins.* Jon and Dr. Hummel call each other by their last names.

2. Jon responds, *It's nice to meet you.* He could also say, *I'm glad to meet you.*

3. The title Doctor (Dr.) is used for people with various academic degrees: Doctors of Philosophy (Ph.D.'s), dentists and veterinarians, among others. As we will see in the second conversation, Dr. Hummel is a Ph.D., not an M.D. (medical doctor).

4. Nan says *See you later* to Jon. *See you later* is an informal good-bye. It does not necessarily mean that she expects to see him later. She says *Good-bye for now* to Dr. Hummel because she expects to see him after the interview.

NEWSLETTER

New Words and Expressions

agree, at home, beach, brother, child (children), computer programmer, good, happiness, happy, hospital, international, kid, laboratory, mean (*v.*), parent, single, sister, teach, there (locative), us, visitor, week, welcome, when

Names

Sydney /sídni/
Anna /ǽnə/
James Richards /dʒeɪmz rítʃərdz/
Drew /dru/
Felicidad Diaz /fɛlísidɑd díaz/

Teaching Suggestions

1. Have students read the newsletter on their own.

2. Ask students to identify the people in the pictures on this page. If students are unsure of family vocabulary (*mother, father, sister, brother,* etc.) refer them to the family tree on page 21.

3. Ask students what MHI means. Elicit other examples of abbreviations.

Additional Information
Vocabulary and Usage

1. *Kid* means *child,* and is used informally.

2. Felicidad Diaz is referred to as *Ms. Diaz.* Traditionally, *Mrs.* was used before the name of a married woman and *Miss* before the name of an unmarried woman. These days, many professional women, both married and single, prefer the title *Ms.* to *Mrs.* or *Miss.* It is frequently used in newspapers and business correspondence.

Names

Ms. /mɪz/

Grammar

Adjectives in English always have the same form. For example: *one other country, two other countries.*

SPEAKING

EXERCISE 1 (individuals, pairs)
Language Focus

simple present, *wh-* questions and short answers with *be* and *do*

New Words and Expressions

come from, make

Teaching Suggestions

1. Go over the example with the class. Then go over 1–6, eliciting answers from students.

2. Students do the exercise in pairs. A asks the questions. B, not looking at the book, gives the answers.

EXERCISE 2 (individuals, pairs)
Language Focus

simple present; asking and answering *yes/no* questions with *do, does, don't, doesn't*

New Words and Expressions

manage

Teaching Suggestions

1. Teach new words as needed.

2. Do the example with the class. Point out that when *does* comes at the beginning of a question, it is not stressed, whereas in the short answer, it is stressed.

3. Have students do the exercise in pairs.

EXERCISE 3 (whole class, pairs)
Language Focus

simple present in *yes/no* and *wh-* questions with *be* and *do*; questions with *who*

Teaching Suggestions

1. On the board write: *Where* and *What,* and elicit some questions and answers about Carole and Jim Richards and Ms. Diaz. Then write *Do* and *Does* to elicit *yes/no* questions and answers.

2. Have the students work in pairs, asking and answering questions using *Where, What, Do* and *Does.*

3. On the board write: *Who,* and elicit questions from the class about people in the Newsletter.

4. Point out to students that the answer can be either the name or the name + *do/does.* Also point out that the verb following *who* is usually singular, even if the answer is plural. For example: *Who comes from Australia? The Richards do.*

5. Have the students work in pairs or in threes. They should take turns asking *who* questions.

6. (Optional) Have the students ask *Where, What* and *Who* questions about each other.

EXERCISE 4 (threes, whole class)
Language Focus

formal and informal greetings, introducing another person formally

MHI Newsletter, No. 5

WELCOME, INTERNATIONAL VISITORS!

MIAMI, July 19. This week we have five visitors from other countries. When you see them, please say hello and welcome them to MHI.

Dr. Paul Hummel is in charge of the research department at the Eisen Company in Basel, Switzerland. He, his wife, Anna, and their two sons live near Basel. Dr. Hummel and his wife are both chemists.

Mr. and Mrs. James Richards are computer programmers from Sydney, Australia. They both work at Drew Laboratories there. They live in an apartment near a beach. Jim says, "We don't have any children, but Carole's younger brother lives with us. He's a good kid." Carole agrees.

Felicidad Diaz comes to us from Mexico. She teaches at ABC Hospital in Mexico City. Ms. Diaz is single. She lives at home with her parents, an older brother and a younger sister. Her name means "happiness" in Spanish, and she is a happy person.

Speaking

1

Complete these questions with *are, is, do* or *does*. Give short answers.

1. Where .... *does* .... Paul Hummel come from? *Switzerland.*
2. Where .... Jon and Nan work? ....
3. Where .... MHI? ....
4. What .... the Eisen Company make? ....
5. How old .... Paul Hummel's sons? ....
6. Where .... Paul Hummel live? ....

2

Complete these questions with *do* or *does, don't* or *doesn't*. Give short answers with *do, does, don't* or *doesn't*.

1. .... *Does* .... Jon Wilkins write the newsletter? *Yes, he does.*
2. .... Paul Hummel come from the United States? ....
3. .... his wife work at the Eisen Company? ....
4. .... the Hummels live in Basel? ....
5. .... their children go to school? ....
6. .... Dr. Hummel manage the research department? ....

3

- Ask and answer questions like the ones in Exercises 1 and 2.
A, ask about Mr. and Mrs. Richards. **B,** ask about Ms. Diaz.

- Ask and answer questions with *who.*

A: Who has two sons?
B: Paul Hummel (does). Who comes from Australia?
A: Carole and Jim Richards (do).

4

Practice the first conversation in this unit. There are three roles.

1. **A** and **B,** you work at MHI. B writes the newsletter. Use your real names. **C,** you are Mr. Richards (in Newsletter).

2. Practice the conversation again. (Switch roles.) This time C is Ms. Diaz.

3. This time C is Mrs. Richards.

5

Find out the missing information about the people in the chart.
Have conversations like this:

A: Where does Timothy work?
B: At Brown's Photo Studios.
A: Oh, that's right. He takes children's pictures.
B: Where do John and Jim work?

A

	Where do they work?	What do they do?
♂ Timothy		
♀ Jeanne	K-D Department Store	
♂ Dan		
♀ Lynn	home	
♀ Christina		
♂ John and ♂ Jim	The ABC Taxi Company	
♂ Tony and ♀ Marie		
♀ Lee	Sam's Used Cars	

B

	Where do they work?	What do they do?
♂ John and ♂ Jim		
♀ Christina	Forrest University	
♀ Lynn		
♂ Timothy	Brown's Photo Studios	
♀ Lee		
♂ Tony and ♀ Marie	R and G Jewelry	
♀ Jeanne		
♂ Dan	WFBS Television	

design(s) jewelry

take(s) children's pictures

manage(s) the sales department

sell(s) cars

announce(s) the news

teach(es) Spanish

drive(s) taxis

write(s) for a newspaper

New Words and Expressions

real, roles, switch (*v.*)

Teaching Suggestions

1. Write the conversation on the board with blank lines where the names should be. Choose three students and help them model the conversation for the class.

2. Have the students practice this conversation in groups of three.

3. When they have practiced the first conversation, write the name *Mrs. Richards* on the board. The third sentence should say: *She comes from Australia.* Have them switch roles.

4. When they have practiced the second conversation, have them switch roles again. Change the name of *Mrs. Richards* to *Ms. Diaz,* and in the third sentence, write: *She comes from Mexico.*

Workbook

You can now assign Exercises A–D.

EXERCISE 5 (pairs)

Language Focus

simple present, third-person singular and plural in questions with *where* and in statements

New Words and Expressions

announce, car, department store, design (*v.*), drive, jewelry, news, photo, sale, sell, studio, take pictures, taxi, television, university, used cars

Teaching Suggestions

1. Teach new words and expressions, as needed.

2. Copy this chart on the board:

/s/	/z/	/əz/
makes	lives	practices
meets	agrees	teaches
works		

Have students say the first one in each group after you and continue saying the others on their own.

Remind students that they worked on the three pronunciations of *s* in Unit 2. (Note: The pronunciation of *s* endings on verbs follows the same phonetic rules as described with nouns.)

3. (Optional) Ask students to add other verbs to the three groups. (The other verbs in the Opening Conversations and Newsletter that belong in the first group are: *wants, asks, likes* and *writes;* the second group: *comes, answers, means, interviews, sees* and *welcomes;* in the third group: *manages* and *changes.*)

4. Tell students to spend a few minutes looking at the chart in their books.

5. This is an information gap exercise. Refer to the introduction for a general presentation of gap exercises. Have the students work in pairs. Go over the example with all the students first. Have the As say the A part and the Bs say the B part.

    T: *Now, Bs, ask the As about John and Jim.*
    Bs: *Where do John and Jim work?*
    As: *At the ABC Taxi Company.*
    Bs: *Oh, that's right. They drive taxis.*

6. Students finish the exercise in pairs.

7. Go over the answers with them by asking, *Who designs jewelry? Who works at Forrest University? Who manages the sales department? Who works at home?* and so on.

8. Refer to the chart in number 2 above. Insert the new verbs from this exercise in the chart.

    T: *Where does* designs *go?*
    S1: *In the second group,* or *With the /z/ group.*

Answers: first column: *takes,* second column: *designs, sells, drives,* third column: *announces.*

9. (Optional) Point out to students that Dan is short for Daniel, Jim is short for James, and Tony is short for Anthony. You may wish to ask them if any of them have shortened names.

Workbook

You can now assign Exercise E.

EXERCISES 6 & 7 (individuals, pairs)

Language Focus

intonation of *or*-questions, *in/on/at* in addresses, simple present, third-person singular, in questions and statements

New Words and Expressions

mailing list, prefecture, state

Names

Guilford /gílfərd/
Attleboro /ǽtəlbəro/
Belmont /bélmɑnt/
Amodeo /ɑmədéɪo/
Deborah /débərə
Audet /odét/
Austin /ɔ́stɪn/
Macko /mǽko/
Gail /geɪl/
Canal /kənǽl/
Makris /mǽkrɪs/
Vernon /və́rnən/

Teaching Suggestions

1. Teach new words and expressions, as needed.

2. Refer to the preposition chart. *You can say, "I live in a house, an apartment, a room." You can also say, "I live in (country)." What else can you say?*
 S1: *I live in (city) or (state/prefecture).*
 T: *I live on a street, an avenue, a boulevard, a road. Can you give me an example?*
 S2: *I live on* ....
 T: *I live at home* or *I live at (example of number + street name). Can you give another example?*
 S3: *I live at* ....
If you have college students, you may wish to teach *on campus* and *in a dormitory.*

3. This is an information gap exercise. Refer to the introduction for a general presentation of these exercises. Have the class break into pairs. Do the example with the class. Then do another example, if necessary:
 T: *As, ask the Bs about Mr. David Albright.*
 As: *Does Mr. David Albright live at 9 or 12 Belmont Avenue?*
 Bs: *At 9 Belmont Avenue.*

4. (Optional) Compare the ways a letter is addressed in the U.S. and in your students' country or countries.

6

Pronunciation

● A question with two choices sounds like this:

Do Dr. and Mrs. Martin Adams live on Guilford Street or Guilford Avenue?

● Practice saying these phrases. Notice how *in, on* and *at* are used for locations.

| at | home
200 Woodland Street
(number and street) | on | Woodland Street
(street name only) | in | a house, an apartment, a room
Miami (a city)
Florida (a state, a prefecture)
The United States (a country) |

7

You're checking your company's mailing list. **A,** you have an old list.
Ask B your questions. **B,** you have a new list. Give A the new information.

A

Adams, Dr. and Mrs. Martin — Guilford Avenue, Attleboro   *Street?*

A: Do Dr. and Mrs. Martin Adams live on Guilford Street or Guilford Avenue?
B: They live on Guilford Street.

1. Ask B your questions.

Adams, Dr. and Mrs. Martin — Guilford Avenue, Attleboro   *Street?*

Albright, Mr.David — 9 Belmont Avenue Attleboro   *12?*

Amodeo, Deborah and John—377 Plain Road, South Attleboro   *Attleboro?*

Audet, Louis — 18 Melrose Street, West Attleboro   *Place?*

2. You have a new list. Give B the correct information.

Macko, Gail and Arthur — 27 Canal Street, West Attleboro

Madden, Frank — Guilford

Makris, Paul and Cindy — 107 North Main Street, Vernon

Mauer, Norman R. — 30 Maple Street, Attleboro

B

Adams, Dr. and Mrs Martin — Guilford Street, Attleboro

A: Do Dr. and Mrs. Martin Adams live on Guilford Street or Guilford Avenue?
B: They live on Guilford Street.

1. Give A the new information.

Adams, Dr. and Mrs. Martin — Guilford Street, Attleboro

Albright, Mr. David — 9 Belmont Avenue, Attleboro

Amodeo, Deborah and John — 377 Plain Road, South Attleboro

Audet, Louis — 18 Melrose Place, West Attleboro

2. You have an old list. Ask A your questions.

Macko, Gail and Arthur — 25 Canal Street, West Attleboro   *27?*

Madden, Frank — Guilford   *Attleboro?*

Makris, Paul and Cindy — 107 Main Street, Vernon   *North Main?*

Mauer, Norman R. — 30 Maple Street, Attleboro   *13?*

21

8

Ask some classmates where they live, where they work and what they do.

- Talk to three other people in your class. Write down the answers.

A: Where do you live?
B: ....
A: (Where) do you work?
B: I work at .... OR I don't have a job.
A: What exactly do you do?

- Work with a partner. Tell your partner the names of the people you talked to. Ask each other about these people.

A: I talked to ...., ... and ....
B: Where does .... live?
A: ....

9

- Practice this conversation:

A: Do you have any brothers or sisters?
B: Yes, I do. I have an older sister and a younger brother.
   OR No, I don't. I'm an only child.
A: What are their names?
B: My sister's name is Ruth. My brother's name is Tony.
A: Where do they live?
B: My sister lives in an apartment in New York. My brother lives at home.

- **A,** ask about B's family. **B,** give true answers. **A,** write down the information B gives you.

10

- Fill in the blanks and practice saying these words:

wife's = her
husband's = his
my wife's and my = our
son's = ...
sons' = *their*
daughter's = ...
daughters' = ...

| engaged | single | divorced |
| married | separated | widowed |

- Practice this conversation:

A: Are you married?
B: Yes, I am. OR No, I'm not.
A: What's your wife's/husband's name?
B: Her/His name's Chris.
A: Do you have any children?
B: Yes, I/we do. I/we have two sons and a daughter. OR No, I/we don't.
A: What are their names?
B: Our sons' names are Matthew and John. Our daughter's name is Amy.
A: How old are they?
B: 13, 11 and 8.

- **A,** ask about B's family. **B,** give true answers. **A,** write down the information B gives you.

- Join another pair of students. Tell them what you know about your partner's family from this exercise and from Exercise 9.

11
Put It Together

Look at the family tree. Talk about your families.

A: Do you have any aunts and uncles?
B: Yes, I have two aunts and one uncle.
A: Where do they live?

Niece, Nephew, Sister, Cousin, Sister-in-law/Brother, Mother/Father, Aunt/Uncle, Grandfather/Grandmother Grandfather/Grandmother

EXERCISE 8 (mixer, pairs)

Language Focus

simple present, all persons; *wh*-questions and statements

New Words and Expressions

job

Teaching Suggestions

1. Teach new words if needed.

2. Go over the first example with the students, and have them do that part of the exercise. Point out that those who don't have a job can also say, *I'm a student, I'm a housewife, I'm retired,* or any other appropriate response.

3. Model the second part with a student and have students practice in pairs.

EXERCISE 9 (pairs)

Language Focus

simple present, *yes/no* and *wh*-questions, short answers and statements, *'s* for possession, possessive adjectives, prepositions in addresses, review of *be*

New Words and Expressions

be an only child

Note: We can say either *Do you have any brothers or sisters?* or *Do you have any brothers and sisters?*

Teaching Suggestions

1. Students read the conversation silently to themselves.

2. Teach new words and expressions as needed.

3. Read the conversation aloud for the students. Divide the class in two groups (one takes A's part, the other B's part) and have them repeat after you.

4. Students practice the conversation in pairs.

5. Students practice the true version of the conversation by first asking you the questions.

6. Students practice the conversation in pairs.

7. (Optional) Students write down the information about their partners.

Workbook

You can now assign Exercises E and F.

EXERCISE 10 (pairs)

Language Focus

possessive adjectives, *'s* for possession, simple present; review of *be*, talking about marital status and family members

New Words and Expressions

divorced, engaged, married, separated, widowed

Teaching Suggestions

1. Teach new words and expressions, as needed.

2. Have the students orally supply the three missing possessive adjectives. (son's = his, daughter's = hers, daughters' = theirs) Write them on the chalkboard.

3. Follow the teaching suggestions given for Exercise 9.

4. In the last part of the exercise, each pair of students joins another pair.

Workbook

You can now assign Exercise G.

EXERCISE 11 (pairs)

Language Focus

same as Exercises 9 and 10

New Words and Expressions

aunt, cousin, grandfather, grandmother, nephew, niece, sister-in-law, uncle

Teaching Suggestions

1. Again, pair students and have them join another pair. Tell the students they should try not to look at their written notes for Exercises 9 and 10. If they have forgotten information, they can ask their partner again, or as a last resort, refer to their notes. Students should have conversations beginning with the exchange suggested in the text.

Note: The family tree has been provided to give students the vocabulary they need to talk about their families. It can also be used for additional language practice. Two optional activities are suggested below.

2. (Optional) Elicit the vocabulary from students.

    T: *Your mother's mother is your* ....
    S1: *Grandmother.*
    T: *Your mother's sister is your* ....
    S2: *Aunt.*

Explain that the rules for the pronunciation of *'s* are the same as they have already learned for *s* at the end of verbs and plural nouns.

(*continued*)

3. (Optional) Elicit possessive words using both names of students and the family tree *(Keiko's, uncle's),* and ask students which *s* sound column they go in:/s/, /z/ or /əz/.

Workbook
You can now assign Exercise H.

If You Have Time

1. Students can describe and discuss a typical family in their country or countries and compare it to their idea of a typical American family.

2. Students can write a newsletter, similar to the one in this unit, about the teachers in their English program. Or they can write a newsletter about the students in the class.

CHECKLIST

Teaching Suggestions

General Notes
—*Have* is irregular in the third-person ending.

—*Do* is irregular in the pronunciation and spelling of the third person.

—Possessive adjectives are the same before plural and singular nouns.

my daughter   *my* daughters

1. Follow the general suggestions for the Checklist page detailed in Unit 1.

2. Students can practice the use of the simple present tense by asking questions and making statements about themselves and their families, where they work and live.

3. (Optional) Students can practice salutations. For example:

T: *How do you introduce a friend to your boss/parents?*
Ss: *Mr.* ...., *I'd like you to meet* ....
T: *You meet your friend on the street. How do you greet him/her?*
Ss: *Hi,* ...., *how's it going?*
T: *What does your friend say?*
Ss: *OK, thanks,* ....

I know how to . . .

USE THESE FORMS

☐ **Simple Present Tense**

I	work	he	works
you	do	she	does
we	have	it	has
they			

questions

(Where) Do you work?
　　　　 Does he

short answers

Yes, I do. 　　　No, I don't.
　　 he does. 　　　　 he doesn't.

statements

I work for a small company.
He works

I don't work.
He doesn't

☐ **Possessives**

possessive adjectives

my, your, his, her, its, our, their
My sister's name is Ruth.

possessive forms of nouns

's: Carol's son is a writer. Carol's son's name is John.
s': Her daughters' names are Joanne and Betty.

USE ENGLISH TO

☐ **introduce someone formally**
Dr. Hummel, I'd like you to meet Jonathan Wilkins.

☐ **greet someone new**
It's nice to meet you.

☐ **greet someone I know informally**
Hi, John. How's it going?
OK, thanks, Nan.

☐ **leave a conversation politely**
Well, I'd better get back to work.

☐ **say goodbye formally**
Goodbye for now, Dr. Hummel.

☐ **say goodbye informally**
See you later, Jon.

☐ **talk about these subjects**
family members　 jobs　 names
where someone lives

☐ **UNDERSTAND THESE EXPRESSIONS**

He'd like to interview you.
(He) changes (his) mind (every day).
(He's) a good kid.
I'd better get back to (work).
(I'm) an only child.
(I'm) in charge of (the research department).
See you later.
What exactly (do you do there)?
Welcome to (MHI).

a family tree

CHECKLIST

🖭 **Listening**

1

A man is showing a friend pictures of his family.
Fill in each person's relation to the man. Use the words from the box.

| grandfather | brother-in-law | grandmother | niece | father | nephew | mother | son |
| parents | daughter | sister | uncle | brother | aunt | sister-in-law | cousin |

1. .... 2. .... 3. .... 4. .... 5. .... 6. ....

2

Jeanne is asking Marie about Marie's family. Mark the statements *T* (true) or *F* (false).

_F_ 1. Marie's husband's name is Mark.

___ 2. Marie and Mark have two children.

___ 3. One of their sons, Terry, is a dancer.

___ 4. Marie's sister lives in an apartment.

___ 5. Mark and Marie's son Bob is a student.

___ 6. Bob doesn't live on campus.

___ 7. Marie has two brothers.

___ 8. Jeanne and her husband have three children.

3

Marina Polis is the fifth international visitor to MHI. Listen to this interview and answer the questions about her. Circle the letter of the correct answer.

1. Where does she work?
   a. at a hospital
   b. at a school

2. What does she do there?
   a. She's a nurse.
   b. She's in charge of supplies.

3. Does she live and work in Athens?
   a. yes
   b. no

4. Does she live in a house or an apartment?
   a. a house
   b. an apartment

5. How many children does she have?
   a. three
   b. one

6. Where's her daughter?
   a. at the University of Michigan
   b. at Miami University

4

Give true answers.

1. ....
2. ....
3. ....
4. ....

5. ....
6. ....
7. ....
8. ....

LISTENING

EXERCISE 1 (individuals)
Language Focus
vocabulary about family relations

New Words and Expressions
show (*v.*), relation

Teaching Suggestions
1. If necessary, review the family tree terms.

2. Play the cassette or read the tapescript.

3. Students do the exercise.

4. Go over the exercise with the students, or have them work in pairs first, and then go over the exercise with them.

5. (Optional) Find out if students recognize the British royal family. Ask if there have been any changes.

Answers: 1. brother and sister-in-law   2. brother and sister-in-law   3. mother and father   4. aunt   5. nephew
6. grandmother

EXERCISE 2 (individuals, pairs)
Language Focus
asking for and giving information about one's family

Names
Marie /mərí/
Mark /mɑrk/
Terry /téri/
Bob /bɔb/
Jeanne /dʒin/

Teaching Suggestions
1. Play the cassette or read the tapescript.

2. Students do the exercise.

3. Work in pairs to check answers. Go over answers. If the answer is False, then ask them for the correct information.

Answers: 1. T   2. T   3. F   4. F   5. T   6. T   7. F   8. T

EXERCISE 3 (individuals, pairs)
Language Focus
simple present tense in questions and statements about occupation, residence, family

Names
Marina Polis /mərínə pólis/

Teaching Suggestions
1. Play the cassette or read the tapescript.

2. Students do the exercise.

3. (Optional) Have them work in pairs to check their answers, then go over the answers with the whole group.

Answers 1. a   2. b   3. a   4. b   5. b   6. a

EXERCISE 4 (individuals)
Language Focus
personal questions based on the language taught in this unit

Teaching Suggestions
1. Play the cassette or read the tapescript.

2. Students do the exercise.

3. Ask students what the questions were.

Answers: Since answers are personal, they will vary for each student.

EPISODE 3 The Moon of India

Key Vocabulary

cruise, enjoyable, evening dresses, fall collections, fashion buyer, full, lifts his wine glass, Mediterranean, mysteries, real estate, sad, seasick, smiles a lot, strangers, vacation homes

Names

Pierre Maurice /piέr mɔrís/
Paris /pǽris/
Mediterranean /mɛdɪtəreínian/
Europe /juárəp/

Teaching Suggestions

1. Have students retell the story up to this point: Someone stole a famous necklace, the Moon of India, from the City Museum in New York. The police think the thief killed his/her partner and is traveling on the *Princess,* a ship. They put a police officer on the ship. We don't know who the thief is or who the police officer is. Christina Jordan, her aunt Agatha Jordan, Frank Adams, Lucy Cardozo and Robert Grant are passengers on the ship. They're sitting at the same table.

2. Follow steps 1–6 of Episode 1.

3. Ask the comprehension questions.

Answers: 1) Robert Grant works in real estate. He travels a lot for his business, because he finds vacation homes for Americans in France and Spain. 2) Lucy Cardozo is a fashion buyer. She's in Europe to buy for the fall collections. 3) They talk about fashion. 4) Frank Adams is a writer. He writes mysteries. 5) Christina is not feeling well. She's seasick.

4. (Optional) Other possible questions. Why does Agatha say again, "I'm forgetful"? Why are Frank Adams' eyes sad?

5. Have students close their books and relate the main points of the episode. Check their understanding of the story as they tell it. Correct any misunderstandings.

6. (Optional) Expansion questions. Do you read mysteries? Do you like French fashion? Would you like a vacation home in France or Spain? Would you like to go on a cruise? Do you think that the people in the story are going to have an enjoyable and interesting cruise? Do you think one of the people at Table 5 is the thief? The police officer? Who?

7. (Optional) Role-play. Students can role-play the dialogues between Robert and Lucy on deck, and the conversation among Robert, Lucy, Agatha and Frank at the table, using role cards as described in Episode 1.

MOON OF INDIA

 Episode Three

People are walking on the deck of the *Princess* before dinner. Robert and Lucy are talking, looking at the sea and the evening sky.

Lucy says, "It's wonderful!"

Robert asks, "Is this your first trip to the Mediterranean?"

"It's my first cruise. And you?"

"No. I travel a lot for business."

"Oh, that's interesting."

The dining room is full. Agatha Jordan enters and finds Table 5. There are three people at the table: two men and a woman.

"Oh dear. Am I late? Please don't get up. I'm Agatha Jordan, Christina's aunt. She isn't coming to dinner. She's a little seasick."

"That's too bad," says one of the men, "I hope she feels better soon." He gives Agatha a big smile. "But I'm very happy to meet you, Mrs. Jordan. I'm Robert Grant."

"And I'm glad to meet you, Mr. Roberts."

"It's Grant, Mrs. Jordan, Robert Grant."

"I'm sorry, Mr. Grant. I'm very forgetful."

Robert Grant introduces the other people at the table. Lucy Cardozo is about 32. She's wearing black slacks and a silk blouse. Frank Adams is in his early 40s. He smiles a lot, but his eyes are sad.

"What do you do, Robert?" asks Frank.

"Real estate. We find houses in Spain and France, usually for Americans who want vacation homes in Europe."

Agatha turns to Lucy, "What do you do, Lucy?"

"I'm a fashion buyer. I'm in Europe to buy for the fall collections. The clothes in Paris this year have some beautiful colors."

"Really," says Agatha. "Who's your favorite designer?"

"My favorite is the Pierre Maurice collection. Pierre makes the most beautiful evening dresses," says Lucy.

"Oh yes. They're wonderful."

Robert sees the waiter coming to their table. "Oh, and speaking of wonderful, here comes dinner!"

Frank smiles, "Well, here we are. Our first evening. Four strangers on a boat with a week together in front of us."

Robert says, "A good idea for one of your stories, Frank, eh?"

"Are you a writer?"

"Yes, mysteries mainly. *The Hour of the Wolf, In the Evening Hours.* Do you know them?"

"Sorry, I don't," says Agatha.

"I don't read many mysteries," says Lucy.

Frank says, "Oh well!" He lifts his wine glass. "To an enjoyable and interesting cruise!"

Comprehension Check

1. What does Robert Grant do? Why does he travel a lot for his business?
2. What does Lucy Cardozo do? Why is she in Europe?
3. What do Agatha and Lucy talk about?
4. What does Frank Adams do?
5. Why doesn't Christina come to dinner?

U N I T 4

Secretary: Good morning, Dr. Lee's office.
Mr. Wolfe: Hello, this is Peter Wolfe. I'd like to make an appointment for a checkup.
Secretary: Can you come in on Monday, the 25th, at 9 AM?
Mr. Wolfe: Well, I work from 9 to 5 every day, but yes, I can.
Secretary: Good. What's your number at work, Mr. Wolfe?
Mr. Wolfe: 257-1310, extension 149.
Secretary: Thank you. We'll see you on the 25th then.

Doctor: Are you having any problems, Mr. Wolfe?
Mr. Wolfe: No, I feel great. I sleep well, eat right, get regular exercise.
Doctor: How often do you exercise?
Mr. Wolfe: Every day.

(later) . . .
Doctor: You're in very good shape, Mr. Wolfe.

Mr. Fox: Hello?
Secretary: Hello, Mr. Fox? This is Dr. Lee's office. We'd like to make an appointment for your annual checkup.
Mr. Fox: Oh, yeah, I got your card.
Secretary: Can you come in on Tuesday the 21st at 10:30?
Mr. Fox: No, I can't. I sleep late in the morning. Is the doctor ever there in the evening?
Secretary: Dr. Lee has evening hours on Thursdays. Can you make it on the 23rd at 7 o'clock?
Mr. Fox: Yeah, OK. That's Tuesday, the 23rd?
Secretary: No, Thursday, the 23rd. We'll see you then.

Doctor: Do you ever exercise, Mr. Fox? Go swimming? Jogging?
Mr. Fox: I can't swim, and I hate jogging.

(later) . . .
Doctor: Well, Mr. Fox, you have bad habits, but you're in good shape for a 50-year-old man.
Mr. Fox: But, Doctor, I'm only 26.
Doctor: I know.

UNIT 4

Unit Language Focus

GRAMMAR: simple present tense, frequency expressions, time expressions, *can* for ability, *how often* questions
COMMUNICATIVE AREAS: saying telephone numbers, beginning a telephone conversation formally and informally, making an appointment on the phone, talking about habits and routines, talking about ability, checking that you understand something

OPENING CONVERSATION

New Words and Expressions

A.M., annual, appointment, bad, be in good shape, can't, card, checkup, eat, evening, ever, exercise, extension (ext.), habit, hate (*v.*), hour, jog, late, make an appointment, make it, man, M.D., Monday, morning, P.M., problem, regular, secretary, sleep, swim, there, Thursday, twice, will, yeah, year

Names

Wolfe /wʊlf/
Fox /fɑks/
Lee /li/

Teaching Suggestions

1. Warm-up. While students look at the picture, ask: *Where is this?* Point to Mr. Wolfe. *How old is this man?* Point to Mr. Fox. *How old is this man?*

2. Personalize: *Do you go to a doctor? When? Is your doctor a man or a woman?*

First Two Conversations

3. Explain that the first conversations are on the phone. Play/ read the conversations. Students look only at pictures.

4. Play/read it again. Students listen and read silently.

5. Teach new words and expressions as needed.

6. Let students ask about vocabulary, grammar, or pronunciation.

7. Students read/repeat the conversations line by line.

Second Two Conversations

8. Follow teaching suggestions 4–6. Did your students get the joke at the end?

9. Explain A.M. and P.M. if necessary, and ask questions.

   T: *When is Mr. Wolfe's appointment?*
   S3: *On Monday the 25th.*

   T: *What time?*
   S4: *At 9:00 A.M.*
   T: *When is Mr. Fox's appointment?*
   S6: *At seven o'clock on the 23rd.*
   T: *Is that A.M. or P.M.?*
   S7: *In the evening (or P.M.).*
   T: *Why in the evening?*
   S8: *Because Sammy sleeps late.*
   T: *Who is in good shape, Mr. Wolfe or Mr. Fox?*
   S9: *Mr. Wolfe.*
   T: *Why is Mr. Wolfe in good shape?*
   S1: *He gets regular exercise.*
   S2: *He sleeps well. He eats right.*
   S3: *He exercises every day.*

10. Ask: *Is Mr. Fox in good shape?*
   S1: *No, he isn't.*
   T: *But the doctor says, "You're in good shape." What else does she say?*
   S2: *For a 50-year-old man.*
   T: *How old is Mr. Fox?*
   S3: *26.*
   T: *So, he's not in good shape. Why?*

11. (Optional): T: *Do you know someone like Mr. Wolfe? A TV star? A friend? Do you know someone like Mr. Fox?*

12. Let students ask questions about vocabulary, grammar, or pronunciation.

Additional Information

Grammar

In Unit 3, the simple present tense was used for general information about people and things. In this unit, it is used for habits and routines: *I usually sleep late in the morning. I never go out on weekends.*

Vocabulary and Usage

1. In writing, a medical doctor is referred to as *(full name), M.D.* For example: *Karen Lee, M.D.* In speech, a doctor is referred to as *Dr.* .... For example: *I'm Dr. Lee.*

2. *Can you come in on Monday?* is short for *Can you come (in) to the doctor's office on Monday?*

3. When the secretary answers the phone, she says, *Dr. Lee's office:* but when she makes the phone call, she identifies the office: *This is Dr. Lee's office.*

4. *I'd/We'd like to* is a polite way of saying *I/We want to.*

5. In the first conversation, the secretary says, *We'll see you on the 25th, then. Then* is conversational. It doesn't refer to a time. In the second conversation, the secretary says, *We'll see you then. Then* refers to Thursday the 23rd.

6. In the previous unit, *have* appeared in the simple present *(we have two children).* The doctor says *Are you having any problems?* because she wants to know about Mr. Wolfe's current situation.

SPEAKING

EXERCISE 1 (whole class, pairs)

Language Focus

simple present, frequency expressions, talking about personal routines

New Words and Expressions

always, be up, breakfast, cereal, coffee, dinner, during, egg, get up, go camping, it depends, juice, month, never, night, noon, o'clock, once, out, parentheses, read, sometimes, time, toast, twice, until, watch, week, weekend

Grammar

Frequency expressions: Some frequency adverbs such as *always* and *never* occur only before the main verb. For example: *I never sleep late.* Some frequency adverbs such as *usually* generally occur before the main verb, but can also occur before the subject or at the end of the sentence. For example: *I usually sleep late* (most common). *Usually I sleep late. I sleep late, usually.* Some frequency adverbs such as *sometimes* usually occur before the subject, but can occur before the verb or at the end of a sentence. For example: *Sometimes I sleep late* (most common). *I sometimes sleep late. I sleep late, sometimes.* In this unit we introduce only the most common position of these four adverbs. We suggest teaching only these positions at this point.

Vocabulary and Usage

1. *Go to bed* and *be in bed:* These have similar meanings. The question is, *When do you go to bed?* The usual answer is, *(I go to bed) at* ...., but the answer can also be, *I'm in bed at* ....

2. *Be up* and *get up* have similar meanings. *Get up* is more common.

3. *Go out in the evening* means *go out for pleasure,* such as to a movie or to a restaurant.

4. In Conversation 4, Mr. Fox responds, *A vacation from what?* We usually take a vacation from work. Mr. Fox doesn't work, so he has no reason to take a vacation.

Teaching Suggestions

First Part (whole class)

1. Teach new words and expressions, as needed.

2. Have students study the examples.

3. Ask them to use the frequency adverbs by answering questions about themselves. For example:

  T: *S1, what do you do in the morning?*
  S1: *I go to work/school.*
  T: *Sometimes? Always? Usually?*
  S1: *I always go to work/school in the morning.*
  OR T: *S1, what do you do every day?*

  OR T: *Think of something you always do, usually do, sometimes do, never do, and then tell the class.*
Help them with unknown vocabulary if necessary.

4. Practice the position of the frequency adverbs with *be* by asking questions like, *Are you ever late for class?* or *Who is always on time for class? Who is always late?* and so on.

5. Go over the questions and answers, reminding them to pay attention to the placement of the adverbs.

Second Part (pairs)

1. Make sure students understand the exercise. Let two students model the first exchange (with your help). When the students finish, ask them the same questions in third person; for example: *When does Mr. Fox usually go to bed?*

2. Ask students the same questions; for example: *Maria, when do you usually go to bed?*

3. (Optional) Students ask each other the same questions.

EXERCISE 2 (whole class, pairs)

Language Focus

asking for and giving phone numbers

New Words and Expressions

area code, phone

Teaching Suggestions

1. Teach new words and expressions as needed.

2. Students read the information silently.

3. Have them practice the model number in chorus.

4. Write the following numbers on the board to give them further practice: *(212) 897-3445 (617) 222-2689 442-8890, ext. 21.* Make up others, if necessary.

5. Discuss how they write and say the numbers in their country or countries.

6. Have them work in pairs to practice asking each other the numbers in the text. Teach *I don't have a phone/work number* as alternatives.

Workbook

You can now assign Exercises A and B. Exercise A introduces *beauty shop, hair cut.*

Speaking

1

Add the words in parentheses ( ), and practice saying these questions and
answers. They're from conversations with Mr. Wolfe and Mr. Fox. Use the chart
below to help you.

When do you go to bed?   *(usually)*
a. Oh, I go to bed at 2:00 or 3:00 AM.   *(usually)*
b. I'm in bed at 11 o'clock.   *(every night)*

When do you usually go to bed?
a. Oh, I usually go to bed at 2:00 or 3:00 AM.
b. I'm in bed at 11 o'clock every night.

1. How much sleep do you get? When do you get up? (usually)
   a. I get eight hours of sleep. (always)
      I get up at 7:00. (usually)
   b. It depends. I'm up at noon. (sometimes)
      I sleep until 3:00 or 3:30. (sometimes)

2. Do you eat a good breakfast? What do you have? (usually)
   a. I have juice, eggs, toast, cereal and coffee. (every day)
   b. I eat breakfast. (never)

3. What do you do in the evening? Do you go out? (ever)
   a. I go out. (five or six times a week)
   b. I read or watch TV. (sometimes)
      I go out during the week. (never)
      On weekends I go out. (about twice a month)

4. Do you take a vacation? (every year)
   a. Yes, I go camping in Alaska for two weeks. (every year)
   b. A vacation from what? I work. (never)
      I'm on vacation. (always)

- **A,** you're Dr. Lee. Ask Mr. Wolfe the questions above. **B,** you're Mr. Wolfe.
  Choose the right answers.

- **A,** this time you're Mr. Fox. **B,** you're Dr. Lee.

2

- American phone numbers look
like this: (223) 555-1310.
Say them like this: *area code two
two three// five five five// one three//
one oh.*

Work numbers often have
extensions, for example: 679-7300
ext. 149.
Say them like this: *six seven nine//
seven three// oh oh// extension one
four nine.*

- Have conversations like these:

At home

A: What's your phone number?
B: ----------------------.
724-3045
(623) 856-9568
your number

At work

A: What's your number at work?
B: ----------------------.
(425) 926-7652
896-2211 ext. 1271
your number

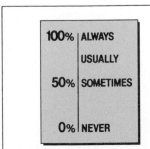

100%	ALWAYS
	USUALLY
50%	SOMETIMES
0%	NEVER

I	'm	always usually never		at home.
			have dinner	
When	Do you	ever usually	exercise?	

Sometimes I	'm exercise			at home.
He exercises		every		day/night.
	(about)	once twice three times	a	week. month. year.

3

● Practice saying these times and days of the week.

AM			PM	
7:30	seven-thirty		3:00	....
8:00	eight/eight o'clock		4:30	*four-thirty*
9:00	....		5:15	....
9:45	....		6:05	six oh five
12:00	(twelve) noon		10:20	....
			12:00	(twelve) midnight

weekdays	the weekend	
Monday	Saturday	M–F = Monday through
Tuesday	Sunday	Friday
Wednesday		Sat, 9–12 = Saturday,
Thursday		from 9:00 to 12:00
Friday		

● Practice this conversation:

B: Hello.
A: Hello. Is this Ellen's Flowers?
B: Yes, it is.
A: Could you tell me when you're open?
B: Monday through Saturday from 10:00 to 3:00.
A: You close at 3:00?
B: That's right.
A: Thank you.

A

1. "Call" these places to find out when they're open. Write down their hours.

   Robert's Hardware

   ....
   ....

   K and D Department Store

   ....
   ....

   Ellen's Flowers

   ....
   ....

2. Answer B's questions. Use the information below.

B

1. Answer A's questions. Use the information below.

2. "Call" these places to find out when they're open. Write down their hours.

   Valley Travel Agency

   ....
   ....

   Hamelman's Bakery

   ....
   ....

   Bush's Drugstore

   ....
   ....

EXERCISE 3 (whole class, pairs)

Language Focus

clock, time, days of the week; using the phone; asking about business hours

New Words and Expressions

bakery, below, call, drugstore, flower, hardware, midnight, open, Saturday, Sunday, through, travel agency, Wednesday, weekday

Names

Robert's /rábərts/
Ellen's /élənz/
Hamelman's /hæmələmənz/
Bush's /buʃəz/

Teaching Suggestions

1. Have the students supply the missing times.

2. Teach new words and expressions as needed.
Note: A hardware store sells tools for building and repairing, and household fixtures, such as electric cords, light bulbs, picture hangers, etc. A drugstore sells soap, toothpaste, and nonprescription medicine such as aspirin; most drugstores have pharmacies, which sell prescription medicine. In the U.S., most small stores are not open on Sunday. Most supermarkets and grocery (food) stores are open on Sundays. Some department stores are open on Sundays.

3. Go over the days of the week. Then write on the board various examples of store hours, for example: M–F 9–12, Tu 10–5, M–Th 8–5:30, etc. Have students supply the meaning. Help with the abbreviations if necessary.

4. (Optional) Ask: *What can you buy at Ellen's Flowers?* (flowers) *At Robert's Hardware?* (hammer, nails, electric cord) *At K & D Department store?* (clothes, kitchen supplies, lamps, etc.) *At Valley Travel Agency?* (airplane and train tickets) *At Hamelman's Bakery?* (bread cakes) *At Bush's Drugstore?* (soap, shampoo, aspirin)

5. Write on the board: *Hamelman's Bakery M–Th 8–5:30, Fri. 8–6:30, Sat. 8–5:30.*

   T: *When does Hamelman's Bakery open on Mondays?*
   S1: *At eight o'clock.*
   T: *Does it open at eight o'clock every day?*
   S2: *Yes.*
   T: *When does it close on Mondays?*
   S2: *At five-thirty.*
   T: *Does it close at five-thirty every day?*

6. Have the students practice the conversation as a whole group or in pairs. Point out that the expression *Could you tell me* .... *?* is polite.

7. Write on the board:
   When do you open on ....? (a specific day)
   When are you open?/Could you tell me when you are open? (the whole week)

8. This is an information gap exercise. In order to make sure the students know what to do, you may want two students (with your help) to model it for the class. Students do the exercise in pairs.

9. (Optional) Tell the students: *It's Saturday.* Ask: *When does Hamelman's Bakery close today?* (5:30) *Does it close at 5:30 every day?* (No, it closes at 6:30 on Fridays.) On the board write: *When does* .... *close today? Does it close at* .... *every day?* Have the students practice similar conversations in pairs.

10. Have a discussion about customary store hours in the students' country or countries.

Workbook

You can now assign Exercises C and D.

EXERCISE 4 (role-play, pairs)

Language Focus

making an appointment on the phone, dates, times

New Words and Expressions

all right, fine, be free

Names

Kathy Miller /kǽθi mílər/
Gage /geɪdʒ/

Teaching Suggestions

1. Teach new words and expressions as needed.

2. Write on the chalkboard:
Kathy Miller
Monday, May 23 Tuesday, May 24 Wednesday, May 25
3:00 meeting
Say: *This is Kathy Miller's calendar. Is she free on Monday at three o'clock?*
S1: *No, she isn't. (She has a meeting.)*
T: *When is she free?*
S2: *On Tuesday and Wednesday.*

3. Students read the conversation silently.

4. Students read the conversation aloud in two groups or in pairs. Point out that *come in on* and *make it on* have the same meaning. Remind them that when they make a phone call it is important to identify themselves; for example: *This is* ....

5. Students work in pairs as described in the instructions.

6. When they have finished, ask the As: *When is your appointment?* Ask the Bs: *When is your appointment?*

EXERCISES 5 AND 6 (whole class, pairs)

Language Focus

pronunciation of *can/can't, can* for ability

New Words and Expressions

backwards, Chinese, difference, dive (*v.*), forward, guitar, motorcycle, piano, sing, song, type (*v.*)

Teaching Suggestions

1. Teach new words and expressions, as needed.

2. Exercise 5: Practice saying *can* and *can't*. Use the examples in the book.

Exercise 6: First Part

3. Have students study the chart.

4. Write some examples on the board. For example:
.... *can/can't speak (language);* .... *can/can't swim.* Have students volunteer information about themselves. For example:
S1: *I can't speak (language).*
S2: *I can play the piano.*
S3: *I can't play the piano.*

5. Check students' pronunciation of *can* and *can't*.

6. Ask questions based on the examples. For example:
T: *Can (S1) speak (language)?*
S4: *No, she can't.*
T: *Can (S2) type?*
S5: *Yes, he can.*
T: *Ask S3 if he (she) can swim.*
S6: *(S3), can you swim?*

Second Part

7. Students work in pairs to ask each other the questions. They can mark the answers on the chart.

Third Part

8. When students are finished, have each pair join another pair. Have A and C form a new pair and B and D form another pair. Have A report to C and B report to D. This way they will all have a chance to speak.

9. Point out how *and* and *but* are used in the examples.

Workbook

You can assign Exercise E.

4

Practice this conversation:

A: Dr. Gage's office.
B: Hello. This is Kathy Miller. I'd like to make an appointment for a checkup.
A: Can you come in on Monday at 3:00?

B: No, that day isn't good for me.
A: Can you make it on Tuesday at 10:00?
B: Yes, that's fine.
A: All right, we'll see you on Tuesday.

A

1. Call Dr. Gage's office and make an appointment at a time when you are free. You are not free at these times: Monday 4–6, Tuesday 12–2, Wednesday 10–12, Friday 12–1

2. Make an appointment for Dr. Gage. He can see people at these times: Tuesday 10–11, Friday 2–3

B

1. Make an appointment for Dr. Gage. He can see people at these times: Tuesday 1–2, Wednesday 10–11, Friday 9–10

2. Call Dr. Gage's office and make an appointment at a time when you are free. You are not free at these times: Monday 3–4:30, Tuesday 9–12, Wednesday 4–5, Friday 3–4:30

5

Pronunciation

Notice the differences between *can* and *can't* and practice saying these sentences.

I can týpe.   I cån't týpe.

In questions and statements, *can* sounds like /**k'n**/.

Can you týpe?   I can týpe.
/**k'n**/   /**k'n**/

In short answers, *can* sounds like /**kan**/.

Yes, I cån.
/**kan**/

Can't always sounds like /**kant**/.

I cån't týpe.   No, I cån't.
/**kant**/   /**kant**/

6

● Look at the words in this chart.

Can you . . . ?	A	B	C	D
dive/swim				
drive a car/motorcycle				
play the guitar/piano				
speak Chinese/Portuguese				
sing a song in English/in your language				
say the alphabet forwards (A-B-C . . .)/backwards (Z-Y-X . . .)				

● Find out what your partner can do, and fill in the chart.

A: Can you swim?
B: Yes, I can.   OR   No, I can't.

● **A** and **B,** join another pair (C and D) and tell each other about yourself and your partner. Then fill in the chart.

C: I can swim, and I can dive. D can swim, but she can't dive.
A: I can swim, but I can't dive. B can't swim, and he can't dive.

7
Culture Capsule

A typical big breakfast in the United States is bacon and eggs, toast with butter and jam, juice and coffee.

Do you usually eat breakfast?
What do you usually have for breakfast?

8

Elizabeth and Lannie Wright are twins. They look alike, but they have different jobs and different habits. They live at home with their mother, Mrs. Ruth Wright.

LANNIE: manages a restaurant   ELIZABETH: trains dogs

Ask and answer questions about Lannie and Elizabeth.
Use the information below.

A: Who works from 4:30 PM to 2:00 AM, Lannie or Elizabeth?
B: Lannie. Who goes jogging every morning?
A: Elizabeth. Who goes shopping in the afternoon?

Schedule

works from 4:30 PM to 2:00 AM   sleeps from 3:00 AM to 11:00 AM
works from 8:00 AM to 3:00 or 4:00 PM   sleeps from 10:00 PM to 5:30 AM

Activities

goes jogging every morning   goes dancing on weekends
goes shopping in the afternoon   takes naps in the afternoon
visits friends during the day   stays home in the evening
goes to baseball games on weekends   takes a vacation in Hawaii
reads in the evening   goes camping in Alaska

9

You want to know more about Lannie and Elizabeth. Ask their mother, Mrs. Wright.

● **A,** ask B (Mrs. Wright), about Lannie. **B,** you're Mrs. Wright. Answer A's questions.

A: When does Lannie usually get up?
B: At 11:00 AM.

1. When does she usually
    - get up?
    - get home?
    - go to work?
    - go to bed?

2. What does she usually do
    - during the day?
    - in the morning/afternoon/ evening?
    - on weekends?

3. Does she ever take a vacation?

● **B,** ask A (Mrs. Wright), about Elizabeth. **A,** you're Mrs. Wright. Answer B's questions.

10
Put It Together

A and **B,** ask each other about a typical weekday and a typical weekend day. Look at the questions in Exercise 9 for ideas. For example: *What time do you get up during the week? When do you usually get up on weekends? . . .*

EXERCISE 7 Culture Capsule (individuals, pairs)

Culture Focus

typical breakfast

New Words and Expressions

bacon, eggs, toast, butter, jam, juice

Teaching Suggestions

1. Have the students read the Capsule and look at the picture.

2. Say the name of each item in the picture and have the students point to the item.

3. Ask various students: *Do you ever have eggs for breakfast? What kind of eggs? Do you ever have bacon and eggs for breakfast? Do you ever have toast for breakfast?* (If appropriate): *What kind of toast? Do you ever have juice for breakfast? What kind of juice? Do you ever have coffee for breakfast? Do you drink regular or decaffeinated?*

4. Ask various students: *What do you usually eat for breakfast? When do you have breakfast? What kind of breakfast can you order in a restaurant in your country?*

5. Have students ask their partners the last questions. *(What do you usually eat for breakfast? When do you have breakfast?)*

6. (Optional) Take a survey of the class: *Who has eggs for breakfast? Who has coffee/tea for breakfast? Who has breakfast at 9:00? Who never eats breakfast?* and so on.

EXERCISE 8 (whole class, pairs)

Language Focus

simple present for habits and routines; questions with *who*; sentence final frequency adverbials (e.g., *every morning*); *in/on/during*

New Words and Expressions

activity, afternoon, alike, baseball, dance, dog, game, stay (*v.*), take a nap, train (*v.*), twins, visit (*v.*)

Names

Elizabeth /əlízəbəθ/
Lannie /lǽni/
Ruth Wright /ruθ ráɪt/

Teaching Suggestions

1. Have students read the introduction and look at the picture.

2. Teach new words and expressions, as needed.

3. Ask students if they know any twins. If they do, ask: *Do they look alike? Do they have the same habits? Do they wear the same kind of clothes?*

4. Ask: *How old do you think Lannie and Elizabeth are?* Have students read over the list of activities. Check if they have any questions. (Students can add activities to the list.)

5. (Optional) Elicit more opinions about Lannie and Elizabeth; for example: *Do they have boyfriends? Do they get along?* Some ways to describe Lannie: *She likes to have fun; she's stylish, lively, outgoing.* (You can present these as questions if you think students won't know these words and you'd like to introduce them.) Some ways to describe Elizabeth: *She's quiet, athletic, a tomboy.*

6. Start the exercise by asking the questions in the example:

> T: *What do you think? Who works from 4:30 P.M. to 2:00 A.M., Lannie or Elizabeth?*
> S1: *Lannie.*
> T: *Why do you think it's Lannie?*
> S1: *Because she manages a restaurant. She works at night.*
> T: *Who goes jogging every morning?*
> S2: *Elizabeth,* and so on.

7. Have the students continue the exercise in pairs.

EXERCISE 9 (pairs)

Language Focus

simple present for habits and routines; *does* .... *ever?*

Teaching Suggestions

1. Do the example with the class.

> T: *Mrs. Wright, when does Elizabeth usually get up?*
> S1: *At 5:30 A.M.*
> T: *That's early! Who can ask another question about Elizabeth?*

Elicit other questions and answers like the example.

2. Students do the exercise in pairs.

3. (Optional) Ask students to think of other questions and use their imagination.

EXERCISE 10 Put It Together (pairs)

Language Focus

asking and answering questions about one's habits and routines

Teaching Suggestions

1. Ask students: *Which questions from 9 can you ask?* (All except *Do you ever take a vacation?*)

2. Ask: *Can you think of other questions to ask?* List the questions on the board. For example: *What do you have for breakfast/lunch/dinner? When/where do you have breakfast/lunch/dinner? Do you ever go dancing?*

3. Have the students work in pairs and do the exercise.

If You Have Time

1. Take a survey of the class. Ask: *Who gets up at* .... *on weekends? Who goes out after work? What does* .... *do during the day? When does* .... *go to bed during the week?*

2. Have each pair join another pair to report and compare, using *I do, too,* and *I am, too.*

Workbook

You can now assign Exercises E and F. Exercise E introduces *music, bike, ride.*

CHECKLIST

Teaching Suggestions

1. Follow the general suggestions for the Checklist page detailed in Unit 1.

2. (Optional) For additional grammar practice, make statements or ask questions about the people in the class, using simple present for habits and routines, frequency expressions and can/can't. Have students use the patterns on the Checklist page as guides.

3. (Optional) From time to time, you may wish to have students review the Checklist part by part and then quiz them orally in class, with books open or closed. For example:

T: *You want to go to the doctor for a checkup. You call the doctor's office. What can you say? How do you make an appointment?*

S1: *I'd like to make an appointment for a checkup,* and so on.

I know how to . . .

USE THESE FORMS

☐ **Simple Present Tense**

The simple present tense describes habits or routines.

How much sleep do you get?
What does he do in the morning?
Do they ever go to the movies?
She goes shopping about once a month.

☐ **Frequency Expressions**

questions

Do you ever	
How often do you	exercise?
When do you usually	

statements

I	'm	always	
		usually	at home.
		never	have dinner

| Sometimes I | 'm | at home. |
| | exercise | |

He exercises		every		day/night.
		once	a	week.
	(about)	twice		month.
		three		year.
		times		

☐ **Time Expressions**

The doctor is here	at 9:00.
	from 9:00 to 5:30.
	until 5:00.
	Monday through Friday.
	on weekdays/weekends.
	in the morning/ afternoon/evening.
	during the day/week.

☐ **Can/Can't** *(expresses ability)*

| I you he, she it we they | can/can't |

questions
Can you swim?

short answers
Yes, I can.
No, I can't.

statements
I can swim.
I can't swim.

USE ENGLISH TO

☐ **ask for and give telephone numbers**
What's your number at work?
Area code (924) 257-1410, extension 149.

☐ **begin a telephone conversation**
Hello?
Hello, Mr. Fox? This is Dr. Lee's office.

☐ **make an appointment**
I'd like to make an appointment for a checkup.
Can you come in on Monday, the 25th, at 9:00 AM?
We'll see you then.

☐ **check that I understand something**
You close at 3:00?
That's right.

☐ **talk about ability**
I can swim, but I can't dive.

☐ **talk about these subjects**
telephone numbers   time
business hours   making appointments
abilities   habits   routines   breakfast   dates

☐ **UNDERSTAND THESE EXPRESSIONS**

Can you make it (on the 23rd)?
Good morning.
Goodbye.
It depends.
Yeah.

AM/PM
an annual checkup

be at home/at work
be up
be in (very) good shape
come in

get home
get up
get (8 hours of) sleep

go jogging/swimming/shopping/dancing
go to bed
go out

sleep late
stay home
take a vacation
take a nap

CHECKLIST

Listening

1

Write the phone numbers as you hear them.

1. .... 4. ....

2. .... 5. ....

3. .... 6. ....

2

Listen to the telephone conversations, and answer the questions.

1. What time does the Public Library open today? ....

2. When does the House of Pizza close tonight? ....

3. When does the Photo Factory open and close today?
....

4. Is the West Side Market open on Saturdays? ....

5. What time does the Steak Out Restaurant close tonight?
.... Is it open on Sundays? .... On Tuesdays? ....

3

Do you hear *can* or *can't?* Circle the correct one.

1. Mary can/can't dance the samba. She can/can't dance the tango.

2. Joseph can/can't speak Portuguese. He can/can't speak Spanish.

3. Terry can/can't type. She can/can't take shorthand.

4. Bob can/can't meet his wife at 3:00. He can/can't meet her at 4:00.

4

Gus Tate plays on the Globals basketball team. Howard Shortell is asking him about his life.

Mark the statements *T* (true) or *F* (false).

Part 1: During the basketball season . . .

—— 1. Gus is never away from home.

—— 2. He usually eats in restaurants and sleeps in hotels.

—— 3. After a game, he goes back to the hotel and goes to bed.

—— 4. He never sleeps until 9:00 or 10:00.

—— 5. He never eats a big breakfast.

—— 6. He exercises every day.

Part 2: After the basketball season . . .

—— 7. Gus and his wife are usually at home.

—— 8. Gus never reads.

—— 9. Sometimes his wife watches TV.

—— 10. He usually gets up early.

—— 11. He goes to work every day.

—— 12. Gus never plays basketball.

5

Give true answers.

1. ....

2. ....

3. ....

4. ....

5. ....

LISTENING

EXERCISE 1 (individuals)
Language Focus
phone numbers

Teaching Suggestions

1. Ask: *How do you write an American phone number? For example, 255-2193?* Have a student write it on the board.

2. Ask: *How do you write a phone number with an area code? For example, (415) 928-3911?* Have a student write it on the board: *(415) 928-3911.*

3. Play the cassette or read the tapescript.

4. The students do the exercise.

5. When they have finished, ask them to dictate the answers to you. Write them on the board.

Answers: 1. 387-5950   2. 357-4815   3. 740-9651
4. 661-6600   5. 924-3434, extension 512   6. 668-2732

EXERCISE 2 (whole class, individuals)
Language Focus

asking about business hours, time, days of the week, phone conversations

Teaching Suggestions

1. Ask students to repeat the names of the places they will hear: *Public Library, House of Pizza, Photo Factory, West Side Market, Steak Out Restaurant.*

2. Play the cassette or read the tapescript. Stop after each conversation to allow students to answer the question pertaining to that conversation.

3. When they have finished, go over the answers with them.

Answers: 1. 9:00   2. 10:30   3. 8:30, 4:45   4. yes   5. 11:15, yes, no

EXERCISE 3 (individuals)
Language Focus
discrimination of *can/can't*

New Words and Expressions

samba, take shorthand, tango

Teaching Suggestions

1. Teach new words and expressions as needed.

2. Review the *can/can't* pronunciation with the students.

3. Play the cassette or read the tapescript.

4. The students do the exercise.

5. Go over the answers.

6. (Optional) Ask students: *Who can do the samba? the tango? Who can type? take shorthand? speak Spanish? Portuguese?*

Answers: 1. can, can't   2. can't, can   3. can't, can't   4. can't, can.

EXERCISE 4 (individuals)
Language Focus

simple present tense for routines and habits

New Words and Expressions

basketball, early, hear, hotel, life, season, team

Teaching Suggestions

1. Teach new words and expressions, as needed.

2. Play the cassette or read the tapescript for each conversation separately.

3. The students do the exercise, one conversation at a time.

4. Go over the answers.

Answers: 1. F   2. T   3. T   4. F   5. F   6. T   7. T   8. F
9. T   10. T   11. T   12. F

EXERCISE 5 (individuals)
Language Focus

personal questions based on the language taught in this unit

Teaching Suggestions

1. Students do the exercise.

2. Ask the students what the questions were.

Answers: Since answers are personal, they will vary for each student.

OPTIONAL WRITING PRACTICE

You are a secretary at a doctor's office. The doctor asked you to make up a questionnaire for the new patients coming to the office for a first visit. Include spaces for name, age, etc., and write out any questions you think should be on this form for the patient to answer.

Name _____

_____

_____

_____

EPISODE 4 The Moon of India

Key Vocabulary

a swim, attractive, college educated, dark corner, died, frightened, hardworking, intelligent, invite someone for a drink, knock (*v.*), lounge, real estate agent, retired, retirement, tired

Names

Edgar /ɛ́dgər/
Estrellas /ɛstréɪʃəs/
Costa del·Sol /kóstə dɛl sól/

Teaching Suggestions

1. Have students retell the story up to this point: Someone stole a famous necklace, the Moon of India, from the City Museum in New York. The police think the thief killed his/her partner and is traveling on the *Princess,* a ship. They put a police officer on the ship. We don't know who the thief is or who the police officer is. Christina Jordan, her aunt Agatha Jordan, Frank Adams, Lucy Cardozo and Robert Grant are passengers on the ship. They sit at the same table. Christina works for a museum in New York, Frank is a mystery writer, Robert Grant finds vacation houses in Spain and France for Americans, and Lucy Cardozo is a fashion buyer. They talk at dinner. Christina doesn't come to dinner. She's seasick.

2. Follow steps 1–6 of Episode 1.

3. Ask the comprehension questions.

Answers: 1) Frank wants to sleep because he wants to write the next day, and Lucy is tired. 2) She goes to her cabin to see Christina. (Christina is not feeling well.) 3) Yes, they are. But they are also good friends. 4) She says she's intelligent, hardworking and attractive. 5) Agatha used to be a schoolteacher. She's retired. Her husband is dead. He left her some money so she doesn't have to work. She has no children. She lives in Vermont. She's happy. 6) He's a real estate agent. He's divorced. His two children live in Idaho. He went to college. He's handsome.

4. (Optional) Other possible questions. What does Frank want to do tomorrow? When are Robert and Lucy going to go swimming? Where does Agatha go before she has a drink with Robert? Why is she frightened when she returns? How is Christina? Why does Agatha say Robert is a good listener? What does Agatha mean when she says, "There's more to you than that, Robert"?

5. Have students close their books and relate the main points of the episode. Check their understanding of the story as they tell it. Correct any misunderstandings.

6. (Optional) Expansion questions. Do you usually need a good night's sleep? When you go out to a restaurant, for example, what do you usually drink? Do you think aunts and nieces (or uncles and nephews) can be good friends? Is Agatha unhappy because she has no children?

7. (Optional) Role-play. Students can role-play the first conversation, and then the dialogue between Agatha and Robert, using role cards as described in Episode 1.

MOON OF INDIA

 ## Episode Four

After dinner, Frank, Lucy, Robert and Agatha are having coffee in the lounge. Robert invites them for a drink.

"No thanks, Robert," says Frank. I have to write tomorrow, and I need a good night's sleep."

Then Lucy says, "I'm feeling a little tired, too." She gets up to leave with Frank and asks Robert, "What about a swim tomorrow?"

"OK, but not too early." Robert turns to Agatha, "What about you? Will you have a drink with me?"

"That would be very nice but first I want to see how my niece is."

"Oh yes, Christina. I hope she's feeling better."

"I think she was just a little tired this evening."

"What can I get you to drink?"

"Mineral water, thank you Robert. I usually don't drink very much."

Robert is waiting on deck outside the lounge for Agatha. He is standing in a dark corner. Agatha returns and he watches her walking along the deck towards the lounge.

"Here's your drink."

Agatha is frightened. "Oh Robert!" She knocks the glass in Robert's hands. "Oh, I'm sorry."

"Don't worry about it. It doesn't matter. How's Christina?"

"She's much better, thank you."

"I'm glad to hear that. She's very nice."

"She's a special young woman: intelligent and hardworking, and . . . attractive, Robert. We're good friends. Once a year we take a trip together in Europe—Italy, Spain or Greece."

"Now tell me about yourself, Agatha."

"My life isn't very interesting. I'm a retired schoolteacher. I live in a little house in Vermont."

"And your husband?"

"Edgar died more than twenty years ago."

"I'm sorry to hear that. Do you have any children?"

"No. I don't."

"That's too bad."

"Is it, Robert? I have a beautiful niece. She's like a daughter to me. And thanks to Edgar, I have plenty of money in my retirement. You see, I'm very happy. I don't usually talk about myself so much, Robert. You're a good listener. But what about you? Tell me about yourself."

"Robert Grant, age 35, college educated, divorced, two children in Idaho. Present occupation: real estate agent for Estrellas Properties, Costa del Sol, Spain. That's me."

"There's more to you than that, Robert, I'm sure."

Robert looks at Agatha and smiles a big smile.

"Christina was right," she thinks. "He's a very handsome man."

Comprehension Check

1. Why don't Lucy and Frank want to stay for a drink after dinner?
2. Where does Agatha go before she has a drink with Frank?
3. Are Agatha and Christina like mother and daughter?
4. How does Agatha describe Christina?
5. What do you know about Agatha now?
6. What do you know about Robert now?

UNIT 5

1. Excuse me? What did you say? I didn't hear you. Oh, yes, I knew James Dean very well. His parents were Mildred and Winton Dean. Jimmy was born right here in Marion, Indiana. That was in, uh, 1931. Times weren't good then. There were no jobs, and his parents didn't have much money. They moved to California in '35. Then Jimmy's mother died, and he came back to Indiana. He grew up in Fairmount, on his uncle's farm.

2. Jimmy and I were in school together. We graduated from Fairmount High in 1949. He didn't like school very much, but he liked sports, and he was good at them. You know, he wasn't especially good-looking. He was short and thin, and he wore glasses. But he had something. Maybe I was a little in love with him then. Later, the whole world was.

3. I met James Dean here in Hollywood in '49. I was in the movie *Giant,* too, but you probably don't remember me. I was never a star like Jimmy. He was a wonderful actor. He died too young. It was a car accident, on September 30, 1955. That was a long time ago, but I still remember him. A lot of people do.

UNIT 5

Unit Language Focus

GRAMMAR: simple past tense of *be* and other verbs (regular and irregular), past time expressions, *in/on* with dates, object pronouns, *what*-questions

COMMUNICATIVE AREAS: talking about past activities and events in people's lives, dates, describing people, asking someone to repeat something

OPENING CONVERSATION

New Words and Expressions

accident, be born, be good at, be in love, but, come back, didn't, die, especially, farm, glasses, good looking, graduate (*v.*), grow up, a long time ago, maybe, move, movie, much, probably, remember, September, short, sports, star, still, thin, uh, was/wasn't, were/weren't, wonderful

Names

James Dean /dʒéɪmz din/
Jimmy /dʒími/
Mildred /míldrəd/
Winton /wíntən/

Teaching Suggestions

1. Warm-up. Ask: *Who is James Dean?* If students know about him, ask, *What did he do? How did he die? What movies was he in?* (East of Eden, Rebel Without a Cause, Giant) *Have you seen them? Why is he famous?* If they do not know who he was, tell them briefly, just enough to identify him.

2. Personalize: *Who is your favorite movie actor or actress? What kind of movies do you like?*

3. Play/read the three interviews through once. Students look only at the pictures.

4. Play/read it again. Students read silently.

OR **4.** Play each interview separately and check comprehension of vocabulary after each one.

5. Teach new words and expressions, as needed.

6. Let students ask about grammar, vocabulary and pronunciation.

7. Students read/repeat the text line by line.

8. Point out the rising intonation of *Excuse me? What did you say?* Have the students do a quick practice in pairs. Ask one student to say something softly. Ask his or her partner to say: *Excuse me? What did you say?*

9. Ask: *Why does the first speaker say "I knew James Dean very well" and not "I know James Dean very well"?* Elicit

Because he is talking about the past; Because James Dean died; etc.

10. Write *Life Events* on the board. Under it write: *was/were born, grew up*
   Ask: *Can you find other examples in the text?*
   Ss: *moved, came back, graduated, died*
Explain the life events listed, as necessary, using yourself, your students or famous people as examples: For example, *I was born in India. Sami grew up in Morocco.*

11. Contrast *was born* and *died* (not *was died*).

12. Note the prepositions in *moved to, graduated from.*

Additional Information

General Notes

It is considered impolite in the U.S. to ask adults when they were born.

Grammar

1. All the verbs except *remember* are in the past tense. On this page there are several irregular pasts: *did, knew, were, was, grew up, came back, wore, had, met.*

2. The last line of the second interview is, *Later the whole world was.* "*Was in love with him,*" is understood here. The last line of the third interview is, *A lot of people do.* "*Do remember him,*" is understood.

Vocabulary and Usage

1. *Times weren't good* in 1931 because of the economic depression in the United States and around the world at that time.

2. In the second interview, the woman says, *He had something.* She means that he was not an ordinary person; he had something special, like a special talent.

3. In conversation, years are often referred to by their last two numbers, for example 1935 becomes *'35* (thirty-five).

4. James Dean is referred to as *Jimmy* by his childhood friends. *Jim* and *Jimmy* are short for *James.*

SPEAKING

EXERCISE 1 (whole class, pairs)

Language Focus

simple past tense of *be* and *do;* past forms of other verbs; *wh-* and *yes/no* questions with the simple past

New Words and Expressions

did (past auxiliary in questions)

Note: Questions beginning with *who* usually take the singular form of the verb. *Who was there? Mr. and Mrs. Jones.* (Exception: If the noun or pronoun following *be* is plural, the verb is plural. *Who were they? Mr. and Mrs. Jones.*)

Teaching Suggestions

First Interview (whole class, pairs)

1. Go over the first few question with the class. Then give students time to complete the questions themselves.

2. Have the students ask and answer the questions on their own. Encourage short answers, as they are more natural. For example:

    S1: *Who were James Dean's parents?*
    S2: *Mildred and Winton Dean.*

3. (Optional) Students think of other questions. For example: *When was James Dean born? Why weren't times good in 1931? When did James Dean move back to Indiana?*

Second and Third Interviews (pairs)

1. Get the students started by having them tell you some of the questions they could ask based on the second interview. For example: *When did James Dean graduate from high school? Did he like school? Did he like sports? What was he good at? Was he good-looking? Was he tall and thin? Did he wear glasses?*

2. Have them do the exercise in pairs. Tell the Bs to close their books. If they don't remember the answer, they should say: *I don't know.*

3. For the third interview ask students some of the questions they could ask. For example, *When did the speaker meet James Dean? Who was in the movie* Giant? *Who was a star? Was James Dean a good actor? When did he die? How did he die?* (In a car accident.)

4. Have them do the exercise in pairs. This time the As should close their books.

If You Have Time

1. Ask questions requiring students to make inferences; for example: *How old is the first speaker? Why did James Dean's parents move to California? Was James Dean a good student? Did he like Indiana?*

2. Ask: *James Dean died in 1955. How old was he?*

3. *Have the students tell you James Dean's story.*

EXERCISE 2 (pairs)

Language Focus

personal questions (*yes/no* and *wh-*) using past tense, *and/but*

Teaching Suggestions

First Part

1. Elicit the questions and possible answers from your students.

2. Students work in pairs and ask and answer these questions.

Second Part

3. When the students are finished, write on the board:
  + and +   − and −
  + but −   − but +
Below it, write:
  She liked school, and she liked sports.
    (Put a "plus" over each clause.)
  She didn't like school, and she didn't like sports.
    (Put a "minus" over each clause.)
  She liked school, but she didn't like sports.
    (Put a "+" over the first clause and a "−" over the second clause.)
  She didn't like school, but she liked sports.
    (Put a "−" over the first clause, and a "+" over the second.)

4. Ask a student, *Who was your partner?*
  S1: *Maria.*
(Point to the blackboard.)
  T: *What can you say about Maria?*
  S1: *She liked school, but she didn't like sports.*
  T: *Was she good at sports?*
  S1: *No.*
Do the same with one or more other students. Then erase the board.

5. Pairs join each other and report.

Workbook

You can now assign Exercises A and B.

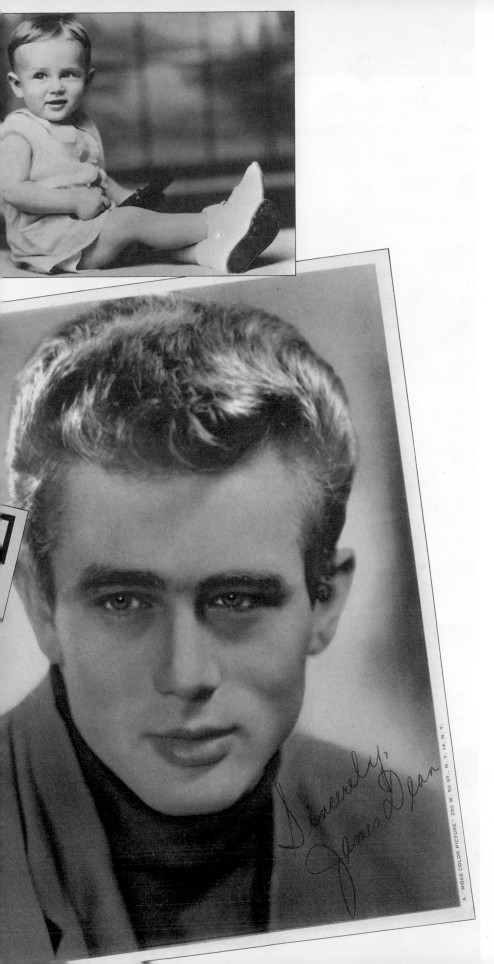

Speaking

1

- First Interview:
Complete these questions with *was,
were* or *did.* Then answer them.

1. Who .... James Dean's
parents?

2. Where .... he born?

3. .... times good in 1931?

4. .... his parents have much
money?

5. When .... they move to
California?

6. .... James Dean grow up in
Fairmount, Indiana?

- Second and Third Interviews:
A, ask B questions about the
information in the second interview.
B, ask A questions about the
information in the third interview.

2

- Ask your partner about his/her life.

A: Where .... you born?
B: In ....
A: .... you grow up there?
B: Yes, ...
    OR   No, ...
    I .... in ....
A: Where .... you go to high
    school?
B: ....
    OR   I'm still in high school.
A: .... like school?
B: ....
A: .... sports?
B: ....
A: .... good at them?
B: ....

- **A** and **B,** join another pair of
students. Tell them about your
partner. Use the information from
Exercise 2.

3

Movie Match

Which movies were these actors and actresses in? Ask questions with *was* and *were*.

A: Was/Were ___(actor or actors)___ in ___(movie)___?
B: Yes, ... was/were.
  OR No, ... wasn't/weren't. Try again!

A

1. Ask B which movies these actors and actresses were in.

   Actors and Actresses

   Barbra Streisand
   Meryl Streep and Robert Redford
   Arnold Schwarzenegger
   Humphrey Bogart and Katharine Hepburn
   Harrison Ford

   Movies

Out of Africa	*Raiders of the Lost Ark*
The Terminator	*The African Queen*
Funny Girl	

2. Answer B's questions.

   Back to the Future: Michael J. Fox
   Butch Cassidy and the Sundance Kid: Paul Newman and Robert Redford
   The Godfather: Marlon Brando
   Superman: Marlon Brando and Christopher Reeve
   Help!: The Beatles

B

1. Answer A's questions.

   Raiders of the Lost Ark: Harrison Ford
   Out of Africa: Meryl Streep and Robert Redford
   The Terminator: Arnold Schwarzenegger
   Funny Girl: Barbra Streisand
   The African Queen: Humphrey Bogart and Katharine Hepburn

2. Ask A which movies these actors and actresses were in.

   Actors

   Marlon Brando
   The Beatles
   Paul Newman and Robert Redford
   Marlon Brando and Christopher Reeve
   Michael J. Fox

   Movies

Butch Cassidy and the Sundance Kid	*Superman*
	Help!
The Godfather	*Back to the Future*

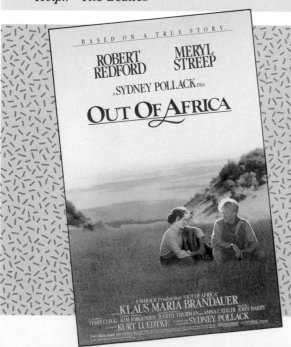

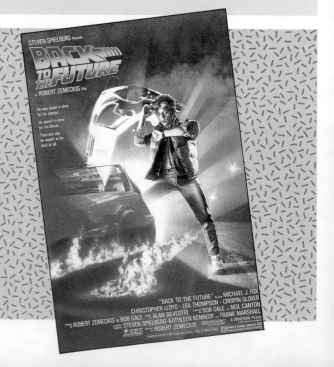

EXERCISE 3 (pairs)

Language Focus

yes/no questions with *was/were*

New Words and Expressions

match (*v.*), try (*v.*), which

Names

Barbra Streisand /bárbrə stráɪzænd/
Meryl Streep /mérəl strip/
Robert Redford /rábərt rédfərd/
Arnold Schwarzenegger /árnəld ʃwórtzənɛgər/
Humphrey Bogart /hʌ́mfri bógɑrt/
Katharine Hepburn /kǽθərin hépbərn/
Harrison Ford /hǽrɪsən fɔrd/
Marlon Brando /márlən brǽndo/
Beatles /bítəlz/
Paul Newman /pɔ́l númən/
Christopher Reeve /krístofər riv/
Michael Fox /máɪkəl fɑks/
Butch Cassidy /butʃ kǽsədi/

Teaching Suggestions

1. Have the students say the names after you.

2. Practice the model conversations, using movies and actors they all know. The first time, give the incorrect movie. The second time, give the correct movie. (Point out that the second time you used the pronoun instead of the actor's name.)

3. This is an information gap exercise. In order to make sure everyone understands the procedure, have two students model the exercise, using movies and actors they all know.

4. Have the students do the exercise in pairs. When they've finished, quiz them, using *who/which*. For example: *Which movie was Christopher Reeve in? Who was in* Out of Africa?

5. (Optional) Have students make up their own quiz, using movies and actors and actresses they know. They can put the actors and actresses in one column and the movies in another.

EPISODE 5 The Moon of India

Key Vocabulary

department, diamonds, disappeared, dive (*v.*), employees, Interpol, investigation, making progress, not sure, police captain, Princess of Aipur, swimming pool, swim suit, wedding present

Names

Barcelona /bɑrsəlónə/
Aipur /ɑípur/

Teaching Suggestions

1. Have students retell the story up to this point: Someone stole a famous necklace, the Moon of India, from the City Museum in New York. The police think the thief killed his/her partner and is traveling on the *Princess*, a ship. They put a police officer on the ship. We don't know who the thief is or who the police officer is. Christina Jordan, her aunt Agatha Jordan, Frank Adams, Lucy Cardozo and Robert Grant are passengers on the ship. They all sit at Table 5. They talk at dinner. Christina doesn't come to dinner. She's seasick. After dinner, Robert Grant invites the others for a drink. Frank and Lucy are too tired. Agatha says yes. First she goes to her cabin to see her niece. She comes back and talks with Robert. She's a retired schoolteacher. Every year, she and Christina take a trip together.

2. Follow steps 1–6 of Episode 1.

3. Ask the comprehension questions.

Answers: 1) The necklace is on the *Princess*. Richard's killer does have it. 2) They think they know, but they're not sure. 3) They think he wants to sell it to someone in Barcelona. 4) Yes, there is. 5) The Moon of India is a beautiful necklace. It has 45 perfect diamonds. It was a wedding present for the Princess of Aipur in 1771. It's worth four million dollars. 6) Yes, because she works at the City Museum.

4. (Optional) Other possible questions. Who is helping the police find the necklace and the killer? Is the necklace worth a lot of money?

5. Have students close their books and relate the main points of the episode. Check their understanding of the story as they tell it. Correct any misunderstandings.

6. (Optional) Role-play. Students can role-play the dialogue between the police captain and Lieutenant Vance, and the conversation on the deck, using role cards as described in Episode 1.

MOON OF INDIA

Episode Five

Back in New York at the police station. The police captain enters Lieutenant Washington's office. Washington is speaking to a newspaper reporter on the telephone. "The investigation is making progress. . . . I can't answer that question. Yes, we're working with Interpol. . . . Yes. . . . No. . . . Yes. . . . Goodbye." Turning to the Captain, "That was the tenth telephone call today."

"Progress on the investigation, I hear."

"Some. . . . We know that Richardson's killer and the Moon of India are on the ship. We think the killer wants to sell it when the *Princess* arrives in Marseilles."

"Who is the killer?"

"We think we know but we're not sure yet."

"We'd better find out soon. The museum wants the necklace back and I want to find the killer."

"We're doing our best, sir. We have one of our best officers on the ship."

Thousands of miles away on the ship, the sun is shining. Agatha, Christina, Frank and Robert are sitting around the swimming pool. Christina is reading a newspaper.

"This is very interesting," she says.

"What is, dear?" asks Agatha.

"The Moon of India is still missing from the City Museum."

"Christina works in the City Museum, Frank."

"Yes," replies Frank, "Christina told me yesterday that her specialty is Egyptian art."

"Do you know the Moon of India, Christina?" asks Robert.

"Yes, but it wasn't in my department, so I didn't see it often. Listen to this." She reads from the paper: "'The famous necklace disappeared from the City Museum the night of April 16. Museum employees discovered the loss early the next morning.' The police, it says, are working day and night."

"What does it say about the necklace?" asks Robert.

"Let's see." Christina reads from the paper again: "'The Moon of India has 45 perfect diamonds. It was a wedding present for the Princess of Aipur in 1771.'"

"Wow!" says Frank.

"The necklace is worth more than four million dollars."

"Four million dollars. That's a lot of money," says Frank.

"Yes," says Robert, "an incredible amount of money."

Lucy arrives in a swimsuit. "Let's go swimming!" She dives into the pool, followed by Robert.

Comprehension Check

1. Where is the necklace? Does Richardson's killer have it?
2. Who is the killer? Do the police know?
3. What do the police think the killer wants to do with the necklace?
4. Is there a police detective on the ship?
5. What do you know about the Moon of India?
6. Does Christina know the Moon of India?

U
N
I
T
6

Harry: Tom! How are you?

Tom: Harry, you look great! How's it going?

Harry: Not bad. It's good to see you. How's your family?

Tom: They're fine.

Harry: How are the kids?

Tom: Well, my boy Danny is taking a course in computers.

Harry: Is he still working at the grocery store?

Tom: Yes, but he wants to change jobs. He has a family now, and he needs to make more money. How about your children? What's Michael doing these days? Is he still living in California?

Harry: Not anymore. He moved to Oregon, and now he's raising sheep.

Tom: Raising sheep? How does he like it?

Harry: Well, it's hard work, but he really likes it.

Tom: And your daughter? She works in New York, right?

Harry: Paula usually works in New York, but she's working on a special project in D.C. this year.

UNIT 6

Unit Language Focus

GRAMMAR: present continuous, *still/anymore*, present
continuous contrasted with simple present, stative verbs
COMMUNICATIVE AREAS: informal greetings and good-
byes; asking about someone's family, work, and other
activities; describing what someone is wearing; talking
about college courses

OPENING CONVERSATION

New Words and Expressions

anymore, boy, college, course, grocery, make money,
project, raise, same here, sheep, special, take it easy, you
know

Names

Tom /tɑm/
Harry /hǽri/
Danny /dǽni/
Michael /mɑíkəl/
Paula /pɔ́lə/

Teaching Suggestions

1. Warm-up: *Where does this take place? Who are these
men? Are they friends? How old are they? Who are they
talking about? Are they married?*

2. Personalize. Ask: *Which picture would you like to be in?
(On a street corner? In a grocery store? In an office? In the
countryside? On a university campus?) Why?*

3. Play/read the conversation. Students look only at
pictures.

4. Play/read it again. Students listen again and read
silently.

5. Teach new words and expressions as needed.

6. Ask the students about the people in the pictures.
 T: *Who is this man?* (Point to Harry or Tom.) *What do
you know about him?* and so on.

7. Students can ask questions about the conversations.

8. Put this example from the conversation on the board:
*Paula usually works in New York, but she's working on a
special project in D.C. this year.* Underline *works* and *'s
working* and label them "simple present" and "present
continuous." Explain that simple present describes general
truths, habits and routines, while the present continuous
describes what's happening now. "Now" can be right this
minute (*Harry and Tom are talking*), or it can mean a
longer period of time (*Danny is taking a course in
computers*).

9. Have students find examples of the present continous in
the conversation and write them on the board. Ask which
refer to right now. (*She's probably waiting for me now*),
and which refer to an extended period (all the others).

10. On the board write: *He wants to change jobs. He
needs to make more money. He really likes it.*

 Explain in these examples that *want, need* and *like* are
talking about what is happening now, but they don't take
-ing. Some verbs in English don't occur in the present
continuous.

11. Students read/repeat the conversation.

12. (Optional) Harry's children live in different places in
the country. Lead your class in a discussion. Do children in
your country move away from the place where their parents
live? Tom's son wants to change jobs, and Harry's son
moved to Oregon and changed his job. Do people in your
country usually change jobs? How often? Harry's wife went
back to college. Do middle-aged people, especially
women, go back to college in your country?

13. (Optional) Divide students in small groups. Have each
group take the conversation about a different child and one
group take the part about Harry's wife. Using the model,
have them imagine different circumstances, jobs, etc., for
each person and rewrite the conversation accordingly. They
then present the new conversation to the class.

14. (Optional) Divide the students into small groups.
Have them expand the conversations to include talk about
Harry and Tom and about Tom's wife and daughter.

Additional Information

General Notes

In the United States it is common for people to move
several times in their adult lives and to change jobs several
times.

Grammar

1. Verbs such as *need, want, like* and *have* (which are
called stative verbs) are usually used to describe states of
being (e.g., *he has a family now; he really likes it*), rather
than specific actions that have beginnings and endings.
Therefore, even when they refer to a current situation, they
do not occur in the present continuous. (However, we say,
*I'm having breakfast. I'm having fun. Are you having any
problems?* In such cases, *have* refers to an action that
begins and ends, and thus has a different lexical meaning
from the stative *have.*)

2. The verbs *work, live,* and *raise* in the conversation
could actually occur in both the continuous and the simple
forms. *Is he still working at the grocery store?* could be,
*Does he still work at the grocery store? Is he still living in
California? He moved to Oregon and now he's raising
sheep,* could be, *Does he still live in California? He moved
to Oregon and now he raises sheep.*

(*continued*)

Present continuous is used for two reasons. First, it sets a more conversational tone because it conveys the sense of *currently.* These men are exchanging news about what is current about their families. Second, it implies that the conditions in question are subject to change; they do not have the permanence associated with the simple present.

Vocabulary and Usage

1. *You look great.* This could only be said among friends.

2. *My boy* is less formal than *my son; the kids* is less formal than either *the children,* or *your kids.*

3. *She works in New York, right?* Using *right* this way is a conversational way to check the correctness of one's statement. It is very informal and used among friends and equals.

4. *D.C.* stands for Washington, D.C. It's an abbreviation for *District of Columbia.* It is not a state.

5. *Take it easy* is a very casual way of saying good-bye.

Workbook

You can now assign Exercises A and B.

SPEAKING

EXERCISE 1 (whole class)

Language Focus

present continuous for immediate present, third-person singular, in questions and answers

New Words and Expressions

can, report, shelf, shop (*v.*), take a walk, watch (*n.*)

Teaching Suggestions

1. Have the students look at the pictures and cues. Use the illustrations in the opening conversation as well, to reinforce the new words.

2. Ask the questions in the exercise. Make sure everyone understands the model. Then you begin, and your students take over.

    T: *What's Danny doing?*
    S1: *Putting cans on the shelf. What's the customer doing?*
    S2: *Shopping. What's Michael doing?*
        And so on.

3. For further contrast of the simple and continuous forms, ask what each person does and is doing. For example,

    T: *What does Danny do?*
    S1: *He works in a grocery store.*
    T: *What's he doing?*
    S2: *He's putting cans on the shelf.*

EXERCISE 2 (pairs)

Language Focus

present continuous for immediate present, third-person singular, in questions and answers; talking about what people are wearing

New Words and Expressions

apron, blouse, boot, dress, hat, high-heeled shoes, jacket, jeans, leather, pants, shirt, sneakers, suit, sweater, tan (*adj.*), tie

Teaching Suggestions

1. Teach the new words as needed by using the illustration or items in the classroom.

2. Point out that a suit for a man is a matching jacket and pants; for a woman it is a matching jacket and skirt. A matching jacket and pants for a woman is called a *pantsuit.*

3. Remind students to use *a* before singular nouns and no article before plural nouns *(shoes, boots, sneakers).*

4. Ask questions about your students' clothing: *Who's wearing (brown boots, a blue dress, etc.)?*

5. Have students do the exercise in pairs.

6. (Optional) Have students ask questions about the pictures, using *who.* For example, S1: *Who's wearing boots?* S2: *Michael.*

7. (Optional) Have students ask each other questions about what they are wearing. For example:

    T: *What's* .... *wearing?*
    S1: ....
    S2: *What's* .... *wearing?*
    S3: .... and so on.

Tom: And your wife?
Harry: Well, she's fine. She went back to college, you know, and now . . . I'd better go! She's probably waiting for me right now.
Tom: OK. It was really good seeing you.
Harry: Same here. Take it easy.

Speaking

1

Look at the pictures. Ask and answer questions about what people are doing.

Danny

A: What's Danny doing?
B: Putting cans on the shelf.

1. Danny
2. the customer
3. Michael
4. Paula
5. Harry's wife

---

wait for Harry, look at her watch
write a report
shop
put cans on the shelf
take a walk

2

Look at the pictures. Ask and answer questions about what people are wearing.

Tom

A: What's Tom wearing?
B: A brown jacket and tan pants.

1. Tom
2. Harry's wife
3. Paula
4. Michael
5. Danny
6. the customer
7. Harry

---

skirt	suit
blouse	tie
sweater	jacket
dress	high-heeled shoes
pants	sneakers
jeans	boots
shirt	hat
apron	

3

A, study the picture of Annie. **B**, study the picture of James. **A**, close your book. **B**, ask A "What's Annie wearing?" **B**, close your book. **A**, ask B "What's James wearing?"

4

A, you're packing for a trip to Alaska. **B**, you're packing for a trip to Hawaii.

● Look at James' and Annie's clothes. Ask and answer questions like these:

A: Do you need a sun hat?
B: Yes, I do.
A: Do you need a jacket?
B: No, I don't.

● Summarize your lists: I need to take . . . .

5

Culture Capsule

In general, Americans like to dress casually. They don't like to wear very formal clothes. In some other countries, people dress formally.

What do teachers in your country usually wear in the classroom?
What do people usually wear in a restaurant?
What do people usually wear in a supermarket?
What do you usually wear in a restaurant? In a supermarket?

6

Do You Remember?

● Describe your partner's clothes. Begin: You're wearing . . .

● **A**, does B remember what you're wearing? Ask questions. **B**, don't look at A. Answer his or her questions.

A: Am I wearing black shoes?
B: Yes, you are.   OR   No, you're not. You're wearing brown shoes.
A: You're right.   OR   Try again!

EXERCISE 3 (pairs)
Language Focus

same as 2

New Words and Expressions

bathing suit, sandals, sunglasses, sun hat, T-shirt, wool

Names

Annie /ǽni/
James /dʒeɪmz/

Teaching Suggestions

1. Use the illustration or articles in the classroom to teach the new words, as needed.

Say the names of the different articles of clothing and have the students point to the illustration as they repeat after you. *Sun hat, bathing suit, gloves, wool hat, sunglasses, T-shirt, wool pants, sandals.*

2. Students work in pairs. Tell them, *You have 30 seconds to study your picture.* After 30 seconds, tell the As: *As Close your books. Bs, ask the As, What's Annie wearing?* After the As have finished, the Bs get a chance to answer. Ask: *Who remembered everything?*

EXERCISE 4 (role-play, pairs)
Language Focus

Simple present of stative verbs: *need, need to*

New Words and Expressions

clothes, summarize

Teaching Suggestions

1. Ask the students: *Is Alaska warm? (No, it's cold!) Is Hawaii warm? (Yes, it is.)*

2. Do one example with them. Then have the students work in pairs and do the exercise. Remind them to summarize their lists after asking and answering the questions.

3. When they have finished, ask the As: *What do you have on your list?* Ask the Bs: *What do you have on your list?*

4. (Optional) Ask students: *When you pack for a vacation, what do you usually take?*

EXERCISE 5 Culture Capsule (whole class)
Culture Focus

American preference for casual clothes

New Words and Expressions

casually, dress (*v.*), formal, in general, running shoes, shorts, supermarket, sweatshirt

Teaching Suggestions

1. Teach new words and expressions, as needed.

2. Have students read the capsule silently.

3. Point to the pictures and ask the students, *What is he/she wearing?*

4. Ask and answer the questions. If your students are multinational, discuss the differences.

5. (Optional) Ask the students, *In general, what do you think of the American style of dressing?*

EXERCISE 6 Do You Remember? (pairs)
Language Focus

present continuous for immediate present, first- and second-person singular

New Words and Expressions

shoes

Teaching Suggestions

1. Have each student take a partner. Tell students to describe what their partner is wearing. (Find out if they need any other clothing vocabulary and supply it.)

2. Demonstrate the second part with a student. Face away from each other and ask: *Am I wearing ....?*

3. Have students do the same.

EXERCISE 7 (role-play, pairs)
Language Focus

present continuous for extended present; stative verb: *like*; talking about; school courses

New Words and Expressions

anthropology, biology, chemistry, child, composition, economics, history, instructor, principle, psychology, register (*v.*), title

Names

Henderson /héndərsən/
Michaels /máíkəlz/
Jones /dʒonz/
Gates /geɪts/
Sage /seɪdʒ/
Fantini /fæntíni/
Moran /mɔrǽn/
Stern /stərn/
Silverman /sílvərmən/

Teaching Suggestions

1. Ask warm-up questions: *You are in your English course. Are you taking other courses? What? When? Who are your teachers?* Have them look at the course list in the book.

2. Teach new words as needed.

3. Explain the course list. The numbers on the side represent course number and section number; for example: *English 101-01* is *English 101, section 1. English 101* is Composition. It meets on Mondays, Wednesdays and Fridays, from 10 A.M. to 10:55 A.M. The instructor is Professor Henderson. (We don't know from reading the schedule if the instructor is a man or a woman.) The class meets in Room 265.

4. Go over the pronunciation of the instructors' names with the students.

5. Ask: *What is English 102?* (Introduction to Literature.) *When does it meet?* (Mondays, Wednesdays and Fridays, from 11:00 to 11:55 in the morning.) *Who is the instructor?* (Professor Michaels.) *Where does the class meet?* (Room 265.) *What is Science 205?* and so on.

6. Divide the class into two sections. Read the instructions in the book. Make sure that students understand they are to choose one more course from the course list. They should also write down the name of the instructor.

7. Have the students fill in the schedule with one more course. Circulate to make sure they are doing this correctly.

8. After they have filled in the schedule, write on the board:

　　How do you like ....?
　　A lot.　　　　　*It's OK.*　　　　　*Not very much.*

9. Ask the As: *How do you like your chemistry course?* Tell them to choose one of the answers. There is no right or wrong answer. *A lot? It's OK? Not very much?* Ask the Bs: *How do you like your European History course? A lot? It's OK? Not very much?*

10. Have two students model the conversation.

11. Have the class do the second part of the exercise in pairs.

Note: The academic year in American universities is usually divided into quarters (*fall, winter, spring* and *summer*) or semesters (*fall, spring,* and *summer semesters* or *terms*). The academic year traditionally starts in September, although in large universities, students can start their courses in any quarter or semester.

12. (Optional) Ask students: *When does the academic year start in your country/countries? What are the course requirements in high school and college?*

Workbook

You can now assign Exercises C–F.

7

	Title of Course	Days	Times	Room	Instructor
English					
101-01	English Composition	MWF	10:00-10:55am	265	Henderson
102-01	Intro to Literature	MWF	11:00-11:55am	265	Michaels
Science					
205-02	Biology	MWF	10:00-10:55am	161	Jones
201-01	Principles of Chemistry	MWF	1:00-1:55pm	160	Gates
Social Sciences					
221	Child Psychology	MWF	2:30-3:30pm	270	Sage
101-01	Intro to Anthropology	MW	3:00-4:20pm	156	Fantini
201-01	Principles of Economics	MWF	10:00-10:55am	151	Moran
201-02	Principles of Economics	T Th	5:00-6:20pm	151	Moran
History					
901-03	European History	T Th	1:00-1:20pm	220	Stern
869-01	History of Mexico	MWF	11:00-11:55am	266	Silverman

Intro = introduction

- **A** and **B**, you're registering for your classes. You each need one more course in your schedule. Look at the course list above, and add one more course to your schedule.

- It's a month later. Have conversations like this:

A: What courses are you taking?
B: I'm taking European History, Biology and ....
A: How do you like your history course?
B: A lot. OR It's OK. OR Not very much.
A: Who's teaching it?
B: ....
A: How do you like ....?
B: ....

A's schedule

	MON	TUES	WED	THURS	FRI
AM					
PM	1-1:55 CHEMISTRY RM 160 Prof GATES / 2:30-3:30 CHILD PSYCHOLOGY RM 270 SAGE		1-1:55 CHEM / 2:30-3:30 CHILD PSYCH		1-1:55 CHEM / 2:30-3:30 CHILD PSYCH

B's schedule

	MON	TUES	WED	THURS	FRI
AM	10-10:55 BIOLOGY RM 161 PROF JONES		10-10:55 BIOLOGY		10-10:55 BIO
PM		1-2:20 EUROPEAN HISTORY PROF STERN RM 220		1-1:20 HISTORY	

8

A and B, you are classmates. A, ask B about the biology and history classes. B, ask A about the chemistry and psychology classes. Use the information from the course list on page 44 and the schedule changes below to answer.

			SCHEDULE CHANGES THIS WEEK		
201-01	Principles of Chemistry	T Th	10:00-11:20	Hawkinson
221-01	Child Psychology	M F	5:00-6:20	Freeman
205-02	Biology	M F	5:00-6:20	Stanley
901-03	European History	M W	3:00-4:20	Millett

biology

A: You know, I'd like to go to your biology class some time. When does it meet?
B: Well, it usually meets on Mondays, Wednesdays and Fridays from 10:00 to 10:55, but this week it's meeting on Monday and Friday from 5:00 to 6:20 in the evening.
A: Where does it meet?
B: Room 161.
A: Who's teaching it?
B: Well, Professor Jones usually teaches it, but this week Professor Stanley is teaching it.
A: Hmm, maybe this isn't a good week to go.

9

● Have conversations like this:

A: What's Mary doing these days? Is she still studying Spanish?
B: Not anymore. Now she's studying Japanese.
A: Studying Japanese?
B: Yes, she wants to travel to Japan.

A, ask questions as in the example.

Mary	live in New York
Peter	study Spanish
John	work as a waiter
Kate	work at the grocery store

B, use this information to answer A's questions.

look for another job	make more money
study Japanese	learn Spanish
live in Mexico	• be an accountant
study accounting	travel to Japan

● A and B, ask each other these questions. Give true answers.

Are you taking any courses? What courses are you taking? When do they meet? How do you like them?

Do you work? What hours do you work? What do you usually do at work? Are you working on any special projects?

10

Pronunciation

Practice this conversation. Ask the questions with real interest.

A: _____(Name)_____! How are you?
B: I'm fine, thanks, _____(Name)_____ How're you?
A: OK. How's your family?
B: Everybody's fine. Yours?
A: Great. How're the kids?
B: Well, my son has a new job.
A: How does he like it?

11

Put It Together

A and B, on a separate piece of paper, write down the information about your life three years ago. Give your partner the piece of paper.

Look at the information about your partner. You haven't seen your partner in three years. You meet again. Find out about your partner.

A: _____(Name)_____! It's good to see you! How are you?
B: I'm fine, thanks _____(Name)_____ How are you? Are you still living in _____?
A: _____.

3 Years Ago

Residence:

Job:

Activities:

Information about family:

EXERCISE 8 (role-play, pairs)
Language Focus

contrasting simple present (habitual) with present continuous (current)

New Words and Expressions

classmate, professor

Names

Hawkinson /hɔ́kɪnsən/
Freeman /frímən/
Stanley /stǽnli/
Millett /mílət/

Teaching Suggestions

1. Have the students study the schedule changes.

2. Have them check or circle the changes that apply to their schedule.

3. Go over the pronunciation of the names.

4. Have two students model the conversation in the book.

5. Ask: *Why shouldn't A go this week?* Ask: *Now, what will B ask A about?* (chemistry)

6. Have the students do the exercise in pairs. Have the As ask the Bs about biology, and the Bs ask the As about chemistry.

7. Have the students switch partners. Have the As ask the Bs about history, and the Bs ask the As about psychology.

8. (Optional): Write: *It usually meets* ...., *but this week it's meeting* .... Ask students if they can think of a temporary change in their lives. Give an example about yourself: *I usually drive to work, but this week I'm taking a taxi;* or *I usually watch* .... *on TV, but this month I'm watching* .... Write students' examples on the board, using the pattern above.

9. (Optional) Lead the class in a discussion of visiting policy in college classes in their country. (In the U.S., students generally don't need permission to visit large lecture classes, but they do need the professor's permission to visit smaller classes.)

EXERCISE 9 (role-play, pairs)
Part One
Language Focus

present continuous, third-person singular; *still/anymore*; stative verb: *want*

New Words and Expressions

accountant, accounting

Teaching Suggestions

1. Have students study the conversation.

2. Have two students model the conversation. Go over the example, and if necessary, show how it is derived from A's and B's columns below.

3. Have students study the cues and think about how they connect.

4. Have students do the exercise. Remind them to take turns as A and B.

5. Teach new words as needed.

Part Two
Language Focus

contrasting simple present with present continuous in talking about one's school or work

Teaching Suggestions

1. Model an example of a question and answer with a student. Have the students do the exercise in pairs. Circulate and check if they need any help with vocabulary or self-expression. Give them enough time to answer the questions in as much detail as possible.

2. When they have finished, ask if they needed any words they didn't know. List new vocabulary on the board.

3. (Optional) If your students are college students, you could have them do an informal survey of the most popular courses.

EXERCISE 10 (pairs)
Language Focus

intonation of questions and answers in informal conversation

New Words and Expressions

everybody

Teaching Suggestions

1. Read the conversation aloud.

2. Have students repeat each line after you. Encourage the students to speak with feeling.

3. Draw attention to the difference in stress and intonation between *How are you?* in the first line and *How're you?* in the second. Point out that *yours* in the fourth line means *your family.*

4. Have students practice the conversation chorally, paying close attention to stress and intonation.

5. Have students practice the conversation in pairs, taking turns as A and B.

6. Finally, have students practice the conversation one more time, this time picking up speed.

(*continued*)

Workbook

You can now assign Exercises G and H.

EXERCISE 11 Put It Together (pairs)

Language Focus

present continuous first-, second-, third-person singular; *still/anymore*

New Words and Expressions

activity, residence

Teaching Suggestions

1. Students read the instructions.

2. Explain, as necessary, *residence* (where you live).

3. Have students brainstorm ideas about possible activities and list them; for example: *sports, hobbies, clubs, courses,* etc.

4. Elicit from students types of information they can give about their families: wife's/husband's job, what sons/daughters are doing, where they are living, etc.

5. On the board, write true information about yourself three years ago: your residence, your job, your activities, and information about your family.

6. Have the students ask you questions about your life three years ago and your life now, using the patterns: *Are you still ....? (Is your husband/wife still ....?)* and so on.

7. Have a student role-play the beginning of the conversation with you.

8. Have the students write down information about themselves on a separate piece of paper, just as you did on the board. Tell them that they can give true information or they can make up information if they want to. Circulate and help them with vocabulary they might need. Remind them to refer to the Checklist if necessary.

9. Students give the information to their partner.

10. They have the conversation.

11. When they have finished, find out if they have any questions about the exercise.

CHECKLIST

Teaching Suggestions

1. See the general suggestions on the Checklist page in Unit 1.

2. (Optional) Make statements or ask questions about the people in the class, using the present continuous and *still/anymore*. Have students use the patterns on the Checklist page as guides.

3. (Optional) From time to time, you may wish to have students review the Checklist part by part, and then quiz them orally in class, with books open or closed. For example:

T: *You're talking to a friend. You want to ask about your friend's family. What do you say?*

Ss: *How's your family?* or *How're your kids?*

T: *You finish talking to your friend. You want to say good-bye. What can you say?*

Ss: *It was really good seeing you,* and so on.

I know how to . . .

USE THESE FORMS

☐ **Present Continuous Tense**

| I | am ('m)
'm not | working |

| he
she
it | is ('s)
isn't | working |

| you
we
they | are ('re)
aren't | working |

questions

What's she wearing?
Are you working at the bank?

short answers

Yes, I am.   No, I'm not.

statements

She's wearing a brown leather jacket.
Danny is taking a course in computers.

The present continuous is used for action happening right now.

What's she wearing?

It is also used for action over an "extended" present time.

What are you doing these days?

Some verbs don't usually take the continuous: be, have, like, need, want.

He likes to speak Japanese.
NOT ~~He's liking~~ to speak Japanese.

The present continuous contrasts with the simple present.

He usually works in D.C., but this year he's working in Boston.

☐ **Still/Anymore**

question

Is he still living in California?

statements

He's still working at the grocery store.
(He's) not (living in California) anymore.

USE ENGLISH TO

☐ **greet someone informally**

Tom! How are you?
Harry, you look great! How's it going?
Not bad. It's good to see you.

☐ **ask about someone's family**

How's your family? How are the kids?/And your husband?
They're/He's fine.

☐ **ask about someone's activities**

What's Michael doing these days?
He's raising sheep.
Raising sheep? How does he like it?

☐ **say goodbye informally**

It was really good seeing you.
Same here. Take it easy.

☐ **talk about these subjects**

clothes   college courses   work   activities

☐ **UNDERSTAND THESE EXPRESSIONS**

How does (he) like (it)?
It's good to see you.
It's hard work.

change jobs
go back to college
make money
pack for a trip
take a course in . . .
work on a special project

CHECKLIST

🔊 Listening

1

Alice is a stranger. She doesn't know the people at the party. Dennis knows some of the people at the party. Listen to this conversation between Alice and Dennis. Match the people in the picture with the names below.

1. Monica ___   2. Joe ___   3. Joan ___   4. Melanie ___

5. Mark ___   6. Fred ___   7. Sue ___   8. Jessica ___

2

Complete the conversations. Choose *a* or *b*.

1. a. Not anymore.
   b. He really likes it.

2. a. Because she wants to change jobs.
   b. She's probably studying.

3. a. Yes, she does.
   b. Very much.

4. a. Yes, I am.
   b. Yes, I do.

5. a. No, he isn't.
   b. Yes, he does.

6. a. On Tuesdays and Fridays.
   b. Not very much.

7. a. She usually eats lunch at 12:00.
   b. She's probably eating lunch.

8. a. Yes, I do.
   b. No, I don't.

3

Give true answers.

1. _____

2. _____

3. _____

4. _____

LISTENING

EXERCISE 1

Language Focus

present continuous second- and third-person singular, talking about what people are wearing

Names

Joan /dʒon/
Fred /frɛd/
Sue /su/
Melanie /méləni/
Joe /dʒo/
Monica /mánıkə/
Mark /mɑrk/
Jessica /dʒésıkə/

Teaching Suggestions

1. Point to a person in the illustration and have the students describe that person. For example: *She's wearing a yellow blouse. He's sitting on the sofa. He's wearing brown pants and glasses. He has blond hair. She's tall,* and so on.

2. Go over the pronunciation of the names so that students know what to listen for.

3. Play the cassette or read the tapescript.

4. Students listen and write the correct letter next to each person's name.

5. Ask: *Which one is Joan?* (*She's wearing* ....) *Which one is Fred?* and so on.

Answers: 1. Monica F   2. Joe E   3. Joan A   4. Melanie H
5. Mark J   6. Fred B   7. Sue G   8. Jessica K

EXERCISE 2

Language Focus

review of present continuous, *still/anymore*, talking about school courses, activities, clothes

New Words and Expressions

because, lunch

Teaching Suggestions

1. Play the cassette or read the tapescript.

2. Students listen and circle the correct response.

3. Check their answers. If there is disagreement, have them listen again.

4. Listen another time. After each segment, have the students respond chorally with the correct response.

Answers: 1. a   2. a   3. b   4. b   5. a   6. a   7. b
8. b

EXERCISE 3

Language Focus

personal questions based on the language covered in the unit

Teaching Suggestions

1. Play the cassette or read the tapescript.

2. Students listen and answer the questions.

3. Ask students what the questions were.

Answers: Since answers are personal, they will vary for each student.

EPISODE 6 The Moon of India

Key Vocabulary

decide, detective, get ready, menu, painting, waiter

Teaching Suggestions

1. Have students retell the story up to this point: Someone stole a famous necklace, the Moon of India, from the City Museum in New York. The police think the thief killed his/her partner and is traveling on the *Princess,* a ship. They put a police officer on the ship. We don't know who the thief is or who the police officer is. Christina Jordan, her aunt Agatha Jordan, Frank Adams, Lucy Cardozo and Robert Grant are passengers on the ship. They all sit at Table 5. They talk at lunch and dinner. Back in New York, Lt. Washington talks to his boss. Interpol (international police) is helping them. The Moon of India and the thief are on the ship. The police think the thief wants to sell the necklace in Barcelona. The next morning on the ship, Christina reads about the Moon of India in the newspaper to the others.

2. Follow steps 1–4 of Episode 1.

3. Students read the episode again.

4. Ask the comprehension questions.

Answers: 1) Frank is happy because he did some good work on his book that afternoon. 2) He wants to write a story about a famous necklace like The Moon of India. It's stolen, and the thief brings it onto a ship and wants to sell it at one of the ship's ports of call. A detective is on the ship. 3) Because each time you look at the dark places in a picture, you see more. 4) His glasses. Frank left his glasses in the Jordans' cabin. 5) Robert Grant.

5. (Optional) Another possible question. Do you think Frank knows that the Moon of India is on the ship?

6. Have students close their books and relate the important points of the episode. Check their understanding of the story as they tell it. Correct any misunderstandings.

7. (Optional) Expansion questions. Frank says, "A good mystery is like a painting." Do you agree with him? What are the dark parts of this story?

 Episode Six

It is the next evening. Agatha and Christina are getting ready for dinner. Christina is looking in the mirror, trying to decide which necklace to wear. There is a knock at the door. It's Frank.

"Are you ladies ready for dinner?"

"Come in, Frank. We'll be ready in a minute."

"Take your time, the night is young."

"You're happy tonight, Frank," says Christina.

"Yes, I did some good work on my book this afternoon."

"Really? Tell us about it."

"Well, you know, that Moon of India story gave me the idea. I'm going to write a story about a famous necklace that is stolen from a museum. The thief takes the necklace on a ship and plans to sell it at one of the ship's ports, but can't because . . . guess why!"

"The police know what's happening," Christina guesses.

"Right. There's a detective on the ship."

Christina asks him, "What happens next?"

Frank walks over to a painting on the cabin wall. "I don't know yet. A good mystery is like a painting. Large parts of it are very dark. But when we look at the painting a second, a third, a fourth time, we see more. When you read a detective story, you need to look into the dark; slowly you begin to see the story."

The dining room is full of people. People are talking and laughing. Waiters are pouring water and bringing large menus to every table. At table five, Frank remembers that he left his glasses in the Jordan's cabin.

"I'll go back and get them for you," offers Christina.

"No, please, you stay here," says Frank, "I'll go and get them."

"OK, here's the key to the room."

Frank walks quickly to the Jordan's cabin, unlocks the door, goes in and gets his glasses. In a hurry to get back to the dining room, he forgets to close the door when he goes out. A few minutes later, Robert Grant comes to the door of the Jordan's cabin. The door is open and he goes inside. A purser watches him go in.

"Christina? Agatha? Anybody home? Hello?"

The purser hears him and enters the room.

"Can I help you, Sir?"

"The door was open," Robert

begins to explain. "I thought they were here."

"I think they are in the dining room, sir."

"Thank you."

"Good evening, sir."

They leave the cabin.

Comprehension Check

1. Why is Frank happy?
2. What is his idea for a story?
3. Why is reading a good mystery like looking at a painting?
4. What did Frank leave in the Jordans' cabin?
5. Who goes into the cabin after Frank?

EPISODE 7 The Moon of India

Key Vocabulary

cafe, contact (*v.*), restaurant, suspect (*v.*), telex

Names

Marseilles /mɑrseí/

Teaching Suggestions

1. Have students retell the last few episodes: The police know that the Moon of India and the thief are on the *Princess.* A police officer is also on the ship. We don't know who they are. Christina Jordan reads about the Moon of India in the newspaper to the others. She's very interested in it because she works at the City Museum. Frank Adams, a mystery writer, is writing a story like the Moon of India. He tells Christina and Agatha about it. At dinner, he goes back to their cabin to get his glasses. Robert Grant also goes to their cabin.

2. Follow steps 1–6 of Episode 1.

3. Ask the comprehension questions.

Answers: 1) The thief. He or she is going to meet someone in Barcelona and is going to call a number in Barcelona. 2) They're going to go to the museum and maybe do some shopping. 3) He's going to contact his office, and then he's going to walk around Barcelona with Lucy. 4) No, she's going to spend the afternoon with him. 5) He wants to stay on the ship and write, because his writing is going well. 6) The police officer. The officer wanted to find the necklace.

4. (Optional) Other possible questions. Was the thief going to meet someone in Marseilles? Who do you think the thief is? Why? Is Barcelona an interesting city? Would you like to go there?

5. Have students close their books and relate the important points of the episode. Check their understanding of the story as they tell it. Correct any misunderstandings.

6. (Optional) Role-play. Students can role-play the dialogues between the thief and the person in Marseilles, and the conversation in the lounge, using role cards as described in Episode 1.

MOON OF INDIA

 ## Episode Seven

Later that evening, someone on the ship makes a phone call to Marseilles.

"Can we meet in Barcelona tomorrow?"

"Barcelona tomorrow? Why? Why not here in Marseilles?"

"Someone was in my room today. I think they're watching me."

"What?"

"Don't worry. They didn't find the necklace. Look, do you want it or not?"

"What time do you arrive in Barcelona?"

"At eight o'clock tomorrow morning."

"All right. In Barcelona, call this number: 223-338."

Back in the lounge, Christina, Agatha, Lucy, Frank and Robert are having a drink.

"What do you want to do in Barcelona tomorrow, Aunt Agatha?"

"We can go to the museum, and maybe do some shopping later."

"What about you, Lucy?"

"I'm going to visit one of the fashion houses in the morning."

"And what about you, Frank?" asks Christina.

"I'm going to stay on the boat."

"Really? Why, Frank?" Lucy asks.

"I don't want to leave the book for a whole day. The writing's going well at the moment."

"Robert, you know Barcelona. Tell Frank how much there is to see."

"Well, there really is a lot—beautiful buildings, gardens, cafes, shops, restaurants, museums . . ."

"Sounds interesting. What are you going to do, Robert?"

"I have to contact my office about some houses near here. In the afternoon, Lucy and I are going to walk around."

"Frank, please come," Christina says. "Maybe you'll get some ideas for your book, and . . ."

"I'm too busy, really."

"Oh, Frank," says Agatha. "Come with us. We'll have a good time and you can explain to us the mysterious meanings of the paintings in the museum."

"All right, I'll go."

Meanwhile, in New York, Lieutenant Washington receives a telex.

"NECKLACE NOT IN ROOM/ SHIP STOPS IN BARCELONA TOMORROW/SUSPECT MAY TRY TO SELL IT THERE/WE NEED TO ACT SOON."

Washington says to his assistant, "So the necklace wasn't in the room. The suspect may try to sell it in Barcelona. We'd better contact Interpol."

Comprehension Check

1. Who makes a phone call to Marseilles? What is going to happen in Barcelona?
2. What are Christina and Agatha going to do in Barcelona?
3. What's Robert going to do?
4. Is Lucy going to spend the whole day with Robert?
5. At first, Frank doesn't want to leave the ship. Why?
6. Who searched the suspect's room? Why?

UNIT 8

Y: Hello, X?
X: Speaking.
Y: This is Y. I'm going to fly to Amsterdam next Monday. I'm going to stay at the Park Hotel. On Tuesday morning I'm going to meet you in the restaurant. We're going to begin Operation Eagle.
X: Very good. See you Tuesday.

Woman: Hello.
Control: Hello. Is 001 there?
Woman: Just a minute, please.
001: Hello.
Control: Hello, 001. This is Control. Could you come to my office right away? Enemy Agents X and Y are going to begin Operation Eagle next week. We need to stop them.
001: What are we going to do?
Control: I'm not sure yet.

Control: All right. Let's go over your assignments. Agent 001, what are you going to do next Monday?
001: At 6:30 AM I'm going to get to the airport. I'm going to drop off a package for 003 at the customs desk. Then at 7:05 AM I'm going to get on Y's plane and follow him to Amsterdam.
Control: 002?
002: I'm going to pick Agent 001 up at the airport in Amsterdam at 8:30 AM. We're going to follow Y to his hotel.
Control: Agent 003?
003: On Monday evening I'm going to pick up a package at the customs desk. Then I'm going to fly to Amsterdam. I'm going to check into Y's hotel. I'm going to put on my disguise there. Then I'm going to turn off the power at 10:00 PM.
Control: And then?
001, 002, 003: We're going to stop Operation Eagle.

UNIT 8

Unit Language Focus

GRAMMAR: *going to* (future), future time expressions, separable and inseparable two- and three-word verbs
COMMUNICATIVE AREAS: asking for someone on the telephone formally and informally, taking telephone messages, talking about future plans, activities at home, on the weekend, vacations

OPENING CONVERSATION

New Words and Expressions

agent, airport, Amsterdam, assignment, check into, customs, desk, disguise (*v.*), drop off, eagle, enemy, fly, follow, get on, get to, go over, just a minute, operation, package, park, pick up, plane (airplane), power, put on, "Speaking" (answer to "Is this so-and-so?"), stop, turn off, yet

Names

001 / o o wán/

Teaching Suggestions

1. Warm-up. Describe the picture: *Two spies are talking on the phone. The spies are having a meeting.* . . . (If necessary, explain *spy* by reference to James Bond.)

2. Personalize: *Do you read books or watch movies about spies? Which ones? Who is your favorite spy?*

3. Play/read the conversation. Students look only at pictures.

4. Play/read it again. Students listen and read silently.

5. Teach new words and expressions as necessary.

6. Have students read the conversation again and let them ask any questions they have about it.

7. Ask: *Who's speaking in the first conversation? Who are Agent X and Agent Y?* (spies; enemies of Control, 001) *Who's speaking in the second conversation? Who is Control?* (001, 2 and 3's boss) *Who is the woman?* (001's wife) *Who's speaking in the third conversation?* (Control, 001, 002 and 003—the "good guys") *What is Operation Eagle?* (we don't know)

8. (Optional) Use the picture to review clothing. Point to each person and ask students to tell you what he or she is wearing.

9. On the board write:

	Monday		Tuesday
Y		(2)	morning (1)
001	6:30 A.M.	(2)	
	7:05 P.M.	(1)	
002	8:30 A.M.	(2)	
003	evening	(3)	
	10:00 P.M.	(1)	

(The numbers in parentheses refer to the numbers of things each agent will do at that time.)

Ask questions about the text. For example: *What's Y going to do on Monday? On Tuesday? What's 001 going to do on Monday at 6:30 A.M.? What's he going to do at 7:05?*

10. Ask other questions about the text: *What's 001 going to drop off at the airport? Who's going to pick it up? What's in the package? Do we know? Who's going to follow Y to Amsterdam? Who's going to follow Y to his hotel?* And so on.

11. Students read/repeat the conversations.

Additional Information

Grammar

1. *Be going to + verb* is used for two purposes. First, for something planned or already decided, as in the conversation on this page; second, for something observable, for which there is evidence, as in Exercise 4. (The modal *will*, while sometimes interchangeable with *going to*, is characteristically used for exerting one's will; for example, making a decision [see Exercise 6], a promise, or a threat.)

2. *the:* In *I'm going to meet you in the restaurant, the* is used because both speakers know which restaurant it is.

Pronunciation and Stress

1. When spoken alone or with a pronoun between the verb and particle, the stress in two- and three-word verbs always falls on the particle. For example: *go óver, pick úp, pick it úp, get ón, take it óff.*

2. When the verb is followed by an object noun phrase, each word in the verb receives equal stress and the phrase stress falls on the object. For example, *pick up the pén, look up these wórds, go over the assígnment.*

SPEAKING

EXERCISE 1 (pairs, whole class)

Language Focus

going to for future plans; separable and inseparable two- and three-word verbs, with and without pronouns

New Words and Expressions

check out of, get off, take off, turn on

Teaching Suggestions

1. Explain that two- and three-word verbs are common in English. Tell students that each one of these verbs needs to be learned as a unit, because the meaning of the whole verb cannot usually be guessed by knowing what the separate parts mean. (Use *turn on* as an example: Mime *turn* and then *turn on* a light.)

2. Ask students to look over the list of verbs. Explain their meanings if necessary. Have them point out that each is paired with its opposite.

3. On the board write:

package	*airplane*
disguise	*power*
hotel	*Agent 001*

Ask students to make sentences using the verbs in the book and the words on the board. Give or write an example, if necessary: *Agent 001 is going to drop a package off at the customs desk.* S2: *003 is going to pick it up.* S3: *Agent 001 is going to get on the airplane at 7:05 A.M.*

   If they use *it/him/her* (a pronoun) with a separable verb, model the separation for them. To contrast, model a sentence with a noun object, separating and then not separating the verb (as in *Pick up the letter* or *Pick the letter up*).

4. Have students study the example. Have two students read it aloud for the class. Point out, if necessary, that A uses a pronoun (in this case, *it*) in the second part of the question, and B always uses a pronoun in his or her response.

5. Have students ask each other the questions in pairs. When they have finished, go over the answers with the class.

Note: the pronoun for 1, 2, 3, 5, 6 and 7 is *it;* for 4 it is *him*.

EXERCISE 2 (role-play, pairs)

Language Focus

two- and three- word verbs, *going to* for future plans

New Words and Expressions

role-play

Teaching Suggestions

1. Tell students to do the exercise without looking at the book and to check themselves afterward by looking at the book.

2. (Optional) Students can role-play Control and the three agents, or do all three conversations for the class.

EXERCISE 3 (pairs)

Language Focus

two-word verbs, review of past tense

New Words and Expressions

clean up, dictionary, father, look up, stereo

Teaching Suggestions

1. Have students study the list of verbs. Explain *clean up, look up* and *stereo,* if necessary.

2. Tell students that one of the verbs is inseparable. *Which one is it? (get on)*

3. Help two students model the example for the class. Show the class where you can find the words to ask and answer the questions about the picture.

4. Elicit another model from the students.
   T: *Look at the first picture. What did the husband say?*
   Ss: *He said, "Pick me up at six-thirty."*
   T: *What did the wife do?*
   Ss: *She picked him up.*

5. Point to the second, third and fourth pictures, asking questions and eliciting answers (as necessary). Have students do the exercise in pairs.

6. Check answers.

If You Have Time

Establish some two-word verbs that can be used in the classroom. On the board write:

hand in	*books*
take out	*assignments/homework*
go over	*briefcase/bookbag*
open up	

Act out the two-word verbs as necessary, telling your students what you are doing. Then give them commands using the two-word verbs. They must act out what you tell them to do.

Workbook

You can now assign Exercises A–C.

Speaking

1

Ask and answer questions about
Agents 001, 002 and 003. Use these
two- and three-word verbs:

Separable

pick up/drop off
put on/take off
turn on/turn off

Pick up *the letter*.
Pick *the letter* up.
Pick *it* up.

Inseparable

get on/get off
check into/check out of

Get on *the plane*.
Get on *it*.

At 6:30/001/package at the airport

A: At 6:30, is 001 going to pick up a
   package at the airport or drop it
   off?
B: He's going to drop it off.

1. At 6:30/001/package at the airport
2. At 7:05/001/Y's plane
3. In Amsterdam/001/Y's plane
4. At 8:30/002/Agent 001 at the
   airport
5. 003/Y's hotel
6. At Y's hotel/003/her disguise
7. At 10:00/003/the power in Y's
   hotel

2

Role-play these conversations.

Conversation 1:
A, you're 001. **B,** ask A "What're you
going to do next Monday?"

Conversation 2:
B, you're 003. **A,** ask B "What're you
going to do next Monday?"

3

Look at the pairs of pictures, and have conversations like this:

A: In picture four, what did the mother say?
B: "Take off your boots."
A: What did the children do?
B: They took them off.

Questions	Answers	
children	clean up	these words in the dictionary
wife	get on	your room
husband	look up	your boots
mother	pick up	me
father	take off	the bus
son	turn off	the stereo
daughter		
teacher		
students		

4

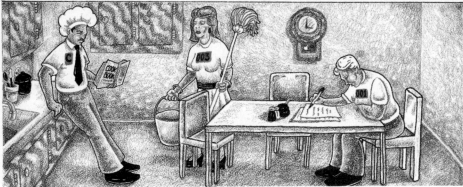

● Look at the picture and find these things:

cookbook	television (TV)	shopping list
vacuum cleaner	laundry bag	bucket

● Have conversations like this:

A: Who's reading a cookbook?
B: Control.
A: What's he going to do?
B: He's going to make dinner.

Questions	Answers	
turning on the TV	Control	go food shopping
reading a cookbook	001	watch TV
making a shopping list	002	make dinner
holding a vacuum cleaner	003	do the laundry
holding a bucket	Agent X	vacuum the bedroom
putting clothes in a laundry bag	Agent Y	wash the floor

● Ask each other questions like this:

A: Who usually does the laundry in your family?
B: I do. Who usually ....?

5

Pronunciation

Use the phrases below and have conversations like this:

A: Who's going to watch TV?

B: 002. Who's going to go grocery shopping?

go grocery shopping

watch TV

make dinner

do the laundry

vacuum the living room

wash the car

6

● Practice this conversation:

A: What're you going to do tomorrow night?
B: I'm going to go to the movies.
  OR I'm not sure yet. Maybe I'll
  ....
  OR I don't know yet.

● Have conversations like the one above. Use these times:

tonight
tomorrow morning/afternoon/night
this/year/Tuesday
next week/month/Saturday
on your next day off/birthday
after class

Here are some possible activities:

go to the movies
paint my apartment
go to Alaska
do my homework
visit friends
watch TV
....
....

● Ask each other about your plans for the weekend. Ask about people, places, times, etc.

EXERCISE 4 (pairs)

Language Focus

going to for activity someone is about to do, review of simple present for habits and routines, review of present continuous

New Words and Expressions

bucket, cookbook, laundry, laundry bag, vacuum cleaner, wash (*v.*)

Teaching Suggestions

First and Second Parts

1. Tell students to look at the picture and find the objects on the list. Go over the pronunciation of the words.

2. Have students study the column labeled *questions*.

3. Help two students model the example.

4. Have students do the exercise in pairs.

5. Check answers.

Note: The *going to* (future) is used in this exercise because there is evidence of the person's next action.

Third Part

1. Have students ask each other the questions about each other.

2. (Optional) Each pair joins another pair and each person reports about his or her partner.

3. (Optional) Ask various students the questions they have just asked each other.

If You Have Time

1. Show students pictures of people about to do something. Students say what the people in the pictures are going to do.

2. Have students mime preparation for doing something or mime something about to happen; for example, someone getting ready to eat, someone about to dive into a pool, someone getting ready to write, someone about to look something up in the dictionary. The other students say what the person is going to do.

EXERCISE 5 (pairs)

Language Focus

sentence stress, *going to*

Teaching Suggestions

1. Go over the stress and intonation of the questions and answers. Point out that the main stress in the first question is on the object. (If they don't know what you mean by *the object* or don't know that grammatical term, show and tell briefly.) Have them exaggerate the stress.

2. Point out that in conversation, they will often hear native speakers pronounce *going to* as *going ta* or *gonna*. If they wish to try out that pronunciation, let them. Practice saying it for them first.

3. Have them do the exercise in pairs.

EXERCISE 6 (pairs)

Language Focus

going to for future plans, future time expressions

New Words and Expressions

plan, tomorrow, tonight, birthday

Note: With *days of the week* and *weekend, this* and *next* are often confusing, even for native speakers. For example, *this Thursday* usually means the Thursday of the current week, but *next Thursday* can mean either the Thursday of the current week or the Thursday of the next week. At this point, it is best to teach that *this* is used for the current week and *next* is used for the next week.

Teaching Suggestions

First and Second Parts

1. Use a calendar to show the meaning of the time expressions. Point to today's date on the calendar and say *today*. Point to the calendar to illustrate the time expressions listed in the book, and have the students give the correct time. Do this randomly so that students won't just read from the book. Expand to times not listed in the book. For example, *this Monday, next Sunday,* etc.

2. Elicit other future time expressions from the students. For example, if your students are full-time students, instead of *on our next day off,* they could say *on our next holiday* or *on our next day off from school.*

3. Have students read the sample conversation. Point out that they use *I'm going to* if they know their plans, and *Maybe I'll* if they are thinking about something but haven't decided.

4. Have students read the instructions and the cues. Elicit other activities and write them on the board. Students can add them to the list in their books.

5. Help two students model the conversation. Model it again, this time with a different time expression.

6. Have students do the exercise in pairs.

7. Have each student say one thing about his or her partner.

Third Part

1. Have students read the instructions.

2. Ask: *What kinds of questions will you ask?* If students need help, give examples: *What're you going to do this weekend? Who are you going to ....? Where (are you*

(continued)

going to ....?)*When (are you going to* ....?)
What're you going to wear? What're you going to eat?

3. Model a conversation with one of the students. The student asks you about your plans for the weekend.

4. Have students do the exercise in pairs.

5. (Optional) Students write down the information about their partners and then report to someone else.

Workbook

You can now assign Exercise D.

EXERCISE 7 (whole class, pairs)

Language Focus

asking for someone on the phone and leaving a message, formally and informally

New Words and Expressions

bye, message

Names

Alex /ǽləks/
Benton /bɛ́ntən/
Ames /eɪmz/
Patty /pǽti/
Greg /grɛg/
Morita /mɔríːtə/
Alan /ǽlən/
Johnson /dʒɑ́nsən/

Teaching Suggestions

1. Practice the informal telephone conversations chorally.

2. Ask: *Why are these conversations labeled informal?* If students can't answer, tell them you know it is informal because Bob uses only his and Alex's first name. *They are probably friends.*

3. Have two students perform the informal conversation.

4. Have two other students perform the conversation. This time, student B uses his or her real name and asks for a friend. Student A can choose to say *Yes* or *No*.

5. Have students work in pairs and practice the informal conversations.

6. Practice the formal telephone conversations chorally.

7. Ask students what the differences are between the informal and the formal conversations. For example, Bob says *Hi* in the first and *Hello* in the second; he uses his first name in the informal conversation and his full name in the second. Note that this material reviews concepts presented in Unit 3.

8. Follow Steps 3–5 above with the new conversations.

9. (Optional) Teach the students—B: *I'm afraid you have the wrong number.* A: *I'm sorry.*

10. Have students study the instructions for the information gap exercise.

11. If you feel the conversation is too long for them to remember, then write cue words on the board.

12. Help two students model the first conversation for the class. A can use his or her real name. Make sure everyone understands the procedure.

13. Have students do the exercise in pairs. Go around the room and check that they are doing it correctly.

Workbook

You can now assign Exercises E and F. (The phrase *Directory Assistance* is introduced in the Workbook.)

7

Practice these telephone conversations:

Informal

A: Hello.
B: Hi, this is Bob. Is Alex there?
A: Yes, he is. Just a minute, please.
B: Thanks.

OR

A: Hello.
B: Hi, this is Bob. Is Alex there?
A: No, he isn't. Can I take a message?
B: Yes. Just tell him I called.
A: OK.
B: Thanks.
A and B: 'Bye.

Formal

B: Hello.
A: Hello. This is Bob Benton. May I please
   speak to Mrs. Ames?
B: Just a minute, please.
A: Thank you.

OR

B: Hello.
A: Hello. This is Bob Benton. May I please speak to
   Mrs. Ames?
B: She's not here right now. Can I take a message?
A: Could you tell her Bob Benton called, please?
B: All right.
A: Thank you.
A and B: Goodbye.

A

1. Make three calls. Call your friends Patty and Greg.
   Then call your teacher, Mrs. Morita.

2. B is going to call three times and ask for Susan,
   Alan and Mr. Johnson. Susan and Alan are home.
   Mr. Johnson isn't. You begin with *Hello*.

B

1. A is going to call three times and ask for Patty,
   Greg and Mrs. Morita. Patty and Mrs. Morita aren't
   home. Greg is. You begin with *Hello*.

2. Make three calls. Call your friends Susan and Alan.
   Then call your teacher, Mr. Johnson.

8
Culture Capsule

In most cities in the United States, you can dial a special telephone number for the following:

	all towns	some towns	your town
☀️ ☁️ the weather 🌧️			
🕐 the time			
👮 the police			
an ambulance ➕			
🔥 to report a fire			
a joke 😃			
🙏 a prayer			
a song 🎵			
$ free financial advice			

Can you phone for information like this in your town/city?

9
Put It Together

Talk to your partner about his or her last vacation and vacation plans for next year. Include these questions:

What did you do last summer?
What are you going to do next summer?

Here are some possible activities:

go	biking	play	golf
	fishing		tennis
	hiking		---------------------
	sailing		take pictures
	swimming		travel to another country
	---------------------		visit family

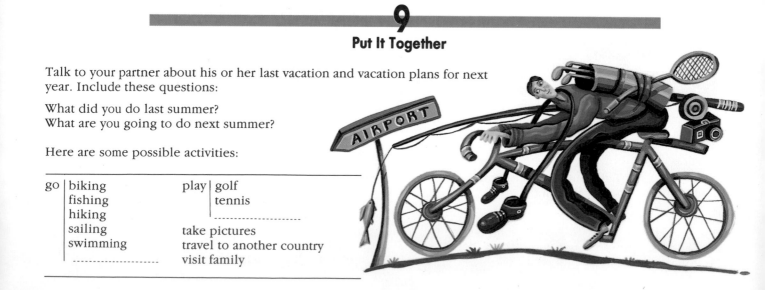

EXERCISE 8 Culture Capsule (whole class)

Culture Focus

special telephone numbers in the U.S.

New Words and Expressions

advice, ambulance, fire, financial, free, joke, police, prayer, report, town, weather

Teaching Suggestions

1. Have students study the chart.

2. Explain, as necessary, *ambulance, joke, prayer, free financial advice.*

3. Tell students to check whether there are special numbers students can call for services in their areas.

4. Ask the students: *Do you have a special telephone number for the weather? What is it? Do you have a special telephone number for the time?* and so on. Ask the students: *Do you have any other special telephone numbers?*

EXERCISE 9 Put It Together (pairs)

Language Focus

talking about future plans, review of past tense

New Words and Expression

bike (*v.*), fish (*v.*), golf (*v.*), hike (*v.*), summer, tennis

Teaching Suggestions

1. Ask the students: *What do you do in the summer? Do you take a vacation? What kinds of things do you do on your vacation?* List their answers on the board. (Note: If your students' principal vacation is in another season, then substitute *winter, fall (autumn)* or *spring* for *summer.*)

2. Tell students to look at the activities shown in the book. Explain vocabulary as necessary.

3. Have them add their own ideas to the list.

4. On the board write:
What did you do last summer? Where?
When? Who with? What?

5. (Optional) Ask students if they can think of other questions to add. Add them to the questions in number 4, above.

6. Ask: *What can you say if your partner had a good or bad summer?* For example, *Sounds great!* or *Sounds terrible!* Write these and any others students think of on the board.

7. Tell them to think about last summer and about next summer. Point out that in talking about next summer, they say, *I'm going to* .... if they're sure, and *Maybe I'll* .... if they're not sure.

8. Have students do the exercise in pairs. Remind them to refer to the Checklist if necessary.

9. (Optional) Ask students to tell about their partners' summers.

CHECKLIST

Teaching Suggestions

1. See the general suggestions in the Checklist page in Unit 1.

2. (Optional) Review *be going to* and future time expressions. Have the class ask questions and give answers about each other, using *be going to* and the future time expressions. For example: *Sami, what are you going to wear tomorrow? What's Maria going to do this weekend? Is Ken going to visit his girlfriend next week?*

3. (Optional) Review two- and three-word verbs. Write the verbs on the board and have the students make statements or ask and answer questions about the class using the verbs. For example, *How many words did you look up this week? Who's going to turn off the lights in the classroom?*

4. (Optional) From time to time, you may wish to have students review the Checklist part by part and then quiz them orally in class, with books closed. For example:

T: *You call a friend on the phone. How do you ask for him/her?*

Ss: *Is .... there?*

T: *You call your teacher on the phone. How do you ask for him/her?* and so on.

OPTIONAL WRITING PRACTICE

You are an assistant to Marie Marshall, a local politician. Today, November 20, Ms. Marshall has a very busy schedule. She has to do many things.

Write out her schedule for her, and leave it on her desk. Use the following words and expressions:

go over	get to	call
clean up	turn on	look up
pick up	get off	drop off
him	going to	get into
		check into

November 20 Day's Events

7:00 _____

8:00 _____

9:00 _____

10:00 _____

11:00 _____

. . .

6:00 _____

62

I know how to . . .

USE THESE FORMS

☐ **Going To Future**

I	am	going to	leave in a
He/She/It	is		minute.
You/We/They	are		

questions
Is he going to get on the plane?
What is he going to do?

short answers
Yes, he is.   No, he isn't.

statements
He is/isn't going to get on the plane.

☐ **Future Time Expressions**

tonight

tomorrow	morning
	afternoon
	night

this	weekend
next	month
	Saturday

on (your) next	day off
	vacation

☐ **Two- and Three-Word Verbs**

separable
Pick *the letter* up. Pick *it* up.
Pick up *the letter*. (Pick ~~up~~ *it*.)

clean up	put on
drop off	take off
look up	turn on
pick up	turn off

inseparable
Get on *the plane*. Get on *it*.
(Get *the ~~plane~~* on.) (Get ~~*it*~~ on.)

check into	get on
check out of	get off

USE ENGLISH TO

☐ **ask for someone on the phone informally**
Hi, this is Bob. Is Alex there?

☐ **ask for someone on the phone formally**
Hello. This is Bob Benton. May I please
   speak to Mrs. Ames?

☐ **give and take a telephone message**
She's not here right now. Can I take a
   message?
Could you tell her I called, please?

☐ **talk about future plans**
What're you going to do tomorrow night?
I'm not sure yet. Maybe I'll go to the
   movies./I'm going to go to the movies.

☐ **talk about these subjects**
activities at home   weekend plans
vacation plans   telephone use

☐ **UNDERSTAND THESE EXPRESSIONS**

I'm not sure yet.
Just a minute, please.

do the laundry
make dinner
go on vacation
go over (an assignment)
right away
stay at (a hotel)
take a message

CHECKLIST

🎞 Listening

1

Listen to each dialogue. Check the correct box.

Someone:

1. ☐ is going to go grocery shopping.
   ☐ went grocery shopping.

2. ☐ is going to wash the car.
   ☐ washed the car.

3. ☐ is going to clean up the house.
   ☐ cleaned up the house.

4. ☐ is going to vacuum the living room.
   ☐ vacuumed the living room.

5. ☐ is going to pick up the kids.
   ☐ picked up the kids.

2

Read these suggestions:

Why don't you . . .?

a. put it on   d. look them up
b. turn it on   e. turn it off
c. clean it up   f. take it off

You're going to hear six conversations. Listen and decide which suggestion completes each conversation.

1. b
2. ....
3. ....
4. ....
5. ....
6. ....

3

These people are going to stay at the Park Hotel in Amsterdam this week: Elizabeth Taylor, Jane Fonda, Sean Penn and Paul McCartney. Which nights are they going to stay there? Write their names in the reservation book at the correct dates.

	MON 25	TUES 26	WED 27	THURS 28	FRI 29	SAT 30	SUN 31
Elizabeth Taylor		⟶		→			
Jane Fonda					⟶		→
Sean Penn	⟶					→	
Paul McCartney					⟶	→	

4

Part 1: You're going to hear five phone conversations. Some have messages, some don't. Check the correct box.

	Message	**No Message**
1.	☐	☐
2.	☐	☐
3.	☐	☐
4.	☐	☐
5.	☐	☐

Part 2: Now listen again and write down the messages. These are the names you're going to hear:

Terry Anderson
Mrs. Kister
Kathy
Sarah McCormack

A MESSAGE FOR
_____
_____
_____ called
☐ Please call back.
Tel. #: _____
_____

A MESSAGE FOR
_____
_____
_____ called
☐ Please call back.
Tel. #: _____
_____

5

Give true answers.

1. _____   3. _____

2. _____   4. _____

LISTENING

EXERCISE 1
Language Focus
understanding whether someone is talking about future or past

Teaching Suggestions
1. Have students read the instructions. They have to decide whether each activity is future or past.

2. Play the cassette or read the tapescript for each item. Students listen and check the correct box after each dialogue.

3. Check answers.

Answers: 1. went   2. is going to   3. cleaned up
4. vacuumed   5. is going to

EXERCISE 2
Language Focus
two-word verbs, review of giving suggestions

New Words and Expressions
dark

Teaching Suggestions
1. Ask students to read the directions.

2. Go over the suggestions with them and review the meanings of the two-word verbs.

3. Go over the first conversation with the class.

4. Play the cassette or read the tapescript, stopping after each item. Students listen, marking their answers.

5. Check answers.

Answers 1. b   2. a   3. c   4. e   5. d   6. f

EXERCISE 3
Language Focus
going to future, future time expressions

New Words and Expressions
reservation

Names
Elizabeth Taylor /əlízəbəθ teílər/
Jane Fonda /dʒeín fɑndə/
Sean Penn /ʃɔn pɛn/
Paul McCartney /pɔl məkártni/

Teaching Suggestions
1. Have students read the directions. Go over the pronunciation of the names.

2. Play the cassette or read the tapescript.

3. Students listen, writing their answers as they hear them.

4. Check answers.

Answers: Sean, Mon.–Fri.; Liz, Tues.–Wed.; Paul, Fri.; Jane, Fri.–Sat.

EXERCISE 4
Language Focus
asking for someone on the phone and leaving a message, formally and informally

Names
Terry Anderson /téri ǽndərsən/
Mrs. Kister /mɪzíz kístər/
Kathy /kǽθi/
Sarah McCormack /sǽrə məkɔ́rmək

Teaching Suggestions
First Part

1. Have students read the directions. Be sure they understand *message*.

2. Play the cassette or read the tapescript.

3. Check their answers.

Answers: 1. message   2. no message   3. message   4. no message   5. no message

Second Part

1. On the board draw an example of a message slip, like the one in the book. Give an example how to fill it in.

3. Go over the pronunciation of the names.

4. Students listen again and fill in the message slips.

5. Check answers.

Answers: Mrs. Kister, Terry Anderson called; Kathy, Terry called. Please call back. Tel. 355-2951.

EXERCISE 5
Language Focus
Personal questions based on language taught in this unit.

Teaching Suggestions
1. Play the cassette or read the tapescript.

2. Students listen to the tape and write their answers.

3. Ask them what the questions were.

Answers: Since answers are personal, they will vary with each student.

64

EPISODE 8 The Moon of India

Key Vocabulary

order (*v.*)

Names

Café Real /kǽfeí reɪǽl/
del Comercio /dɛl komérsio/
Plaza /pláza/
Avenida Iberia /avɛnída ibéria/
Rua Goya /rúa gója/
Malaga /málaga/

Teaching Suggestions

1. Have students retell the last few episodes: The police know that the Moon of India and the thief are on the *Princess*. A police officer is on the ship and searches the thief's room, but does not find the Moon of India. The thief planned to meet someone in Marseilles to sell the necklace and then changed the meeting to Barcelona, because of the room search. On the ship, Christina, Agatha, Lucy, Frank and Robert talk about their plans for Barcelona. Frank wants to stay on the ship and write, but Christina and Agatha persuade him to come into Barcelona with them. Lucy and Robert are going to spend the afternoon together.

2. Follow steps 1–6 of Episode 1.

3. Ask the comprehension questions.

Answers: 1) They are going to meet at the Café Real at 2 o'clock. 2) No, it isn't. He visited Spain five years ago with his wife. 3) He leaves the café because he is sad, thinking about his wife. 4) The thief and the buyer. 5) The meeting doesn't take place, because someone followed the thief.
6) No. We don't know who watched Lucy or who followed the thief. Probably the police (Interpol) followed the thief.

4. (Optional) Other possible questions. What is Robert going to do before he meets Lucy? Does Frank speak Spanish? When was Frank in Barcelona? Is he married? Is the Café del Comercio near the Plaza Real? Does Lucy meet Robert at 2:00? Does the buyer trust the thief?

5. Have students close their books and relate the important points of the episode. Check their understanding of the story as they tell it. Correct any misunderstandings.

6. (Optional) Role-play. Students can role-play the dialogues between Lucy and Robert and the two phone conversations, using role cards as described in Episode 1.

▣ Episode Eight

It is April 24. The ship is in Barcelona. Robert and Lucy are getting ready to leave the ship.

"Where are we going to meet this afternoon?" she asks.

Robert is thinking of something else but replies, "Oh. Uh. The Cafe Real at 2:00. It's the biggest cafe in the main square."

"OK, the Cafe Real. But can we meet before 2:00?"

"No, I have to see a few people this morning. Look, I have to hurry to make my first appointment. There's a taxi. I'll meet you in town, OK?"

Later that morning, Agatha, Christina and Frank stop at a cafe. They find a table outside. A waiter arrives and Frank orders two coffees and a tea in Spanish.

"I didn't know you spoke Spanish, Frank!" says Agatha.

"I can order coffee in lots of different languages."

"Is this your first visit to Spain?" Christina asks.

"No, about five years ago, we were here on vacation. It was spring . . . I was married. My wife died two years ago."

"Oh, I'm sorry, Frank."

There is a long silence. "Excuse me, I think I need a little walk."

In a phone booth near the cafe, someone is dialing 223-338. A man answers. "Very good, you're in Barcelona."

"Where are we going to meet?"

"At the Cafe del Comercio."

"I need directions."

"Where are you now?"

"Near the Plaza Real."

"Walk two blocks down Avenida Iberia and turn left on Rua Goya. It's in the middle of that block."

"Do you have the money?"

"Yes, of course."

It is now 2:00 PM. Lucy arrives at the Cafe Real to meet Robert. He is not

there. She orders a coffee. The cafe is busy and she doesn't see the man watching her from the door of the cafe. Finally Robert arrives. The man at the door sees him and leaves.

"Sorry I'm late. . . ."

In the late afternoon, the passengers return to the ship. There is another telephone call to the man at 223-338.

"Where are you? Where is the necklace?"

"I'm back on the ship. Someone followed me. The necklace is in a safe place. Meet me in Malaga."

"I'm beginning to think you don't have it."

"Don't worry, I do."

"All right. We'll meet in Malaga. And bring the necklace."

Comprehension Check

1. In Barcelona, where are Lucy and Robert going to meet? When?
2. Is this Frank's first visit to Spain?
3. Why does Frank leave the cafe?
4. Who plans to meet at the Cafe del Comercio?
5. Why doesn't the meeting take place?
6. Do you know who watched Lucy? Do you know who followed the thief?

UNIT 9

12:20 PM

Woman 1: Excuse me, how can I get downtown from here?
Woman 2: You can go by taxi, by bus or by local train.
Woman 1: How often do the buses run? Do you know?
Woman 2: Yes, every half hour.
Woman 1: How long does it take?
Woman 2: About forty-five minutes.

Woman 1: When's the next bus?
Clerk 1: There's one in ten minutes, at 12:30.
Woman 1: How much does it cost?
Clerk 1: One way is $6.50. Round trip is $12.
Woman 1: Then, I want to go to Milton. Do I have to change buses?
Clerk 1: Yes. Change at the downtown station.

Man: Can you suggest a good downtown hotel?
Clerk 2: You could try the Century. It's very nice.
Man: How much is it for two people?
Clerk 2: Let me see . . . $75 a night.

UNIT 9

Unit Language Focus

GRAMMAR: *have to* (for obligation), *could* (for suggestions), *can* (for possibility), *by* (means)
COMMUNICATIVE AREAS: asking for and giving information about public transportation, asking for and giving advice, asking for and giving (subway) directions, hesitating

OPENING CONVERSATION

New Words and Expressions

could, cost (*v.*), downtown, have to, how long, how often, let me see, local, one way, round-trip, run (*v.*), station, suggest

Names

Milton /mílton/
Century /séntʃəri/

Teaching Suggestions

1. Warm-up. Ask: *Where is this? People are waiting. Why are they waiting? What kind of information can you get at an information booth? What time is it?* Describe the picture: *This is an airport. A young woman is carrying an overnight bag. There are two people in the information booth wearing uniforms.*

2. Personalize: *Where's the nearest airport? Did you ever go there? How did you get to the airport? Do you know any airports in any other cities or countries?*

3. Play/read the conversations. Students look only at the picture.

4. Play/read it again. Students listen and read silently.

5. Teach new words and expressions, as needed.

6. Tell students to pay special attention to the pronunciation of *have to* /hæftə/ and *want to* /wæntə/ in the conversations. Remind them of the pronunciation of *can* /kən/ when it comes in the middle of a sentence.

   Remind students that the information questions have falling intonation and the *yes/no* questions have rising intonation. They can see the contrast in the third line of the conversation.

7. Let students ask questions about grammar, vocabulary, or pronunciation.

8. Students read/repeat the conversations.

9. Ask questions about the conversations: *Can you get downtown by taxi? How often do the buses run? When's the next bus? So, what times do the buses leave? Is there a bus at 5 o'clock? Do you think the bus is expensive? How long*

does the bus take from the airport to downtown? So, when will the twelve-thirty bus arrive downtown? Do you think the Century hotel is expensive?*

10. Students practice the conversations in pairs.

Additional Information

Grammar

Downtown is never preceded by the prepositions *to, in* or *at.* Examples: *She's going downtown. He's downtown already. I'm going to stay downtown for a while.* In order to use these prepositions, you would have to say *the downtown area.* Exception: *the bus from the airport to downtown.*

Vocabulary and Usage

1. *run/take:* These are idiomatic uses associated with transportation and time. *Trains and buses run. It takes an hour to read the newspaper.*

2. *how long does it take: It* could be interpreted as referring to *the bus;* in fact, *it* is a non-referential *it,* similar to *it's raining, it's crowded* (an expletive).

SPEAKING

EXERCISE 1 (role-play, pairs, whole class)

Language Focus

asking about transportation, *how often*, *how long*

New Words and Expressions

fare

Names

Cambridgeport /keímbrɪdʒport/
Rockport /rákport/
Naperville /néɪpərvɪl/

Teaching Suggestions

1. Have students study the schedule. Go over the pronunciation of the towns. If necessary, explain that *fare* means *price* and is used for buses, taxis, etc. You may wish to use the schedule to review clock time.

2. Tell the students: *You are at the airport. You want to go downtown. It's twelve-twenty.* (just as in the picture)

3. Have the class work in pairs to try to figure out the conversation.

4. When they are ready, divide the class into two groups. One group reads A's part, and the other group reads B's part. The conversation should sound like this:

A: *How often do the trains run? Do you know?*
B: *Yes: before midnight, every forty-five minutes; after midnight, every two hours.*
A: *How long does it take?*
B: *Thirty-five minutes.*

EXERCISE 2 (role-play, pairs, whole class)

Language Focus

asking about transportation: *when, how much, Do I have to change?, one way/round trip*

New Words and Expressions

clock

Teaching Suggestions

1. Ask: *Now what time is it?* (two forty-five P.M.)

2. Have the class work in pairs to try to figure out the conversation.

3. When they are ready, the class works in two groups again. One group reads B's part and the other group reads A's part. The conversation should sound like this:

B: *When's the next train?*
A: *There's one in fifteen minutes, at three o'clock.*
B: *Do I have to change for Cambridgeport?*
A: *No, you don't.*
B: *How much does it cost?*
A: *One way is $7. Round-trip is $13.*

4. The class works in pairs to complete the exercise.

5. (Optional) When they have finished, have two different pairs model the conversation about Milton and Naperville.

EXERCISE 3 (whole class, pairs)

Language Focus

intonation of items in a series

New Words and Expressions

item, period, question mark, series, subway

Names

Westfield /wéstfild/
Livingston /lívɪŋstən/
Morristown /mɔ́rɪstɑun/
Woodvale /wúdveɪl/
Linden /líndən/
Summit /sʌ́mɪt/

Teaching Suggestions

1. Students practice the model sentence several times.

2. (Optional) You can model the intonation by saying: *ta͡ ta, ta͡ ta, ta ta͡.*

3. Tell students to change the order of the items in the model sentences, keeping the intonation pattern the same; e.g., *You can go by bus, by local train, or by taxi.*

4. Divide the class into pairs. Tell them to follow the instructions, first adding the question marks and periods, and then matching the questions and answers.

5. (Optional) Have different pairs of students model the questions and answers.

Workbook

You can now assign Exercises A–C.

Speaking

1

A and **B,** ask and answer questions about the train schedule.

A: How often .... the trains run? Do you know?
B: Yes, before midnight ...., and after midnight ....
A: How long ....?
B: ....

2

● Now look at the clock and ask about the next train.

B: When's ....?
A: There's one in ...., at ....
B: .... change for Cambridgeport?
A: ....
B: How much does it cost?
A: One way is ....

● **A,** ask about the next train. You want to go to Milton.

● **B,** ask about the next train. You want to go to Naperville.

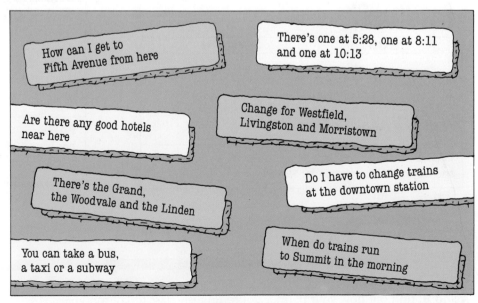

LOCAL TRAINS

All trains go to Cambridgeport and Milton. Change at downtown station for Rockport and Naperville.

Leave airport

6 a.m. – 12 midnight — every forty-five minutes
12 midnight – 6 a.m. — every two hours

Fare: $7.00 one way, $13.00 round trip

A.M.		P.M.	
Leave airport	Arrive downtown	Leave airport	Arrive downtown
12 midnight			
2:00	12:35	12 noon	12:35
4:00	2:35	12:45	1:20
6:00	4:35	1:30	2:05
6:45	6:35	2:15	2:50
7:30	7:20	3:00	3:35
	8:05	3:45	4:20

3
Pronunciation

● Say items in a series like this: You can go by taxi, by bus or by local train.

● Look at the sentences below. **A,** your sentences are yellow. **B,** yours are blue. Find the questions and answers in your color. Add question marks (?) and periods (.).

How can I get to Fifth Avenue from here

There's one at 5:28, one at 8:11 and one at 10:13

Are there any good hotels near here

Change for Westfield, Livingston and Morristown

There's the Grand, the Woodvale and the Linden

Do I have to change trains at the downtown station

You can take a bus, a taxi or a subway

When do trains run to Summit in the morning

● Now ask and answer the questions. **B,** answer A's questions and **A,** answer B's.

4

A and **B**, have conversations like this:

A: Excuse me, how .... Coselville from here?
B: You have to take .... There aren't any ....
A: When .... run?
B: At 8:43 AM, ... and ....
A: How long ....?
B: About ....
A: How much ....?
B: One way ....
A: .... change on the 8:43?
B: .... (Change at) ....

DESTINATION COLESVILLE

BUS		TRAIN
lv.	arr.	
8:43 a.m.*	10:55 a.m.	
10:30 a.m.	12:30 p.m.	
4:50 p.m.*	7:02 p.m.	
*Change at Newton		

FARE
one way: $5.50   round trip: $11.00

A

1. Ask B about Greenville.

2. Answer B's questions about Libertyville.

DESTINATION LIBERTYVILLE

BUS		TRAIN
lv.	arr.	
3:31 a.m.	7:31 a.m.	
6:16 a.m.*	10:30 a.m.	
2:27 p.m.*	6:45 p.m.	
*Change at Unionville		

FARE
one way: $12.25   round trip: $24.50

B

1. Answer A's questions about Greenville.

DESTINATION GREENVILLE

BUS	TRAIN	
	lv.	arr.
	12:00 p.m.	9:06 a.m.*
	2:23 p.m.	11:17 a.m.*
	10:45 p.m.	7:48 p.m.
	*Change at Balesville.	

FARE
one way: $8.50   round trip: $15.50

2. Ask A about Libertyville.

5

A and **B**, find out how your partner got to English class today/tonight.
Did he/she walk? Take a bus? A train? How long did it take? How much did it cost?

EXERCISE 4 (whole class, pairs)

Language Focus

asking about public transportation: *how long, how much, one way/round trip; have to; can* for possibility

New Words and Expressions

destination

Names

Colesville /kólzvıl/
Newton /njútən/ or /nútən/
Greenville /grínvıl/
Balesville /béılzvıl/
Libertyville /líbərtivıl/
Unionville /júnjənvıl/

Teaching Suggestions

1. Have students study the first schedule. Go over the pronunciation of *Colesville* and *Newton*. If necessary, teach the meaning of *destination: I want to go to Colesville. Colesville is my destination.*

2. Have students read the times and fares aloud.

3. Have students work in pairs to try to do the sample conversation.

4. When they are ready, go through the conversation line by line with the whole group, eliciting as much as possible from students. The conversation should go like this:

A: *Excuse me, how can I get to Colesville from here?*
B: *You have to take the bus. There aren't any trains.*
A: *When do the buses run?*
B: *At 8:43 A.M., 10:30 A.M. and 4:50 P.M.*
A: *How long does it take?*
B: *About two hours, or Let me see . . . , or It depends. . . .*
A: *How much does it cost?*
B: *One way is $5.50 and round-trip is $11.00.*
A: *Do I have to change on the 8:43?*
B: *Yes. Change at Newton.*

5. Divide the class into two groups, and have one group read A's part and one group read B's part.

6. (Optional) Have students work in pairs again, until they feel comfortable with the conversation.

7. Go over the pronunciation of the names in the two other schedules.

8. Have students work in pairs and complete the exercise.

9. (Optional) Have different pairs model the conversation for the class.

EXERCISE 5 (pairs)

Language Focus

talking about means of transportation, *how long, how much*

Teaching Suggestions

1. Have students read the instructions and do the exercise in pairs.

2. (Optional) Have students think of other questions they might ask; for example: *Was it crowded? Did you get a seat? Can you usually get a seat? Did you enjoy the ride?*

3. After students have completed the exercise, ask various students to report what their partners told them. Find out who has the longest commute, who pays the most money, if anybody walks, and so on.

4. (Optional) Have students talk about other trips: going to work, downtown, from the local airport to the downtown area.

EXERCISE 6 (pairs)
Language Focus

asking for and giving directions for taking the subway, imperative mood

New Words and Expressions

(train) line, stop, thank you anyway, toward, I'm sorry

Names

Aquarium /əkwéərijəm/
Oak Grove /ok grov/
Wonderland /wándərlænd/
Copley Square /kápli skweər/
Harvard /hárvərd/
Symphony /símfəni/
Bowdoin /bódən/
Washington /wáʃɪŋtən/
Alewife /eɪʟwɑɪf/
Arborway /árbərweɪ/

Teaching Suggestions

1. Write the place names on the board. Go over their pronunciation with your students. Find out if students know where Boston is.

2. Tell students to locate *Oak Grove* on their subway map. Then ask them to locate *Aquarium*. Tell them that *Aquarium* is on the Blue Line. Explain that an aquarium is a place where people can see fish and sea animals. (Note that students should say *Aquarium* and not *the Aquarium*, when referring to the subway stop.)

3. Tell the class to read A's part. You will read B's part. When you read, tell students to look at the subway map, locating the lines and places you mention. Check that they are able to follow the directions.

4. Ask: *Why does B say, "Go toward Wonderland"?* (because A shouldn't go toward Bowdoin).

5. Have two students model the alternate conversation (the one where B doesn't know the answer).

6. Review the ordinal numbers. Ask: *What's the second stop after State? the third?* and so on.

7. Do an example with the class.
Say: *You want to go to the airport. What will B say?*
Ss: *Take the Orange Line to State. Then change to the Blue Line and go toward Wonderland. Get off at Airport. That's the third stop.*

8. Divide the class into pairs. Tell the As to locate Harvard and Symphony. Tell the Bs to locate Government Center and Copley. (Copley Square is an expensive shopping area in downtown Boston, Harvard University is one of the best universities in the States, Symphony Hall is a large and famous concert hall where the Boston Symphony plays, Government Center is the place where the Boston city government is located. [If students don't understand

government, give examples of cities where their government is located.])

9. Have the pairs do the second part of the exercise.

10. When they have finished, have different pairs model the conversations.

11. (Optional) If there is a subway or commuter train in your students' town/s, then have them role-play asking for and giving directions. In each pair, one student is a local resident, and the other is a foreigner. Make a list of places a foreigner might ask directions to. The students can use that list.

Workbook
You can now assign Exercise D.

EXERCISE 7 (role-play, pairs)
Language Focus

asking for and giving advice, asking about cost

New Words and Expressions

hometown, stay

Names

Harold Johnson's /hǽrəld dʒánsənz/
Epcot /épkɑt/
Atlanta Holton /ætlǽntə hóltən/
Carlson /kárlsən/

Teaching Suggestions
First Part

1. Go over the pronunciation of the hotels with the students.

2. Help two students model the example conversation. Point out that they say: *You could try the (name of a hotel),* because it is a proper noun and there's only one hotel of that name.

3. Have students do the exercise in pairs. Tell them to begin by suggesting the most expensive hotel. (Atlanta, Georgia, is a big city in the South. Orlando, Florida, is the home of Disney World.)

4. Have two students perform the conversations about Orlando and Atlanta for the class.

5. Ask them if they think these hotels are reasonable or expensive compared with prices in their country.

Second Part

1. Students should think about hotels in their city. If they don't know any hotels, tell them to make up some names and places. In giving the prices, they can say, *It's about (price).*

6

● Look at this subway map of Boston, and practice these conversations:

A: Excuse me, how can I get to the Aquarium?
B: Take the Orange Line to State. Then change to the Blue Line and go toward Wonderland. Get off at Aquarium. That's the next stop.
A: Thank you very much.

OR

A: Excuse me, how can I get to the Aquarium?
B: I'm sorry, I don't know.
A: Thank you anyway.

● **A**, ask about Government Center and Copley Square. **B**, ask about Harvard University and Symphony Hall.

Reproduced by Permission of MBTA,
James F. O'Leary, General Manager

7

● Practice this conversation:

A: Can you suggest a good hotel in New York?
B: You could try the Plaza. It's very nice.
A: How much is it for one person/two people?
B: $300 a night/$500.
A: That's not bad. OR A: That's kind of expensive.
                          B: Well, you could try the Traveler's Inn. It's OK.

A

Ask B about hotels in Atlanta. Then answer B's questions about hotels in Orlando.

WHERE TO STAY IN ORLANDO	one person	two people
High House	$130	$160
Harold Johnson's	$90	$125
Epcot Town House	$70	$90
Sunset Inn	$50	$70

B

Answer A's questions about hotels in Atlanta. Then ask A about hotels in Orlando.

WHERE TO STAY IN ATLANTA	one person	two people
Atlanta Holton	$85	$115
Holly Inn	$65	$100
Center City Hotel	$45	$70
Carlson Hotel	$29	$40

● You're going to visit your partner's home town. Ask about hotels there.

8
Culture Capsule

In many places in the United States public transportation isn't very good. Not many trains or buses run from outside cities (the suburbs) to downtown. Most people have cars, and they like to drive. They drive to work, drive to go grocery shopping and drive their kids to school. Most people like to drive to work alone. There's a "rush hour" every morning from 7:01 to 8:59, and every evening from 4:30 to 7:30. In New York, the average commuter spends 81 minutes a day—or 310 hours a year—going to and from work!

Is public transportation in your country good? What kinds are there between cities? From outside cities to the downtown area? Inside cities? Do most people have cars? Do they drive to work? Do they drive alone or with other people? Are there rush hours? When are they?

9
Put It Together

Think about past trips to other cities or countries. Write down the name of one place and any information you remember. How long did you stay there? How did you get there? How long did the trip take? Did you stay in a hotel?

Ask your partner about his or her trip. Begin: *Where did you go? Were you on business or vacation?*

2. Ask students what other questions they can ask about the hotels. For example, *Where is it? Does it have a restaurant? Is it near a subway stop? Is it near stores?* List the questions on the board.

3. Have students do the exercise in pairs.

EXERCISE 8 Culture Capsule (whole class, individuals)
Culture Focus

public transportation in the U.S.

New Words and Expressions

average, commuter, inside, minute, outside, public transportation, rush hour, spend, suburb

Teaching Suggestions

1. Read the Culture Capsule aloud to the students or have them read it silently.

2. Teach new words and expressions, as needed.

3. Ask the questions of individual students.

4. Have the students work in pairs and ask and answer the questions.

5. (Optional) If your students are from different countries, compare the information about public transportation systems and driving. If your students are from the same country, compare their answers with the information about the United States.

EXERCISE 9 Put It Together (individuals, pairs, whole class)
Language Focus

asking for and giving personal information about travel, transportation and hotels

Teaching Suggestions

1. Have the students read the first paragraph. Ask them if they can think of other questions to ask. Write their questions on the board.

2. Have students take a few minutes to think about the questions and to write down information. They can refer to the Checklist page for help.

3. Students do the exercise in pairs.

4. (Optional) If your class is small, you can have the whole class discuss their answers and help each other with information. They can then share the information with the rest of the class.

Workbook
You can now assign Exercises E and F.

CHECKLIST

Teaching Suggestions

1. See the general suggestions in the Checklist page in Unit 1.

2. (Optional) To reinforce the grammar content of the unit, you may wish to have students review the Checklist and then quiz them orally in class, with books open or closed. For example, for *have to:* students ask questions and give answers about local transportation. *(I have to take a bus or walk to work. There aren't any trains.)* Or they can talk about regulations at school or at work; for example: *We have to wear uniforms. We have to take five courses.* To practice: students ask and answer questions about local transportation.

3. (Optional) From time to time, you may wish to have students review the Checklist part by part and then quiz them orally in class, with books closed. For example:

T: *You are at the information booth at the airport. You need advice about a hotel. What do you say?*

Ss: *Can you suggest a good hotel?*

T: *What will the person answer?*

Ss: *You could try the* ...., *and so on.*

OPTIONAL WRITING PRACTICE

Read the introduction to the students and then copy the parts of the following letter on the board.

Your cousin is going to visit you for your birthday. She needs to take a bus from her town to your town, changing buses once along the way. When she gets to your town, she will need to walk three blocks to your house. In this letter, tell her what she needs to know.

Dear Cousin,

    I'm so happy you are going to visit me. I checked the bus schedule and found out that the buses leave_____

_____

_____

When you get to_____

_____

_____

I can't wait to see you.

                       Love,

I know how to . . .

USE THESE FORMS

☐ **Have to** *(expresses need)*

questions
Do I have to change trains?

short answers
Yes, you do.   No, you don't.

statements
You have to change at. . . .
You don't have to (change trains).

☐ **By**
You can go by | taxi.
| bus.
| train.
| plane.

USE ENGLISH TO

☐ **ask for and give advice**
Can you suggest a good hotel?
You could try the Century.

☐ **suggest possibilities**
You can go by taxi, by bus or by local train.

☐ **ask for information about public transportation**
How often do the buses run? Do you know?
How long does it take?
How much does it cost?
Do I have to change buses for Milton?

☐ **hesitate**
Let me see. . . .

☐ **ask for and give directions**
Excuse me, how can I get to the Aquarium?
Take the Orange Line to State. Then change to . . . , and go toward . . . . Get off at . . . , the next stop.

☐ **talk about these subjects**
public transportation   travel   hotels

☐ **UNDERSTAND THESE EXPRESSIONS**
How much is it?

every two hours
one way
round trip

CHECKLIST

📼 Listening

1

Sue Thompson is going to take a business trip to Nashville. Her assistant, Max Martin, makes two phone calls for her. He's new, and he makes a lot of mistakes. Correct Max's memos.

Part 1: Max calls the bus station.   Part 2: Max calls a travel agent.

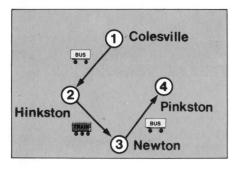

MEMO

To: Sue

You have to go to Nashville by bus. There aren't any trains. There are three buses a day, except Sundays.

Leave	arrive Nashville
10:24 a.m.	12:36 a.m.
1:18 p.m.	3:41 p.m.
5:01 p.m.	9:11 p.m.

You don't have to change on the 1:18 but you do on the others. There's a thirty-minute wait between buses. The round-trip fare is $16.36.

M.M.

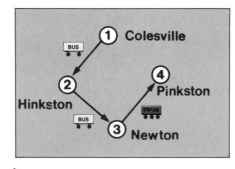

MEMO

To: Sue

The Hotel Magee in Nashville is $85 a night for two people. Would you like a reservation?

M.M.

2

Complete the conversations. Choose *a* or *b*.

1. a. Yes, you can.
   b. You can take a taxi, a bus or a local train.

2. a. It takes half an hour.
   b. Every two hours, between 10:00 AM and 5:00 PM.

3. a. About 45 minutes.
   b. Every hour.

4. a. $4.50.
   b. That's kind of expensive.

5. a. One way.
   b. Yes, it is.

6. a. There aren't any others.
   b. No, you don't.

7. a. At 2:47.
   b. Yes, there is.

8. a. Every hour, between 6:00 AM and 9:00 PM.
   b. At 4:47.

3

Wilfred Klutz gets on a bus at Colesville. Listen and decide which picture describes his trip.

a. ____   b. ____   c. ____

4

Give true answers.

1. ....   3. ....

2. ....   4. ....

LISTENING

EXERCISE 1

Language Focus

asking for and giving information about public transportation, asking for and giving advice

New Words and Expressions

assistant, business trip, decide, memo, mistake, travel agent

Names

Nashville /nǽʃvɪl/

Teaching Suggestions

1. Have students study the instructions.

2. Teach new words as needed.

3. Have students listen to the tape and figure out the correct information.

4. Check answers.

First Part

Buses leave at 9:17, 1:18 and 7:01. They arrive in Nashville at 11:36, 3:41 and 9:11. You have to change on the 1:18 only. There's a 15-minute wait between buses. The round-trip fare is $29.

Second Part

The Hotel Magee is $85 a night for one person.

EXERCISE 2

Language Focus

have to, asking for and giving information about public transportation

Teaching Suggestions

1. Have students read the instructions and the choices for each item.

2. Play the cassette or read the tapescript, stopping after each conversation.

3. Students listen to the tape and circle the correct response.

4. Check answers.

Answers: 1. b   2. b   3. a   4. a   5. a   6. b   7. a   8. b

EXERCISE 3

Language Focus

have to, asking for and giving information about public transportation

Names

Hinkston /híŋkstən/
Pinkston /píŋkstən/
Newton /njútən/

Teaching Suggestions

1. Go over the pronunciation of the names in the pictures.

2. Have the students review the information in each picture. For example: In the first picture it says he takes a bus to Hinkston and then changes to a train. He takes the train to Newton and then changes to a bus for Pinkston.

3. Students listen to the tape and choose the correct picture.

4. Answer: b

EXERCISE 4

Language Focus

questions about transportation

Teaching Suggestions

1. Students listen to the tape and give true answers.

2. Ask them what the questions were.

Answers: Since answers are personal, they will vary with each student.

EPISODE 9 The Moon of India

Key Vocabulary

brush against, costume, costume ball, fill out, form, gold, mask, receipt, safe (*n.*), shape, steal (*v.*), suitcase, unpack

Teaching Suggestions

1. Have students retell the last few episodes: A police officer is on the ship and searches the thief's room, but does not find the Moon of India. The thief planned to meet someone in Marseilles to sell the necklace and then changed the meeting to Barcelona, because of the room search. The ship arrives in Barcelona. Lucy and Robert agree to meet at 2:00 in a café. Agatha, Christina and Frank go into Barcelona together. They stop in a café. Frank tells them about his wife. She died two years ago. The thief gets directions to the meeting place from the buyer. Lucy waits in the café at 2:00. Someone is watching her. Robert arrives late. The passengers go back to the ship. The thief calls the buyer from the ship. Someone followed the thief, so the thief didn't go to the meeting place. They decide to meet in Malaga.

2. Follow steps 1–4 of Episode 1.

3. Students read the episode again.

4. Ask the comprehension questions.

Answers: 1) No, she isn't. She's finding her costume for the Costume Ball. 2) She finds the Moon of India. 3) She takes it to the purser (and he puts it in the ship's safe). 4) Who put the necklace behind the painting? Was it Christina? 5) Yes, she does. 6) (Students will give individual answers.)

5. (Optional) Other possible questions. How does she find the Moon of India? What does Christina think about the Moon of India? Who do you think put the Moon of India behind the painting? Why?

6. Have students close their books and summarize the episode. Check their understanding of the story as they tell it. Correct any misunderstandings.

7. (Optional) Expansion questions. Imagine you found the Moon of India, like Agatha. What would you do with it?

8. (Optional) Role-play. Students can role-play the dialogues between Agatha and the purser and Agatha and Christina, using role cards.

MOON OF INDIA

🔊 Episode Nine

It is April 25. Agatha is in her cabin. She's unpacking one of her suitcases to get her costume for the Costume Ball the next night. She takes out a long, dark blue dress, a mask and a hat the shape of the moon. She plans to go to the ball as the "Queen of the Night." She turns the dress around to look at it, and it brushes against the painting on the wall. The painting moves, and she sees something behind it. She looks more closely. It's a necklace! She takes the necklace from behind the painting and looks at it.

The Moon of India. From Christina's Museum, she thinks. Agatha sits down and puts her face in her hands. *What's the Moon of India doing here?* she thinks. *What should I do?* Then she gets up and puts the necklace in a small box. Quickly she walks to the purser's office.

"I want to put this in the ship's safe."

"Certainly, Madam. Please fill out this form."

Agatha fills out the form. The purser takes the box and puts it in the safe. He smiles as he gives Agatha a receipt.

"When do we arrive in Malaga?"

"The day after tomorrow, Madam, in the morning."

"Thank you very much," Agatha is only half listening.

"Is there anything else I can help you with?"

Agatha's mind is filled with questions, but she can't ask them now. "Well . . . not right now, thank you. Good night."

"Good night."

Christina returns to the cabin. It's almost dark. There's only a dim light on the table between the beds. Christina is very quiet. She thinks her aunt is asleep.

"Is that you, Christina?"

"You're still awake! Oh, I had a wonderful time talking with Frank. He's really an interesting man."

"That's nice, dear."

"Did you choose your costume?"

"What costume?"

"Your costume for the Costume Ball tomorrow night. Are you all right, Aunt Agatha?"

"Oh, I'm fine. Christina, did you ever see the Moon of India?"

"Yes. It's beautiful."

"What does it look like?"

"It's incredible. All diamonds and gold. It's . . . it's one of the most beautiful things in the world. I understand why somebody wanted to steal it."

"You do?"

"I'd love to have it. Well, I'm going to bed now. Good night, Aunt Agatha."

"Sleep well, my dear."

Comprehension Check

1. Is Agatha getting dressed for the Costume Ball?
2. What does she find behind the painting?
3. What does Agatha do with it?
4. What questions fill Agatha's mind?
5. Does Christina know a lot about the Moon of India?
6. Do you think Christina stole it?

SPEAKING

EXERCISE 1 (whole class)

Language Focus

the negative imperative

New Words and Expressions

no passing, sign

Teaching Suggestions

1. Teach new words and expressions as needed.

2. Go over the meaning of the signs with students.
   T: *What does the first sign mean?* Model answer: *Don't turn left here.*
   S1: *Don't turn left here.*
   T: *S2, ask S3 what the second sign means.*
   S2: *What does the second sign mean?*
   S3: *Don't park here,* and so on.

3. (Optional) Explain that people also say: *You can't turn left here.*

4. (Optional) Ask students to think of traffic signs used in their country or countries. Have them draw these on the board and (if appropriate) have other students ask them what the signs mean.

EXERCISE 2 (whole class, pairs)

Language Focus

giving directions

New Words and Expressions

block, Thai

Teaching Suggestions

1. Teach the meaning of *block* if your students don't know it, using the illustration in the book.

2. Explain the directions by using the map on the previous page. T: *You're on the corner of Park and 4th Street. Go past the Thai (/tai/) restaurant on your left. What's the next corner?* Model the answer and the way the corner is described: *Park and Third. Turn left on Third Street and go one block. Where are you?* If students haven't gotten the idea, model for them again: *Third and Main. Go one more block. Where are you?* Ss: *Third and High.* T: *Turn left and go to the next light. Where is it? Turn onto Sixth Street and turn left at the next stop sign. Where are you?* Model the answer: *On Main Street, between Fifth and Sixth.*

3. (Optional) Point out that they can say *Turn left on Fifth Street,* or *Turn left onto Fifth Street.*

4. (Optional) If you can move the chairs and desks in the classroom, you can use the classroom to give directions. Arrange the chairs so that there is one main street and two cross streets. Students can practice giving directions to each other.

5. (Optional) Draw a simple map on the board and label it. Have students give you directions. You trace the directions on the board.

6. Have students practice by giving the same directions the driving instructor gave.

7. Students practice in pairs, devising other ways to get to the driving school. When students are ready, ask various pairs to give the directions they thought of.

EXERCISE 3 (pairs)

Language Focus

giving and following directions

New Words and Expressions

bookstore

Names

Jay's /dʒeɪz/

Teaching Suggestions

1. Go over the names of the stores on the map. Tell students they can also use the Thai restaurant.

2. Model the exercise. Tell students where to start. Give directions to a store on the map. Students follow the directions and tell you which store it is.

3. Students do the exercise. They should do it several times, choosing different stores and different starting points so that they can learn the directions and understand them easily.

4. (Optional) Have individual students give directions to various stores, and have the whole class guess the stores.

5. (Optional) If your students are all from the same area, have them work in pairs, giving directions to places they both know. Their partners must guess the place. If they are from different areas, have them make up the names of new stores and place them on the map. They tell their partners the names of the stores, and their partners ask for directions to them.

Driving Instructor: All right, Mr. Klutz, that's enough for today. Why don't we go back to the driving school now?

Wilfred Klutz: OK. Uh, could you tell me where it is?

Instructor: It's on Park Street between 5th and 6th.

Klutz: Oh, yes, I remember. But how can I get there?

Instructor: Go straight ahead to the next light. Turn right on Main Street.

②

Instructor: No, Mr. Klutz! You can't turn left here! You have to turn right. Right, turn right!

③

Instructor: How fast are you going now, Mr. Klutz?

Klutz: 45.

Instructor: The speed limit here is 25 miles per hour.

④

Instructor: Mr. Klutz! You just went through a red light!

Klutz: Sorry.

⑤

Instructor: You'd better slow down, Mr. Klutz. There's another red light ahead. Look out for that car!

Klutz: Where do I go now?

Instructor: Go past the shopping center on your right. Then turn left at the next stop sign. The school's on the next corner, on the left.

⑥

Klutz: Can I park here?

Instructor: No, you can't. You can park over there. And please do.

Speaking

1

Tell Mr. Klutz what these signs mean:

Don't turn left here.

1.   2.

3.   4.

2

Tell Mr. Klutz another way to get to the driving school. Use these phrases to help you.

Turn left/right on (to) .... street.

Turn left/right at the next light/ corner/stop sign.

Go past .... on your left/right.

Go straight ahead (for .... blocks) (to ....).

Go to the next light/corner/stop sign.

3

A, give directions to a store on the map. Don't tell B the name of the place. **B,** follow A's directions until you get to the store. Which store is it?

EPISODE 10 The Moon of India

Key Vocabulary

ballroom, compliments of, gangster, gun, ladies' room, realistic, spill, spy, tray, trench coat

Names

Cleopatra /kliopǽtrə/
James Bond /dʒeɪmz bɑnd/
Al Capone /æl kəpón/

Teaching Suggestions

1. Have students retell the last few episodes: The thief tries to meet someone in Barcelona to sell the necklace. But someone follows the thief, so the meeting doesn't take place. In Barcelona, Robert is late for his 2:00 meeting with Lucy. Someone is watching Lucy. Frank, Agatha and Lucy are in Barcelona together. At a café, Frank leaves them because he remembers his wife. They took a trip to Barcelona five years ago. She died two years ago. That night, Agatha is in her cabin. She is holding a costume. The costume brushes against a painting in their room. Behind the painting is the Moon of India. She is very upset. She thinks maybe Christina put it there. She puts it in a box and takes it to the purser. He puts it in the ship's safe.

2. Follow steps 1–6 of Episode 1.

3. Ask the comprehension questions.

Answers: 1) Because her specialty is Egyptian art. Cleopatra was an Egyptian queen. 2) James Bond. 3) No, he isn't. He spills a drink on Agatha's dress. 4) No, she meets Lucy. Lucy is dressed like a gangster. 5) Agatha is frightened because Lucy has a gun. It looks like a real gun. 6) The thief. Because the necklace isn't there.

4. (Optional) Other possible questions. Why does Agatha go to the ladies' room? Is Lucy's gun real?

5. Have students close their books and summarize the episode. Check their understanding of the story as they tell it. Correct any misunderstandings.

6. (Optional) Expansion questions. Have you ever been to a costume party? What did you wear? or, Imagine you're invited to a costume party. What would you wear?

7. (Optional) Role-play. Students can role-play the conversations among Frank, Christina and Agatha, and the dialogue between Lucy and Agatha, using role cards.

MOON OF INDIA

Episode Ten

The next evening Christina and Agatha are sitting in the lounge, just outside the ballroom where the music and dancing are beginning. Christina is wearing a Cleopatra costume. Agatha smiles as she looks at Christina. *A beautiful woman,* she thinks. *Could she possibly . . . ?*

A man wearing a hat and a trench coat enters the lounge. He looks like a spy.

"Is that Frank?" asks Christina. "Frank!" she calls.

Frank replies in a deep voice, "Sorry darling, guess again."

"James Bond!" says Agatha.

Frank looks at the two women. He continues in his deep voice, "Now, let me guess. Christina, you're the beautiful Cleopatra, Queen of Egypt, and you, Agatha, you're. . . ."

"The Queen of the Night."

"Of course. You both look wonderful."

Robert, in a waiter's uniform enters carrying a tray of drinks. The others don't see his face, only his white uniform and the drinks.

"Compliments of the Captain."

"That's very nice." Christina then sees it is Robert and laughs.

"Robert, where did you get that costume?"

"One of the waiters. I gave him ten dollars to borrow it. It looks good on me, don't you think?" He spills a drink on Agatha's dress. "Oh Agatha, I'm sorry."

"Don't worry, Robert. Excuse me, I'll just go and put some water on it."

Agatha walks down the hall. She opens the door to the ladies room and sees someone wearing a man's suit. "Oh, excuse me," and she begins to go out.

"Agatha. It's all right. It's me, Lucy."

"Lucy!"

"It's my Al Capone gangster suit." Lucy's jacket is open, and while she is looking in the mirror, Agatha sees that she is carrying a gun. The gun looks real and Agatha is frightened.

"It's a very nice costume, dear, very realistic," Agatha says.

In the ballroom, people are dancing. Robert, Christina and Frank are standing by the door.

"Where's Lucy?" Robert asks.

"I didn't see her," Christina replies.

"Maybe she's dancing. You see the woman in the black mask? Is that Lucy?" Frank suggests.

Robert wants to take a closer look, and invites Christina to dance. There are many people on the dance floor. The music and dancing continue for hours.

While most people are enjoying the ball, one person quickly enters the Jordan's cabin, looks behind the painting for the necklace, doesn't find it, throws the painting down and leaves the cabin.

Comprehension Check

1. Why do you think Christina chose a Cleopatra costume?
2. Who does Frank look like?
3. Is Robert a good waiter?
4. Does Agatha meet a man in the ladies room?
5. Why is Agatha frightened?
6. Who throws down the painting in Agatha and Christina's room? Why?

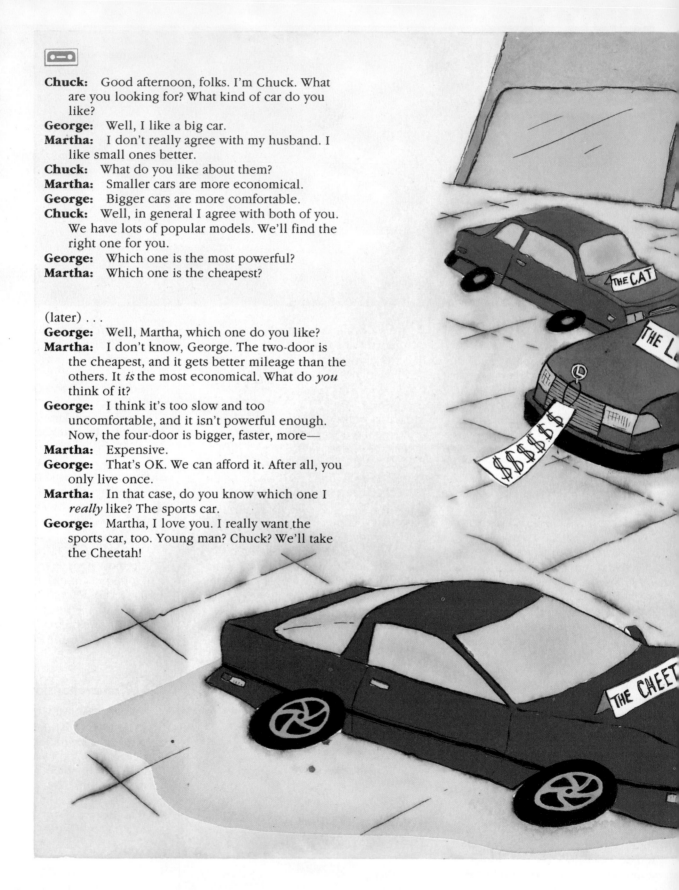

UNIT 11

Chuck: Good afternoon, folks. I'm Chuck. What are you looking for? What kind of car do you like?

George: Well, I like a big car.

Martha: I don't really agree with my husband. I like small ones better.

Chuck: What do you like about them?

Martha: Smaller cars are more economical.

George: Bigger cars are more comfortable.

Chuck: Well, in general I agree with both of you. We have lots of popular models. We'll find the right one for you.

George: Which one is the most powerful?

Martha: Which one is the cheapest?

(later) . . .

George: Well, Martha, which one do you like?

Martha: I don't know, George. The two-door is the cheapest, and it gets better mileage than the others. It *is* the most economical. What do *you* think of it?

George: I think it's too slow and too uncomfortable, and it isn't powerful enough. Now, the four-door is bigger, faster, more—

Martha: Expensive.

George: That's OK. We can afford it. After all, you only live once.

Martha: In that case, do you know which one I *really* like? The sports car.

George: Martha, I love you. I really want the sports car, too. Young man? Chuck? We'll take the Cheetah!

UNIT 11

Unit Language Focus

GRAMMAR: adjective comparisons (comparatives, superlatives), too/enough
COMMUNICATIVE AREAS: asking for and giving opinions; making comparisons; agreeing and disagreeing; understanding measurements of size, weight and speed; showing concern

OPENING CONVERSATION

New Words and Expressions

afford, after all, big, cheap, cheetah, comfortable, economical, folks, in that case, get good mileage, kind (n.), model, popular, powerful, slow, sports car, two-door, four-door, than, uncomfortable, You only live once

Names

Chuck /tʃʌk/
George /dʒɔrdʒ/
Martha /márθə/

Teaching Suggestions

1. Warm-up. Ask: *Where is this? Which one is the salesman? What's he doing? What are the people doing? Which cars do you think the older people will buy?*

2. Personalize: *Do you like big or small cars? Why? Do you or your family have a car? What kind? How old is it?*

3. Play/read the conversation. Students look only at the picture.

4. Play/read it again. Students listen and read silently.

5. Teach new words and expressions, as needed.

6. Students read/repeat the conversation.

7. Let students ask questions about grammar, pronunciation or vocabulary.

8. Teach the comparative. On the board write *small cars* and *big cars.* Off to the side list the adjectives *economical, cheap, powerful, fast* and *comfortable.* ·

Ask: *What does Martha think about small cars?* Ss: *They're more economical. They're cheaper.*

Write ....*er (than)* and *more* .... *than.* Explain: *We use* -er *with all one-syllable adjectives. We use* more *with adjectives of three or more syllables. For two-syllable words we use* -er *if they end in* y *and* more *if they don't.* Ask students to make the comparative form of the remaining adjectives on the board. Explain that we use this form when comparing two things.

Ask: *What does George think about big cars?* Ss: *They're more comfortable. They're more powerful. They're faster.*

9. Teach *too/enough* by using pictures or stick figure drawings of one person wearing something *too small/not big enough* and another person wearing something that's *too big.*

Have students use *too/enough* to talk about the cars: On the board write *four-door* and *two-door.* Then list the adjectives *slow, powerful, uncomfortable, expensive, economical.* Ask: *What does George think about the two-door?* Answer for the students: *It's too slow.* Ask: *What else does he think about it?* Elicit: *It's not powerful enough.* Ask about Martha's opinion and elicit similar responses.

10. Teach the superlative. On the board write *sports car, four-door* and *two-door.* Then write in a list: *economical, cheap, big, expensive.* Say: *Compare the three. What can you say about the two-door?* Answer for them: *It's the most economical. What else can you say?*

On the board write *the* ....*est* and *the most* .... Ask: *When do we use* the ....*-est and when do we use* the most? Review the rule given for the comparative in Teaching Suggestion 8 above. Explain that we use this form when comparing three or more things.

Have students practice the superlative, making statements about the three cars. Begin: *What can you say about the four-door?* Ss: *It's the biggest.*

11. Ask: *At first, which car does Martha like the best? What about George? Which car do they really like the best? Which car are they going to buy?*

12. Have the students practice the conversation in pairs.

13. (Optional) Have the students role-play the conversation for the class.

Additional Information

Grammar

1. *What kind of car* vs. *What kinds of cars:* He says *What kind* and not *What kinds,* because most people are looking for one type of car.

2. *What kind* vs. *Which one: What kind* establishes the category or type. *Which* asks about specific ones within those categories. For example: *What kind of car do you like? I like sports cars. Which one do you like? I like the* .... *(name of specific model).*

Vocabulary and Usage

1. *Good afternoon* is not usually used in everyday conversation. It is used by sales people and by people on TV, such as newscasters and talk-show and variety-show hosts. Chuck is a salesman, so he says, *Good afternoon.*

2. *Folks* is an informal way of saying *people.*

3. *I'm Chuck* (*Chuck* is short for *Charles*): It is common for salespeople and service personnel to refer to themselves by their first names in the United States.

SPEAKING

EXERCISE 1 (pairs)
Language Focus
comparisons of two and three things

New Words and Expressions
gallon, heavy, kilometers, light, liters, miles per gallon, price, seating capacity, seconds, weight

Teaching Suggestions
First Part

1. Have students study the chart. Use the information in the illustration and in the conversion chart to teach the new words and expressions.

2. Have students read the conversion chart. For example: *One pound equals point four five kilograms.*

3. To prepare the students for the exercise, go over the information in the illustration. Ask: *How much does the Cheetah cost? The Leo? The Cat? Which one is more expensive/cheaper? How much does the Leo weigh? The Cat? So which one is heavier/lighter?* And so on.

4. Help two students model the example conversation.

5. Continue the example, comparing the sports car and the four-door. Have students study the list of adjectives, and point out that they will use *more* .... with only one of the adjectives. Which one?

6. Have students do the exercise in pairs.

7. Have students close their books. Ask them the same questions about the models.

Second Part

1. Tell students that this time they are going to compare all three cars.

2. Help two students model the example conversation. Point out that they can also say, *Which is the fastest?* (and omit the *one*).

3. Have students do the exercise in pairs.

4. Have students close their books, and ask them questions about the three models.

EXERCISE 2 (pairs)
Language Focus
too, not .... *enough,* expansion of comparatives, giving opinions, agreeing, disagreeing and giving reasons

New Words and Expressions
disagree, reasons

Teaching Suggestions

1. Have students read the instructions and example sentences.

2. Ask for some reasons why someone might think big cars are better, and list them on the board. For example:

big cars	small cars
more powerful	not powerful enough
more comfortable	not comfortable enough
	OR too uncomfortable

3. Ask for some reasons why small cars are better, and list them. For example:

big cars	small cars
not economical enough	more economical
OR too uneconomical	get better mileage
too big and heavy	smaller and lighter

4. Erase the information on the board. Have the students do the exercise.

5. When they have finished, ask individual students which they think are better and why. Ask if their partners agreed or disagreed with them.

Workbook
You can now assign Exercises A–C.

	The Cheetah	The Leo	The Cat
price	$18,190	$12,400	$8,678
weight	2900 lbs.	3200 lbs.	2400 lbs.
0-60 m.p.h.	6 secs.	18 secs.	16 secs.
miles per gallon	14	22	28
seating capacity	2	6	4

Speaking

1

Note:

1 lb. (pound)	=	.45 kilograms
60 seconds	=	1 minute
1 mile	=	1.6 kilometers
1 gallon	=	3.8 liters

● Ask and answer questions comparing two models:

A: Which is heavier, the two-door or the four-door?

B: The four-door. Which one ....?

Use these words:

expensive – cheap	fast – slow
heavy – light	big – small

● Ask and answer questions comparing three models:

A: Which one is the fastest?

B: The sports car. Which one ....?

2

Which do you think are better, big cars or small cars? Agree or disagree with your partner. Give reasons. Use these words:

powerful	economical
comfortable	(un)comfortable
cheap	

A: I think small cars are better. They .... than big cars.

B: I agree. Big cars are too ....

OR I don't agree. Small cars are too ....

They're not .... enough.

Big cars are .... than small cars.

3

Practice reading this out loud.

1. The three tallest mountains are Everest, Kanchenjunga and K2.
2. The three largest islands are New Guinea, Borneo and Greenland.
3. The three biggest lakes are Lake Superior, Lake Victoria and the Caspian Sea.
4. The three longest rivers are the Mississippi, the Nile and the Amazon.

Note:

1 sq. mi. (square mile) = 259 hectares   1,000 = one thousand
1 ft. (foot) = .305 meters   1,000,000 = one million
   1,000,000,000 = one billion

A

The Three Tallest Mountains
Everest (Asia)
Kanchenjunga (Asia)
K2 (Asia)

The Three Largest Islands
New Guinea (South Pacific)
Borneo (South Pacific)
Greenland (North America)

Lakes
Lake Superior 31,820 sq. mi.
Lake Victoria 26,828 sq. mi.
The Caspian Sea 170,000 sq. mi.

Rivers
The Mississippi 3,872 mi. (long)
The Nile 4,145 mi. (long)
The Amazon 4,000 mi. (long)

B

Mountains
Everest 29,108 ft. (tall)
Kanchenjunga 28,208 ft. (tall)
K2 28,268 ft. (tall)

Islands
New Guinea 317,000 sq. mi.
Borneo 287,000 sq. mi.
Greenland 840,000 sq. mi.

The Three Biggest Lakes
Lake Superior (North America)
Lake Victoria (Africa)
The Caspian Sea (Asia/Europe)

The Three Longest Rivers
The Mississippi (North America)
The Nile (Africa)
The Amazon (South America)

1. Ask B questions to find out the tallest mountain and the largest island. For example: *What's the tallest mountain in the world?* Write 1 next to the answers.

2. Answer B's questions.

3. Ask B questions about the other two mountains and islands. For example: *Which is taller, Everest or K2?* Mark the answers 2 and 3.

4. Answer B's questions.

1. Answer A's questions.

2. Ask A questions to find out the biggest lake and the longest river. For example: *What's the biggest lake in the world?* Write 1 next to the answers.

3. Answer A's questions.

4. Ask A questions about the other lakes and rivers. For example: *Which is bigger, Lake Superior or Lake Victoria?* Mark the answers 2 and 3.

EXERCISE 3 (pairs)

Language Focus

comparatives and superlatives, large numbers in measurements

New Words and Expressions

square mile, hectare, foot, meter, million, billion, lake, sea, mountain, island, river

Names

Lake Superior /leɪk supíərijər/
Lake Victoria /leɪk vɪktóriə/
Caspian Sea /kǽspiən si/
Mississippi /mɪsɪsípi/
Nile /nɑɪl/
Amazon /ǽməzɔn/
Everest /ɛ́vərəst/
K2 /kei tu/
Kanchenjunga /kǽntʃɛnjúŋə/

Teaching Suggestions

1. Teach new words and expressions, as needed.

2. Model the four sentences for the students in order to go over the pronunciation of the names in this exercise. Then let them repeat each one after you.

3. Have students read the Note about square miles, feet and large numbers aloud. For example: *One square mile equals two hundred and fifty-nine hectares.*

4. This is an information gap exercise. Help two students model an example to make sure everyone understands the procedure. After B answers A, A puts **1** next to Everest, **2** next to K2 and **3** next to Kanchenjunga.

5. Have students work in pairs. A asks B about the mountains and islands, and B asks A about the lakes and rivers.

6. (Optional) Students can make reverse comparisons; for example: *Which is smaller/shorter?*

7. (Optional) When they have finished, ask various As and Bs for the information *(how big, tall, long)* so that they have more practice with long numbers. If you do this, practice the pronunciation of the numbers in the book first.

8. (Optional) On the board write the names of several major cities in the students' country or countries. Have them ask questions about them. *Which is bigger?*

9. (Optional) Have the As close their books and have the Bs ask the As, *Where's* .... ? For example, *Where's Lake Victoria? In Africa.*

EXERCISE 4 (pairs)

Language Focus

too and *not* .... *enough;* review of *can't* for inability and impermissibility

New Words and Expressions

figure out, hot, keep up with, move (*v.*), pizza, problem, reach, smart, What's the matter?, What's wrong?

Teaching Suggestions

First Part

1. Have students study the illustration and example conversation.

2. Teach new words and expressions, as needed.

3. Help two students model the example conversation. *What's the matter? What's wrong?* Show a sad face. Reverse roles and say, *What's the matter?*

4. Have the class do the exercise in pairs. Tell the Bs to ask about numbers 1 and 3, and the As to ask about 2.

5. (Optional) Have students cover the captions and try to do the exercise without the cues.

6. After students have done the exercise once, tell them to act out the situation and practice the conversation again.

7. (Optional) Have students describe the situation, using the third person. For example: *Those shoes are too small. She can't wear them.*

Second Part

1. Have students study the illustration and example conversation.

2. Teach new words and expressions, as needed.

3. Follow steps 3–5 for the First Part, except this time, tell the As to ask about numbers 1 and 3 and the Bs to ask about 2.

4. (Optional) Have students figure out other ways to give the information in both parts of the exercise. For example, in the first example conversation, the person could say, *These shoes aren't big enough.* In the second example conversation, the person could say, *I'm too slow.*

Workbook

You can now assign Exercises D and E.

EXERCISE 5 (pairs)

Language Focus

giving opinions, agreeing and disagreeing, expansion of comparatives with *which* and *who*

New Words and Expressions

beautiful, best, better, cold, enjoyable, funny, healthy, important, ocean, rich, salary, worse, worst

Teaching Suggestions

First Part

Note: For a general question with *who,* the verb is always singular unless it is immediately followed by a plural noun or pronoun. Compare: *Who are they?* with *Who's right, the students or the teacher?*

1. Teach new words and expressions, as needed.

2. Have students read the questions. Make sure they understand the vocabulary. Ask them if they can add other questions. (Or you might want to add other questions.) List those questions on the board.

3. Help two students model the example conversation.

4. Have the class work in pairs to do the exercise.

5. When they have finished, take a vote of their opinions for each question.

6. (Optional) Go back to the example. Ask: *Why is a vacation in the mountains more enjoyable?* List possible reasons on the board: *It's cool. I like trees. The ocean is far away. I can't swim.* Ask: *Why is a vacation at the ocean more enjoyable?* List possible reasons: *I enjoy swimming. I like the sound of the ocean.* Have two students model the example conversation, this time giving personal reasons for their opinion. When they have finished, discuss the reasons they gave.

Second Part

1. Have students study the list of adjectives. Have them add other adjectives, or add ones you feel are appropriate. Remind them that they can also use the ones in the example questions.

2. Have students think of questions they could ask, and list some of the questions on the board. For example, *Which is more interesting, a trip in your country or a trip in another country? Who is more popular, Princess Diana or Queen Elizabeth? Which is better for you, hot weather or cold weather?*

3. Have the students do the exercise in pairs. Remind them to try to give reasons for their opinions.

4. Finally, have various pairs ask the class some of their questions.

Workbook

You can now assign Exercise F.

4

● Have conversations about these pictures.

these shoes/small/wear

A: What's the matter?   OR   What's wrong?
B: These shoes are too small.
   I can't wear them.

1. this pizza/hot/eat

2. this sofa/heavy/move

3. these gloves/
   expensive/afford

● Have conversations about these pictures.

keep up with/those people/fast

A: What's wrong?   OR   What's the matter?
B: I can't keep up with those people.
   I'm not fast enough.

1. see/that movie/old

2. reach/those cookies/
   tall

3. figure out/
   that problem/smart

5

Ask your partner these questions.
Agree or disagree with his/her answers.

A: What do you think? Which is
   more enjoyable, a vacation at the
   ocean or a vacation in the
   mountains?
B: A vacation in the mountains.
A: I agree (with you). Which
   ----------------------?
   OR   I don't really agree (with
   you). I think a vacation at the
   ocean is more enjoyable. Which
   ----------------------?

1. Which is better, hot weather or
   cold weather?
2. Which is the easiest, chemistry,
   biology or psychology?
3. Who's more famous, Elvis Presley
   or James Dean?
4. Who's smarter, men or women?
5. Which is more important, an
   interesting job or a good salary?

● Use these words and make up
your own questions:

good	*good*	*bad*
bad	good	bad
————	better	worse
	best	worst

healthy	*healthy*
funny	healthy
easy	healthier
————	healthiest

rich	*rich*
hot	rich
old	richer
small	richest

beautiful	*beautiful*
comfortable	beautiful
interesting	more beautiful
popular	most beautiful
————	

6

Ask your partner his/her opinion on these questions. Agree or disagree.

A: Who's the best tennis player in the world?

B: I think it's ....

A: I think so, too.

OR   Really? I don't think so. I think it's ....

1. What's the fastest car?

2. .... popular song in your country right now?

3. .... famous man/woman from your country?

4. .... powerful person in the world?

5. ....?

7
Culture Capsule

Sports are very popular in the United States, both to watch and to play. The most popular sports to watch are: football, baseball, basketball, bowling, golf and tennis.

What are the most popular sports in your country?
Which sports do you like to watch?
Which sports do you like to play?

8
Put It Together

A, B and C, you each want to buy a house.

A, you have three children. You can afford to pay $130,000.

B, you're single. You have a lot of money. You collect modern art. You can afford to pay $500,000.

C, you and your wife/husband are retired. Your children are married and don't live with you anymore. You like to garden. You can afford to pay $120,000.

old – new	modern – old-fashioned
big – small	interesting – boring
attractive – ugly	expensive – cheap

● Ask your partners these questions. Use the words above to help you.

Which house do you like best?
What do you like about it?
Why do you like it better than the others?

● Ask the same questions, but give true answers.

EXERCISE 6 (pairs)

Language Focus

superlatives, giving opinions, agreeing and disagreeing

New Words and Expressions

player

Teaching Suggestions

1. Have students study the instructions and ask them to think of other, similar questions. Be sure that the questions are ones that elicit opinions and are not ones about established facts (*What's the biggest city in the world?* is not appropriate, for example). For example: *Who's the most powerful woman/man in your country? What are the most important courses in school? What's the best language to know? Who is the most important person in a person's life?* List the questions on the board.

2. Help two students model the example. Then have them or another pair of students ask one of the questions on the board. Ask them to give reasons.

3. Have students do the exercise in pairs. Then ask various pairs to give their answers to some of the questions and their reasons for their answers.

EXERCISE 7 Culture Capsule (whole class, pairs)

Culture Focus

popular sports in the U.S. and students' home countries

New Words and Expressions

football, basketball, bowling, golf

Teaching Suggestions

1. Teach new words as needed.

2. Have the students read the Culture Capsule silently, or read it to them.

3. Point out the difference between *football* and *soccer* in the U.S. Ask: *Is football here like American football, or is it different? Can you touch the ball with your feet? In the U.S. that game is called soccer.*

4. Ask your students the first question.

5. (Optional) Add more questions to the list. For example: *Which do you like better, ... or ....? Why? Did you play .... in high school?* With the second question in the Student Book, point out that they can say, *Do you mean on TV or at a real game?*

6. Have students ask and answer the questions in pairs.

7. Finally, make a survey of the class: the most popular sports to watch and to play.

Workbook

You can now assign Exercises G and H.

EXERCISE 8 Put It Together (role-play, threes)

Language Focus

comparatives and superlatives, *too* and *not enough,* giving opinions and reasons, large numbers

New Words and Expressions

art, attractive, ugly, modern, old-fashioned, boring, collect, retired, garden (*v.*)

Teaching Suggestions

1. Have students look at the illustrations and adjective lists and read the instructions.

2. Teach new words and expressions, as needed.

3. If appropriate, have students figure out the value of the houses in local currency.

4. Ask students about the houses, using the list of adjectives (except for *attractive, ugly, interesting,* or *boring,* which involve personal opinion). For example: *Which house is the oldest? Which one is the newest? Which one is the most modern? Which one is the most old-fashioned?*

5. Divide the class into groups of three and have them decide who is A, B and C. Tell them to decide which house they like the best and to think of their reasons. Remind them that they can refer to the Checklist for assistance.

6. Have them answer the questions within their groups.

7. Then ask the As, Bs and Cs the three questions in turn.

8. Finally, have them answer the questions again, this time giving their personal opinions.

9. When they have finished, ask the class, *Who likes the gray house? Why? Who likes the white house? Why? Who likes the red house? Why?*

CHECKLIST

Teaching Suggestions

1. See the general suggestions in the Checklist page in Unit 1.

2. (Optional) Grammar practice: On the board write some of the adjectives learned in the unit. Have the students ask and answer questions with *Which* and *Who* about themselves, the class or other topics/people, using these adjectives. Then write on the board *too* and *not enough,* and have students use the adjectives on the board to make sentences with *too* and *not enough.*

3. (Optional) From time to time, you may wish to have students review the Checklist part by part and then quiz them orally in class, with books open or closed. For example:

T: *You're talking about cars with your friends. How do you ask their opinions about a car?*

Ss: *What do you think of it?* OR *What do you like about it?*

T: *Someone says, I like big cars. They're more comfortable. You agree. What do you say?*

Ss: *I agree.* OR *I think so, too.*

And so on.

OPTIONAL WRITING PRACTICE

You live in the U.S., and you have a car you want to sell. Write an advertisement for it. Your advertisement can be either for a newspaper, or a sign you will put up all over town (in the supermarket, on telephone poles, on bulletin boards). You decide. But be sure to write an ad that will sell your car!

_____

_____

_____

_____

_____

_____

_____

I know how to . . .

USE THESE FORMS

☐ **Adjective Comparisons**

To compare two things use the comparative.
Small cars are faster than big cars.
Big cars are more expensive than small cars.

To compare three or more things, use the superlative.
The two-door is the cheapest of all the cars here.
It isn't the most comfortable.

Add -er *or* -est *to adjectives of one syllable* (tall   taller   tallest) *or adjectives ending in* -y (easy   easier   easiest).

Spelling

Words ending in -y *change the* y *to* i *before adding* -er *or* -est.
easy   easier   easiest

Words ending consonant-vowel-consonant double the final consonant.
big   bigger   biggest

Use more *or* most *before words of three or more syllables* (more powerful) *or words of two syllables not ending in* -y (most modern).

irregular comparisons
good   better   best
bad   worse   worst

☐ **Too/Enough**

It's too slow and uncomfortable, and it isn't powerful enough.
This pizza is too hot. I can't eat it.

USE ENGLISH TO

☐ **ask someone's opinion**
What kind of car do you like?
What do you like about them?
Which one do you like?

☐ **give an opinion**
I like big cars. Bigger cars are more comfortable.
I think it's too slow.

☐ **agree**
I agree (with you)./I think so, too.

☐ **disagree**
I don't really agree with you.
Really? I don't think so. I think . . . .

☐ **show concern**
What's the matter?/What's wrong?

☐ **talk about these subjects**
speed   weight   size   quantity
large numbers   cars   sports
geography   houses

☐ **UNDERSTAND THESE EXPRESSIONS**

Good afternoon.
It gets good mileage.
That's OK.
We can afford (to buy) it.
You only live once.

after all
in general
in that case
miles per gallon

CHECKLIST

▣ Listening

1

Listen to the conversation and check the correct answer.

1. Which is smaller?
   ___ Monaco   ___ San Marino

2. Which is faster?
   ___ an antelope   ___ a cheetah

3. Which is taller?
   ___ Sears Tower
   ___ the World Trade Center

4. Which has the biggest population?
   ___ Shanghai   ___ Tokyo

5. Which is the heaviest animal?
   ___ a hippopotamus
   ___ an elephant

2

Which picture is correct, according to the conversation? Circle a or b.

1.   a.   b.

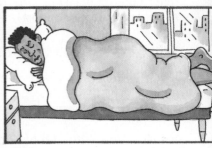

2.   a.   b.

3.   a.   b.

4.   a.   b.

3

Give true answers.   1. ....   2. ....

                        3. ....   4. ....

LISTENING

EXERCISE 1

Language Focus

comparatives and superlatives

New Words and Expressions

antelope, elephant, hippopotamus, population

Names

Sears /sɪərz/

Teaching Suggestions

1. Familiarize students with the new words by having them look at the illustrations while you pronounce the words.

2. Preview the exercise by asking the students to guess the answers. For example, ask them: *Which do you think is smaller, Monaco or San Marino? Which do you think is faster, the antelope or the cheetah?* and so on.

3. Play the cassette or read the tapescript.

4. Have students do the exercise. Then ask them: *Which is smaller, Monaco or San Marino?*

5. (Optional) Have students listen again and write down the actual numbers. Then ask questions about each picture. For example, *How big is Monaco?* Sl: *Smaller than one square mile.*

Answers:

1. Monaco (smaller than one sq. mi.)

2. cheetah (65 m.p.h.)

3. Sears Tower (1,454 ft. tall)

4. Tokyo (11,694,000 people)

5. elephant (16,000 lbs.)

EXERCISE 2

Language Focus

too, not enough

Teaching Suggestions

1. Preview the listening exercise by having the students describe the situation in each picture. For example, in the first picture, the sweater is too small; in the second picture, the sweater is too big.

2. Play the cassette or read the tapescript.

3. Have students do the exercise. Then ask them which pictures fit the conversation they heard.

Answers: 1. b   2. b   3. a   4. a

EXERCISE 3

Language Focus

personal questions based on the language covered in the unit

Teaching Suggestions

1. Play the cassette or read the tapescript.

2. Have students do the exercise and then ask if they remember the questions. Ask various students what their answers were.

Answers: Since answers are personal, they will vary with each student.

EPISODE 11 The Moon of India

Key Vocabulary

arrest, magnificent, police identification card, scream

Teaching Suggestions

1. Have students retell the last few episodes: Agatha is in her cabin unpacking a costume for the Costume Ball. She holds up the costume and bumps into a painting on the wall. Behind the painting is the Moon of India. She takes it to the purser to put in the ship's safe. She asks herself, "Did Christina put it there?" At the Costume Ball, Agatha sees a gun in Lucy's costume. She's frightened. During the ball, someone goes to Agatha's cabin. It's the thief. The thief looks for the necklace behind the painting. The necklace isn't there. The thief throws the painting on the floor.

2. Follow steps 1–4 of Episode 1.

3. Students read the episode again.

4. Ask the comprehension questions.

Answers: 1) She thinks someone has come into her room to look for the necklace. 2) She knows Lucy isn't a fashion buyer, because Lucy didn't know that Pierre Maurice died ten years ago. 3) Yes, she does. Because Lucy has a gun. 4) Because Lucy tells her and shows Agatha her police identification. 5) They're talking about the Moon of India. 6) He invites her to his cabin for a drink. It's his last night.

5. (Optional) Other possible questions. Are you surprised that Lucy is a police officer? Was Lucy's gun real? Why does Robert say, "It still is magnificent"? Do you think Christina should have a drink with Robert in his cabin?

6. Have students close their books and summarize the episode. Check their understanding of the story as they tell it. Correct any misunderstandings.

7. (Optional) Expansion questions. Are there women police officers in your country?

8. (Optional) Role-play. Students can role-play the dialogues between Agatha and Lucy and Robert and Christina, using role cards.

Episode Eleven

Agatha leaves the ball and returns to her cabin. She sees the painting on the floor. She stands for a moment in the doorway. Suddenly, there is somebody behind her. Agatha screams and then sees it is Lucy.

"What's the matter, Agatha?"

"Somebody was in here."

"You should. . . ."

"Please. I think you know about this."

"Agatha, what are you talking about?"

"You're not a fashion buyer. I know that. Pierre Maurice, the designer we talked about the first night, died ten years ago. And why are you carrying a gun? I saw a gun under your jacket this evening."

"It's part of my costume."

"And you put the Moon of India in our room. But you won't get it back."

"I am looking for the necklace, Agatha. You see, I'm a police officer." She shows Agatha her police identification card. "I'm on this cruise to find the necklace and

arrest the person who stole it."

"But if you're not the thief, Lucy, who is?"

On deck, Robert and Christina are talking. "Your job must be very interesting, Christina."

"Yes it is. The City Museum has one of the best Egyptian collections in the country."

"And it had the Moon of India."

"Yes, it was magnificent."

"It still is magnificent."

"Yes, of course. It still is magnificent, wherever it is."

They watch the ocean and the stars. Robert takes Christina's arm. "Would you like to come to my cabin and have a drink?"

"It's a little late, Robert."

"I'm leaving early tomorrow. This is my last night. Let's just have one drink."

"All right, but I can't stay long."

Comprehension Check

1. What does Agatha think when she sees the painting on the floor?
2. How does Agatha know that Lucy is not a fashion buyer?
3. At first, does Agatha think Lucy stole the necklace? Why?
4. How does Agatha learn that Lucy is a police officer?
5. What are Robert and Christina talking about on the deck?
6. Why does Robert invite Christina to his cabin?

UNIT 12

Rick: Hi, Jane. What's wrong? You look depressed.

Jane: Hello, Rick. I just filled out a questionnaire in this magazine. I'm a boring person.

Rick: No, you're not. Why do you say that?

Jane: Well, for example, which do you like better, Walt Disney or James Bond movies?

Rick: That's easy. James Bond movies. In fact, Sean Connery's my favorite actor. Who's yours?

Jane: Mine's Woody Allen, and I like Walt Disney movies. Where do you like to eat out?

Rick: At any foreign restaurant, I guess. I like to try new things.

Jane: Would you rather watch TV or go out in the evening? I'd rather watch TV.

Rick: Really? I'd rather go out.

Jane: See? I'm boring. What do you think? Will your life be different in five years?

Rick: Probably. I hope so anyway. What about you?

Jane: Probably not. I'll have the same job, live in the same place. . . . What would you like to do for your next vacation?

Rick: I don't know. I'd **like** to go to an exciting place, like the Amazon or Mt. Everest.

Jane: Do you think you will?

Rick: I doubt it, but maybe someday. You've got to have dreams.

UNIT 12

Unit Language Focus

GRAMMAR: *will* for future possibility, *would like to, would rather*, possessive pronouns, embedded questions with *Do you think*
COMMUNICATIVE AREAS: talking about likes, dislikes, preferences, future possibilities, desires, hopes and doubts; agreeing and disagreeing

OPENING CONVERSATION

New Words and Expressions

completely, depressed, doubt, dream, exciting, fill out, foreign, have got to, hope, magazine, mine, point, questionnaire, rest (*v.*), score, someday, unusual, would rather, in fact

Names

Burger King /bə́rgər kıŋ/
James Bond /dʒeımz bánd/
McDonald's /mıkdánəldz/
Rick /rık/
Walt Disney /wɔlt dízni/
Woody Allen /wudi ǽlən/
Sean Connery /ʃɔ́n kánəri/

Teaching Suggestions

1. Warm-up. Ask: *What's the woman doing? What's the man doing? Do you think they're friends? What're they thinking about?* Describe the picture: *There is a woman. She's eating lunch. Her name is Jane. There's a man. He's jogging. The two of them are talking. . . .*

2. Personalize: *The woman's eating lunch in the park. Do you ever eat lunch outside? Her lunch is from McDonald's. Is there a McDonald's near here? McDonald's is called a fast-food restaurant. Are there some fast-food restaurants in this area?*

3. Have students read the questionnaire before listening to the conversation. Have them name some Walt Disney and James Bond movies.

4. Teach new words and expressions, as needed. Explain that *would rather* means *prefer to.*

5. Have students calculate Jane's score (10). Ask: *According to the questionnaire, is Jane a boring person or an exciting person?* Ask if they agree with the basis for deciding who is boring and who is exciting.

6. Play/read the conversation. Students look only at the picture.

7. Play/read it again. Students listen while reading silently.

8. Teach new words and expressions, as needed. Explain that *have got to* means *have to.*

9. Point out the emotions expressed in this conversation. For example, Rick sounds concerned when he says, *You look depressed,* and emphasizes his disagreement when he says, *No, you're not.* Jane sounds unhappy when she says, *I'll have the same job, I'll live in the same place. . . .*

10. Tell students they will often hear Americans pronounce *You've got to* as *You've gotta* in conversation.

11. Ask students if they know who Sean Connery and Woody Allen are. If they don't, explain that Sean Connery is famous for playing James Bond. Woody Allen is very funny and intelligent, but you wouldn't describe him as good-looking.

12. Let students ask questions about grammar, pronunciation and vocabulary.

13. Students read/repeat the conversation.

14. (Optional) Have students figure out Rick's score.

15. Have students role-play Rick and Jane in pairs. Looking only at the questionnaire, Rick asks Jane questions. Make sure the students change each pair of statements in the questionnaire to a question. If necessary, list the beginnings of the questions on the board: *Which do you like better? Where do you like to .... ? Would you rather .... ? Will your life .... ? What would you like to .... ?*

16. Ask students: *What does Rick mean when he says, "You've got to have dreams?"*

Additional Information

Grammar

1. *will:* This unit focuses on the future possibility or predictive use of *will.* For example, *I'll probably/I probably won't ....: Maybe someday I'll ....; Will your life be different?*

2. *In five years:* This is a more common way to say *five years from now.* Similar examples: *Vacation starts in two weeks. This will be ready in three days.*

3. *any restaurant: Any* is a determiner here and means *it doesn't matter which (restaurant).*

4. *like to* vs. *would like to: Like to* is used for a person's current preference based on habit or custom; *would like to* is used to express a desire.

Vocabulary and Usage

1. *See?* This means, *Do you see? I am/was right.*

2. *I hope so anyway: Anyway* means *In any case.*

SPEAKING

EXERCISE 1 (pairs)

Language Focus

will for future possibility, *would rather, like to* vs. *would like to*

Teaching Suggestions

1. Have students fill out the questionnaire for themselves.

2. Have them work in pairs and ask each other questions based on the questionnaire.

3. Have students calculate their scores. Ask them if they agree with the results.

4. Ask various students the questions in the questionnaire. Or, alternatively, ask the questions this way: *Who likes Walt Disney movies better than James Bond movies? Who likes to eat out at McDonald's?* And so on.

EXERCISE 2 (pairs, mixer)

Language Focus

asking about favorites, possessive pronouns, possessive forms of nouns, *who/what* questions

Names

Meryl Streep /mérəl stríp/
Arturo's /ɑrtúroz/
Alicia's /ɑlísiɑz/
Joan Collins /dʒon kɑ́lɪnz/
Jessica Lange /dʒésɪkə lǽŋ/

Teaching Suggestions

First Part

1. Have students read the instructions. Have them give examples of actors and actresses, movies, books, and singers. Ask them if they would like to add anything to the categories. List their ideas on the board. They can write them in the book, if they wish. Have students take a moment to decide their answers for each category.

2. Choose three students to model the three possible conversations. Ask: *Whose favorite actress is Meryl Streep?* Choose two volunteers. Ask: *Whose favorite actress is Jessica Lange?* Choose one volunteer. Ask: *Who does* not *have a favorite actress?* Choose one volunteer. Help them model the three example conversations. (Choose actresses more familiar to the class if necessary.)

3. Have students do the first part of the exercise in pairs. Make sure they understand when to use *What* instead of *Who*, and the pronoun *It* instead of *He* or *She* in their answers.

Second Part

1. Have students read the instructions. Then see if they can supply the missing possessive pronouns.

2. Now the students are going to ask various classmates about their favorite actors and actresses. Tell them they should do this as a mixer, going quickly from one person to another.

OR **2.** Have students write the categories from the first part down one side of a piece of paper. Tell them they are going to ask various classmates about their favorite actors and actresses, books, sports, and so on. They should write the name of the classmate they interview at the top of a column and fill in the appropriate information. This should also be done as a mixer.

3. When students have finished gathering the information, have them read the example questions and answers. Start students out by asking the question a few times and having them supply the answer. Always ask about two people (one man and one woman) at the same time so that students use *his/hers* naturally. (Note: If you have single-sex classes, students will have to practice the possessive in a different form: *Maria's is Joan Collins. Kimi's is Elizabeth Taylor.* If you have a large class, have students take over and ask the question about people they were unable to interview. If you have a small class, and the students have interviewed everyone in the class, then you should ask all the questions.)

4. (Optional) Do a chain drill based on the information gathered above. One student starts: *My favorite (color) is (red). What's yours?* S2: *Mine's (blue.) What's yours?* S3: *Mine's* ...., and so on. Then do another drill to practice other pronouns. S1 starts: *My favorite (same as in previous drill) is (same).* Then she looks at another student and asks: *What's hers (his/theirs)?* and points to the student (or students) in question. S2: *Hers is* .... *(His is* .... *Hers is* .... *and hers/his is* ....*)*

Workbook

You can now assign Exercises A and B. The word *coats* is introduced in B.

ARE YOU BORING OR EXCITING?

Do you agree with these statements?

Answer Yes or No.

YES 1. I like Walt Disney movies better than James Bond movies.
NO 2. I like James Bond movies better than Walt Disney movies.
YES 3. I like to eat out at McDonald's and Burger King.
NO 4. I like to eat out at foreign restaurants.
YES 5. I'd rather watch TV than go out in the evening.
NO 6. I'd rather go out than watch TV in the evening.
YES 7. My life probably won't change very much in five years.
NO 8. Maybe someday my life will be completely different.
YES 9. For my next vacation, I'd like to stay home and rest.
NO 10. For my next vacation, I'd like to go to an unusual place like Antarctica.

SCORING:

For 1, 3, 5, 7, and 9, give yourself 2 points for each No and 1 point for each Yes.
For 2, 4, 6, 8, and 10, give yourself 2 points for each Yes and 1 point for each No.

Is your score 16-20? You're an exciting person!
Is your score 10-15? You're boring! You need help!

Speaking

1

A, ask Jane's questions. **B,** give true answers. Then figure out your scores.

2

● Have conversations like these. Use *Who* for people. Use *What* for things.

A: Who's your favorite actress?
B: Meryl Streep.
A: She's mine, too.

OR

A: Who's your favorite actress?
B: I don't have one. Who's yours?
 OR Jessica Lange. Who's yours?
A: Mine's ....

| actor | book | color | singer |
| actress | sport | movie | |

● Find out the favorites of other people in your class. Then ask and answer questions about them.

A: Who are Arturo's and Alicia's favorite actresses?
B: His is Joan Collins. Hers is Elizabeth Taylor.

my - ....
your - ....
his - ....
her - ....
our - ours
their - theirs

3

Listen to music

classical *Bach, Mozart*
popular *John Denver, Billy Joel*
jazz *Ella Fitzgerald, Dizzy Gillespie*

Play sports

basketball   tennis   baseball

Go to movies

cartoons *Mickey Mouse*
westerns *The Good, the Bad and the Ugly*
thrillers *Psycho*

● Ask your partner what he/she likes. Have conversations like these:

A: Do you like to listen to music?
B: Yes, I do.
A: What kind of music do you like?
B: ----------------------.

OR

A: Do you like to listen to music?
B: Not especially. Do you?
A: ----------------------.

● Have conversations like this:

A: Would you rather listen to music or play sports?
B: I'd rather play sports (than listen to music).
A: I would, too.
   OR   I'd rather listen to music.

4

Pronunciation

Practice these conversations:

A: Do you like jazz?

B: Yes, I do.

C: I do, too.   OR   Really? I don't.

OR

A: Do you like jazz?

B: Not especially.

C: I don't either.   OR   Really? I do.

5

● **A, B** and **C,** ask each other about what you each like, and fill in this chart. Use a √ if your classmate likes something. Use an X, if he or she doesn't. Follow the example in Exercise 4.

	A	B	C
jazz			
classical music			
baseball			
westerns			

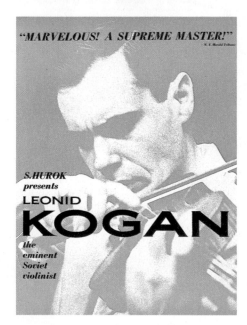

● Find a partner from a different group. Use the information above and have conversations like this about the people in your first group.

A: Would -------------------- like to go to the jazz concert?
B: Probably. She likes jazz. Would -------------------- like to go to the violin concert?
A: Probably not. He doesn't like classical music.

EXERCISE 3 (pairs)

Language Focus

talking about likes and preferences, what kind of

New Words and Expressions

cartoons, classical, jazz, music, thriller, western, not especially

Names

Bach /bɑk/
Mozart /mótsɑrt/
John Denver /dʒɑn dénvər/
Billy Joel /bíli dʒoəl/
Ella Fitzgerald /élə fɪtsdʒérəld/
Dizzy Gillespie /dízi gɪléspi/

Teaching Suggestions

First Part

1. Have students read over the categories of music, sports and movies. Use the examples of composers, performers and movies next to each category to teach the new words. If students don't recognize the names in the book, provide names they are familiar with.

2. Ask students to provide additional examples in each category. Ask them if they want to add any other types of music (for example: rock, folk), movies (horror movies, love stories) or sports to the chart. Write their ideas on the board. Ask if they want to add another category; for example: *read books, read magazines, go out to restaurants, go to plays.*

3. Have students read the example conversation. Explain that *not especially* means *not really* or *not very much.*

4. Help three students model the two possible conversations for the class (Student A and two Student Bs).

5. Have students work in pairs. They should talk on at least three topics.

6. (Optional) You can ask various students about their partners. For example, *Does S1 like to go to movies?* S2: *Yes, she does.* T: *What kind?* S2: *Horror movies.*

Second Part

1. Have two students model the conversation for the class. Point out that they can also ask questions about one area, like, *Would you rather listen to jazz or to classical music?*

2. Have students do the exercise in pairs. When they are finished, ask various students about their partners. For example: T: *Would S1 rather listen to jazz or to classical music?* S2: *Jazz,* or *I don't know. I didn't ask her (him).*

EXERCISE 4 (whole class, threes)

Language Focus

stress and intonation

Teaching Suggestions

1. Help students practice the model conversations a few times chorally, first using the responses in the left column and next using the responses in the right column. Make sure they use the right stress and intonation, exaggerating at first, in order to get a feeling for it.

2. Have students practice the model conversations in groups of three, first exaggerating the stress and intonation, then trying to say it quickly and normally, as in conversation.

3. (Optional) Have one or more groups say the conversation for the class.

EXERCISE 5 (threes, pairs)

Language Focus

agreeing and disagreeing with someone's likes and dislikes

Teaching Suggestions

First Part

1. Have each group decide who is A, B and C. Have one group serve as a model, and go through the exercise with them. *Do you like jazz? . . .*

2. Have the groups do the exercise. Tell them to take turns being the first to ask the questions.

3. (Optional) Students can add other categories to the chart for further practice.

Second Part

1. Divide the class into pairs so that students who were together for the previous part of the exercise are not together now. If you have an even number of students, the easiest way to do this is by having the As pair up with As, the Bs with Bs, and the Cs with Cs. Have students study the instructions.

2. Help two students model the example conversation for the class. Explain that each person is going to give true information. They are going to ask each other questions about the people on their charts.

3. Have students do the exercise in pairs.

Workbook

You can now assign Exercises C and D.

EXERCISE 6 (pairs)

Language Focus

possessive pronouns, review of prepositions of location, possessive form of nouns

Teaching Suggestions

1. Have students read the instructions and look at the seating plan. Begin the exercise with them: *You are A. What is your partner's seat number?*

    S1: *B3.*
    T: *What is your brother's seat number?*
    S2: *C2.*

2. Have students work in pairs and figure out the seat numbers. Point out that they can say either, *His is C2,* or *C2 is his.* Their conversation could go like this:

    A: *B3 is yours.*
    B: *Right. And your brother's?*
    A: *His is C2.*
    B: *And your sister's?*
    A: *Hers is C1.*
    B: *And her husband's parents?*
    A: *Theirs are D1 and D2.*

3. Go over the answers by asking questions similar to step 1.

    T: *Which is A's sister's seat number?*
    S2: *C1.*
    T: *So C1 is hers. And her husband's parents'?*
    S3: *D1 and D2 are theirs.*

4. (Optional) Have two students model the whole dialogue.

5. (Optional) Each pair rearranges the seating plan and passes the plan to the next pair. They then practice the dialogue again with the new information.

EXERCISE 7 (whole class)

Language Focus

stress in two-syllable words

New Words and Expressions

stress

Teaching Suggestions

Note: The word *different* is almost always pronounced as a two-syllable word. In dictionaries a three-syllable pronunciation is also given.

1. Have students read the explanation and practice the stress in the two words *boring* and *yourself.*

2. On the board write *boring,* and next to it, *yourself.* Say each word for the students, or have them say each word and tell you whether it belongs with *boring* or with *yourself.*

3. Ask students to find other two-syllable words in the book. (They can look at the opening conversation of the previous unit.) As they say each word, have them indicate whether it belongs with *boring* or with *yourself.*

EXERCISE 8 (pairs)

Language Focus

talking about future possibilities with *will;* embedded questions with *Do you think you'll* .... *someday?;* talking about future hopes and doubts

New Words and Expressions

I doubt it, moon, North Pole, peace, perfect, someday, world war

Teaching Suggestions

First Part

1. Have students read over the instructions and example. Model the example with a student.

2. Teach new words and expressions as needed.

3. Have two students model another example for the class. *Will there be peace in the world someday?* Have students do the exercise.

4. When students have finished the exercise, ask them these questions: *Who hopes to visit Antarctica someday? Who hopes people will live to be 150 someday? Who hopes to be famous someday?*

5. (Optional) Expand on the questions: *Why do/don't you want to visit Antarctica? Why do/don't you hope people will live to be 150 someday?*

6. Have students add one of their own questions to the list. Put several on the board.

Second Part

Follow the same procedure as for the first part.

6

Figure it Out!

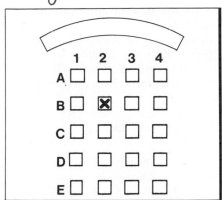

	1	2	3	4
A	☐	☐	☐	☐
B	☐	☒	☐	☐
C	☐	☐	☐	☐
D	☐	☐	☐	☐
E	☐	☐	☐	☐

You have five tickets to the theater. Your seat number is B2. Your partner's (B's) seat is on your right. Your brother's seat is behind yours. Your sister's seat is on his left. Her husband's parents' seats are behind them. Figure out the seat numbers and tell your partner. Use *yours, his, hers* and *theirs*.

A: -------------------- is yours.
B: Right. And your brother's?
A: -------------------- is --------------------.

7

Pronunciation

In words of two syllables, the stress is usually on the first syllable:

bŏring

Sometimes it's on the second syllable:

yoursĕlf

Where's the stress in these words? Practice saying them after your teacher.

depressed	rather
different	Hello
ticket	maybe
foreign	evening
someday	

8

● **A,** ask questions. **B,** give true answers. Have conversations like this:

you visit Antarctica

A: Will you visit Antarctica someday?
B: I hope so.   OR   I hope not.

1. you visit Antarctica
2. there will be peace in the world
3. we have another world war
4. people live to be 150
5. you be famous
6. I be very rich
7. --------------------

● Continue with conversations like this:

you'll drive across the U.S.

A: Do you think you'll drive across the United States someday?
B: Maybe someday.   OR   I doubt it.

1. you'll drive across the U.S.
2. people will live on the moon
3. you'll go to the North Pole
4. our English will be perfect
5. I'll be a movie star
6. --------------------

Mike Quon 1985

9
Culture Capsule

When television was new, only big cities in the United States had TV stations, or channels. Now almost everyone in the U.S. has a wide choice of channels. There are "regular" channels and cable channels. New York City, for example, has 7 regular channels. And one cable company there offers 34 more. Regular channels are free, but people pay for cable channels, usually every month.

These are some popular cable channels on American TV:

A&E Arts and Entertainment
(plays, concerts, dance)
*CNN Cable News Network
DIS The Disney Channel
(for children)
ESN Eastern Sports Network
*HBO Home Box Office
(movies)
*TMC The Movie Channel
*SHO Showtime
(movies)
MTV Music Television
(popular music videos)

*24 hours a day

How many TV channels can you get in your town or city? Do you have to pay for the "regular" ones? Does your town or city have cable TV? What kinds of programs can you get on it?

Do you have a TV at home? Which American cable TV channels would you like to watch? What do you like to watch on TV?

10
Put It Together

• **A** and **B**, write a questionnaire to find out your classmates' likes and dislikes and hopes for the future. Below are some possible subjects and questions. For more ideas, see the questionnaire on the first page of this unit.

Possible subjects

music   food
sports   vacations
movies   TV

Possible questions

Who's/What's your favorite ....?
Do you like (to) ....?
Would you rather .... or ....?
Would you like to .... someday?

• Work with another pair of students (C and D). **A,** ask C the questions on your questionnaire. **C,** ask A. **B,** ask D. **D,** ask B.

EXERCISE 9 Culture Capsule (whole class and/or pairs)

Culture Focus

television in the U.S., types of cable channels

New Words and Expressions

arts, cable, channel, entertainment, free, offer, program, TV station, wide choice, video

Teaching Suggestions

1. Have students read the Culture Capsule information silently, or read it aloud to them.

2. Teach new words and expressions as needed. Explain *TV stations or channels, cable channels and regular channels.* Give examples of *channels* or *stations* your students know. Distinguish between *cable channels* and *regular channels,* if applicable. If not, point out that there are no cable channels in the area, and explain that cable channels come through cables under the ground.

3. If your students all come from the same city or town, then ask the first group of questions of the whole class. If your students come from different cities (which have different TV systems) or countries, then they can ask each other the questions in pairs. Have them report differences and similarities to the whole class.

4. Use the second group of questions to lead a discussion of television likes and dislikes.

Workbook

You can now assign Exercises E–G.

EXERCISE 10 Put It Together (pairs)

Language Focus

talking about favorites, preferences, desires, likes and dislikes

New Words and Expressions

dislikes, hope (*n.*), possible

Teaching Suggestions

1. Have students read the instructions.

2. Teach new words as needed.

3. Give students time to think of other subjects or questions to include. For example, the other questions in the questionnaire on the first page of the unit are: *Would you like to* ....? *Will you* .... *someday/in* .... *years? Will your life be* .... *someday/in* .... *years?* List students' ideas on the board.

4. Divide students into pairs and have them make up their questionnaires. Tell them they each need to have their own copy of the questionnaire. Circulate to provide help as necessary and to check the accuracy of their questions.

5. When they have completed their questionnaires, have each pair join another pair. Each of the four people will ask one of the people in the group the questions from their respective questionnaires.

6. When they have finished, ask them: *What were the most difficult questions? What were the most interesting questions? The funniest questions?*

7. (Optional follow-up) Have the whole class write up a questionnaire whose questions they will ask students from other English classes. They can choose a theme and decide on a scoring system.

CHECKLIST

Teaching Suggestions

1. See the general suggestions in the Checklist page in Unit 1.

2. (Optional) For additional grammar practice, have students ask and answer questions and make statements about themselves using *will,* embedded questions with *Do you think you'll* ...., *would like to* and *would rather.*

3. (Optional) From time to time, you may wish to have students review the Checklist part by part, and then quiz them orally in class, with books open or closed. For example:

> T: *You're talking about music with a friend. You want to tell her what you like and dislike. What can you say?*
> S1: *I like jazz.*
> S2: *I don't like classical music,* and so on.

OPTIONAL WRITING PRACTICE

You are PSYCHO, an astrologer who writes a newspaper column answering questions from readers. You receive the following letter from a reader. Write your answer for the column.

Dear PSYCHO:
I was born on August 3, 1966, at 4:18 A.M. Please tell me about myself and my future. At present I am,
$\qquad$ BORED AND LONELY

Dear Bored and Lonely:

_____

_____

_____

_____

_____

_____

I know how to . . .

USE THESE FORMS

☐ **Will**

I	will ('ll)
you	will not (won't)
he, she, it	
we	
they	

questions
Will your life be different in five years?
Where will you live?

short answers
Yes, it will.   No, it won't.

statements
You'll be famous.
Maybe I'll have the same job.
I probably won't see Mt. Everest.

☐ **Embedded Questions**

Do you think + *Will you* eat out tonight?
Do you think *you will* eat out tonight?

☐ **Would Like To/Would Rather**

I	would ('d)
you	
he, she, it	
we	
they	

questions
Would you like to be famous?
Would you rather go out or watch TV?

short answers
Yes, I would.   No, he wouldn't.

statements
I'd like to go to a concert.
He wouldn't like to go to a play.
I'd rather go out (than watch TV).

☐ **Possessive Pronouns**

mine, yours, his, hers, ours, theirs
Sean Connery's my favorite actor. Who's
yours?
Mine's Woody Allen.

USE ENGLISH TO

☐ **talk about likes and dislikes**
Do you like to listen to music? What kind of
   music do you like?
I like jazz. I don't like popular music.

☐ **talk about desires**
What would you like to do for your next
   vacation?
I'd like to go to an exciting place.

☐ **talk about preferences**
Would you rather watch TV or go out?
I'd rather watch TV.

☐ **agree with someone**
I do, too./ I would, too./ I don't, either.

☐ **disagree with someone**
Really? I do/ don't/ would/ wouldn't.
I'd rather go out.

☐ **talk about future possibilities**
Do you think you'll go to the moon?
Probably (not)./ Maybe./ I doubt it.
I hope so/ not.

☐ **talk about these subjects**
hopes for the future   favorites
entertainment   sports   music   TV

☐ **UNDERSTAND THESE EXPRESSIONS**

Not especially.
You look (depressed).
You've got to have dreams.
Why do you say that?

eat out
fill out
go out

CHECKLIST

🔊 Listening

1

Listen to the questions. There are two correct answers for each question. Choose the one that gives **your** true opinion.

You will hear, "1. Do you like Walt Disney movies?"
The correct answer can be *a* or *b*.

1. a. Yes, I do.
   b. Not especially.
   c. Yes, I would.
   d. No, I wouldn't.

2. a. Yes, I do.
   b. Not especially.
   c. Yes, I would.
   d. No, I wouldn't.

3. a. Yes, I would.
   b. No, I wouldn't.
   c. I'd rather watch TV.
   d. I'd rather go out.

4. a. Yes, I would.
   b. No, I wouldn't.
   c. I hope so.
   d. I hope not.

5. a. Yes, I do.
   b. No, I don't.
   c. Probably.
   d. Probably not.

6. a. I hope so.
   b. I hope not.
   c. Yes, I would.
   d. No, I wouldn't.

7. a. I hope so.
   b. I hope not.
   c. Yes, I do.
   d. Not especially.

8. a. I'd rather play sports.
   b. I'd rather listen to music.
   c. Maybe someday.
   d. I doubt it.

2

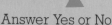

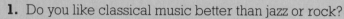
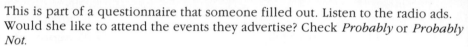

WHAT ARE YOU LIKE?

Answer <u>Yes</u> or <u>No</u>

<u>YES</u> **1.** Do you like classical music better than jazz or rock?
<u>YES</u> **2.** Do you like to eat at foreign restaurants?
<u>YES</u> **3.** In general, would you rather go to a movie than a sports event?
<u>YES</u> **4.** Would you like to go to the moon someday?

This is part of a questionnaire that someone filled out. Listen to the radio ads. Would she like to attend the events they advertise? Check *Probably* or *Probably Not.*

	Probably	**Probably Not**
1.	☐	☐
2.	☐	☐
3.	☐	☐
4.	☐	☐
5.	☐	☐

3

You will hear people talk about their likes and dislikes. Choose the appropriate response for each.

1. a. It's mine, too.
   b. Really? I don't.

2. a. I don't, either.
   b. I do, too.

3. a. Mine is tennis.
   b. Probably.

4. a. I would, too.
   b. Really? I don't.

5. a. Really? I'd rather play sports.
   b. Really? I'd rather go to the movies.

6. a. Really? I do.
   b. Really? I don't.

7. a. Probably not.
   b. I would, too.

4

Give true answers.

1. _____   4. _____

2. _____   5. _____

3. _____   6. _____

LISTENING

EXERCISE 1

Language Focus

questions and answers about likes, desires, preferences; hopes for the future and future possibilities

Teaching Suggestions

1. Ask various students what their answer is to the example question. There are four choices in their books, and two answers are possible. If all students provide the same answer (a or b), then use yourself as a contrast.

2. Play the cassette or read the tapescript.

3. Have students do the exercise.

4. Stop after each question and ask, for example: *Who likes to eat out at foreign restaurants? Who would rather watch TV?* Alternatively, you can ask, for example: *For number 2, who answered* a? *Who answered* b?

Answers: 1. a *or* b 2. a *or* b 3. c *or* d 4. a *or* b
5. c *or* d 6. c *or* d 7. a *or* b 8. c *or* d

EXERCISE 2

Language Focus

like to vs. *would like to, would rather, probably (not)*

Teaching Suggestions

1. Explain that *What are you like?* means *What kind of person are you?*

2. Have students read the questionnaire.

3. Play the cassette or read the tapescript.

4. Have students listen and do the exercise.

5. Check their answers. Ask them what each ad was about.

Answers: 1. Probably 2. Probably not 3. Probably
4. Probably not 5. Probably

EXERCISE 3

Language Focus

expressing likes and dislikes, agreeing and disagreeing about likes and dislikes, possessive pronouns

Teaching Suggestions

1. Play the cassette or read the tapescript.

2. Have students do the exercise.

3. Check their answers.

Answers: 1. a 2. b 3. a 4. b 5. a 6. a 7. b

EXERCISE 4

Language Focus

personal questions based on the language covered in the unit

Teaching Suggestions

1. Play the cassette or read the tapescript.

2. Have students do the exercise.

3. Ask them what the questions were.

4. (Optional) Ask various students what their answers were.

Answers. Since answers are personal, they will vary with each student.

EPISODE 12 The Moon of India

Key Vocabulary

crazy, get hurt, hostage, instructions, valuable

Teaching Suggestions

1. Have students retell the last few episodes: Agatha finds the Moon of India behind a painting in her room. She takes it to the purser to put in the ship's safe. She asks herself, "Did Christina put it there?" At the Costume Ball, Agatha sees a gun in Lucy's costume. She's frightened. During the ball, someone goes to Agatha's cabin. It's the thief. The thief looks for the necklace behind the painting. The necklace isn't there. The thief throws the painting on the floor. Agatha returns to her cabin. She sees the painting on the floor. Lucy comes up behind her. Agatha screams. She thinks Lucy is the thief because she has a gun, and because she isn't really a fashion buyer. Lucy is a police officer. She shows Agatha her identification. Robert Grant and Christina are on the deck talking about the Moon of India. Robert invites Christina to his cabin for a drink. It's his last night. She accepts.

2. Follow steps 1–4 of Episode 1.

3. Students read the episode again.

4. Ask the comprehension questions.
Answers: 1) Because he thinks she has the Moon of India. He's the thief, and he wants it. 2) Robert stops her. 3) Because it was in Christina and Agatha's cabin. If Christina doesn't have it, then Agatha has it. 4) He tells her to bring him the necklace. 5) Because he'll kill Christina if she doesn't. 6) Yes, she is.

5. (Optional) Other possible questions. Christina says, "You're the second person. . . ." What does she mean? Who's the second person? Robert says, "Don't play games with me." What does he mean? Do you think Agatha should give the necklace to Robert? How can Lucy help Agatha?

6. Have students close their books and summarize the episode. Check their understanding of the story as they tell it. Correct any misunderstandings.

7. (Optional) Role-play. Students can role-play the dialogues between Robert and Christina and the phone call between Robert and Agatha, using role cards.

Episode Twelve

Robert turns the lights on in his cabin and offers Christina a seat. "Make yourself comfortable. What would you like to drink?"

"Some cognac, please."

Robert gives Christina the drink and sits down next to her. "Now tell me more about the Moon of India."

"Why are you so interested in the Moon of India?"

"Don't you know?" Robert's voice is cold.

"No, I don't know. It's very strange. You're the second person. . . ."

"What did you say? Who's the other person?"

"It's not important, Robert. Aren't you going to make yourself a drink?"

"Don't play games with me, Christina. You know about the Moon of India. Who's the other person?"

"You're frightening me, Robert. What's the matter? I don't understand. I think I'd better leave."

Christina gets up and walks to the door. Robert moves in front of her.

"Robert, let me go."

"Where is the necklace?" Robert takes a gun from his pocket. "Where is the necklace?" he repeats.

"I don't know what you're talking about. You're crazy."

"So, it's the old lady. She found the necklace. Not you."

"What are you talking about?"

"I'm talking about the Moon of India. Your aunt has it and I'm going to get it from her. But you'll have to stay with me until I do."

In the Jordan's cabin, Agatha is explaining to Lucy what happened. They are looking at the picture.

"Yesterday, I found the necklace behind the painting. Tonight, when I returned from the ball, I found the painting on the floor."

Suddenly the phone rings.

"Agatha, this is Robert Grant. You have something I want. Bring the necklace to my cabin right away or you'll lose something very valuable. Here, listen."

"Agatha, it's me, Christina. Please do what he asks. He has a gun and he'll use it."

"You have ten minutes," says Robert.

"I'll need more time. The necklace is at the purser's. Give me twenty minutes."

"Twenty minutes and no more. And don't say a word to anyone." The phone cuts off.

Agatha turns to Lucy, "That was Robert. He stole the necklace. He's holding Christina as a hostage. If I don't give him the necklace, he's going to kill her."

Lucy takes Agatha's hand. "Don't worry. Follow my instructions and Christina won't get hurt."

Comprehension Check

1. Why does Robert ask Christina about the Moon of India?
2. What happens when Christina tries to leave the cabin?
3. How does Robert know that Agatha has the necklace?
4. On the phone, what does Robert tell Agatha to do?
5. Why does Agatha say she will do it?
6. Is Lucy going to help Agatha?

U N I T 13

Cathy: Would you like to come to dinner on Saturday, Jay?

Jay: I'd like to, Cathy, but I'm going to be out of town. Thanks for the invitation.

Cathy: Sure. We'll try again sometime.

Cathy: Are you going to be around for the weekend, Steve?

Steve: I probably will.

Cathy: Would you like to come to dinner at our house on Saturday?

Steve: Sure! That would be really nice.

Cathy: Great.

Steve: What time?

Cathy: Oh, about 6:00.

Steve: Thanks a lot, Cathy. I'll see you then.

Don: Come on in, Steve. Here, I'll take your coat.

Liz: Hi, Steve. I'm Cathy and Don's niece, Liz.

Steve: Hi, Liz. It's nice to meet you.

Cathy (from the kitchen): Make yourself comfortable, Steve. Dinner won't be ready for a while.

Don: Cathy, could you pass the potatoes, please? . . . Thanks.

Cathy: Would anyone like anything else? More meat? Vegetables?

Liz: Nothing for me, thanks. I'm saving room for dessert.

Steve: I'll have some more meat. It's delicious. I always have room for dessert.

UNIT 13

Unit Language Focus

GRAMMAR: *will* and *going to* for future; *will* for promising, offering help and expressing decisions; *could* for requests; review of *have to*

COMMUNICATIVE AREAS: inviting someone, accepting and refusing invitations; welcoming someone; dinner at someone's house; offering, accepting and refusing food; ordering in a restaurant; offering help; holidays

OPENING CONVERSATION

New Words and Expressions

a while, be around, coat, Come again, Come in, company, dessert, enjoy, Good night, invitation, Make yourself comfortable, nothing, out of town, pass (*v.*), potato, ready, save room for, That would be really nice, We'll try again sometime

Names

Cathy /kǽθi/
Jay /dʒeɪ/
Steve /stiv/
Liz /lɪz/
Don /dɑn/

Teaching Suggestions

1. Warm-up. Ask: *What do you think the woman is saying to the man on the phone? Is she inviting him to dinner? How many people are at the dinner? What are they eating? What are they wearing?* Describe the pictures.

2. Play/read the conversation. Students look only at the pictures.

3. Play/read it again. Students listen while reading the conversation silently.

4. Teach new words and expressions as needed.

5. Point out the rising question intonation in *More meat? Vegetables?*

6. Let students ask questions about grammar, pronunciation and vocabulary.

7. Have students close their books, and ask them questions about the conversations.

> *Who does Cathy invite first? Does he say yes? Why not? Who does she invite next? Does he accept?*
> *What is the invitation for? What time?*
> *Who is Don? About how old is he? Describe him. Who is Liz? About how old is she? Describe her.*
> *When Steve arrives at Don and Cathy's house, what does Don do and say? What does Steve bring Don and Cathy? What does Cathy say?*

> *At dinner, Don wants some potatoes. What does he say to Cathy? Cathy asks, "Would anyone like anything else?" Liz says, "Nothing for me, thanks." Why does she say that? Does Steve say, "Nothing for me, thanks?" What does he say? What kind of pie does Steve want?*
> *When Steve and Liz leave, what do they say? What do Don and Cathy say?*

8. Personalize: *Do you often invite people to your house for dinner? Whom do you invite? In your country, how do you greet people when they come to your home? Do you have any special phrases? When you go to someone's house, do you bring something? What do you bring? In your country, what do you say after eating in someone's house? What do you say when you leave?*

9. Students read/repeat the conversation.

10. Divide students into fours and have them practice the conversation.

11. (Optional) Have different groups of four role-play the conversation for the class.

Additional Information

General Notes

In the U.S. (and many other countries), it is polite but not always expected for guests to bring a gift for their hosts. Often, upon being invited, a guest will ask, *Can I bring something?* The host or hostess will say *No.* The guest may still choose to bring something, such as a bottle of wine or flowers. However, if the guest is a very good friend, and the occasion is informal, the host or hostess might ask the guest to bring something.

Grammar

Will has a variety of uses. In the last unit, the predictive future possibility and probability meanings of *will* were presented. In this unit, the Opening Conversation focuses on making an offer: *I'll take your coat;* promising: *We'll try again sometime;* and making a decision: *I'll have some more potatoes.* In addition, the Conversation reviews probability: *I probably will.*

Later, Exercise 5 contrasts *will* and *be going to: I'm going to have the steak.* (I've made my decision and am telling you my plan.) *I'll probably have the steak.* (I still haven't decided.) Exercise 6 introduces the formulaic use of *will* in ordering food: *I'll have the steak. Will* is used here, even though the decision has already been made.

Vocabulary and Usage

Good night is only used to say *good-bye* at night, never to greet someone (*Good evening* is used as a greeting).

SPEAKING

EXERCISE 1 (whole class, pairs)

Language Focus

will for offers of help, promises, expressing decisions, probable future; *would* for invitations, offering something; *could* for requests

Teaching Suggestions

1. Review the functional and situational language used in this exercise.

On the board write: *invitation.* Under it write: *Would you like to* .... ? Ask students to respond *yes* and *no* politely to this invitation. Ss: *Sure! That would be really nice,* or, *I'd like to, but* ....

On the board write: *Offer/ask for help.* Have one student come to the front of the class and pile lots of books in his or her hands. Say to the class: *I want to help S1. What should I say?* Model or elicit: *I'll help you.* Write this on the board, below *offer.* Now take all the books from S1. Say: *I need help. What should I say to S1?* Model or elicit: *Could you help me?* Write this on the board below *ask for help.*

On the board write: *at the dinner table.* Explain: *I'm Cathy, and I want to offer more food to my guests. What should I say?* Model or elicit: *Would anyone like anything else?* or *Would you like some* .... ? Write this on the board, below *at the dinner table.* Ask: *What should my guests say?* Ss: *Nothing for me, thanks,* or, *I'll have some* .... Write this on the board.

2. Have students work in pairs to figure out the correct answers and practice the conversations. Then ask various pairs to read the conversations.

EXERCISE 2 Pronunciation (whole class)

Language Focus

stress in words of three syllables

New Words and Expressions

celebrate, holiday

Teaching Suggestions

1. Have students read the explanation silently and the examples aloud.

2. Have students try to figure out, without speaking, where the stress falls on the words in the exercise. On the board write the two example words: *Saturday   November*

3. Have students say each word in the exercise and indicate if it belongs with *Saturday* or *November*. Point out that *vegetable* is usually pronounced as a three-syllable word /vétʃtəbəl/ or /védʒtəbəl/, although in dictionaries it is also listed as a four-syllable word /védʒətəbəl/; *restaurant* is pronounced in two ways: /réstərɑnt/ and /réstərənt/.

(later) . . .

Cathy: Would you like some pie? We have apple and peach.

Steve: Yes, thank you. Could I have a little of each?

Steve: Thank you very much. It was a wonderful dinner, and I enjoyed the company.

Don and Cathy: We enjoyed it, too. Come again!

Liz: It was nice meeting you, Steve.

All: Good night.

Speaking

1

Fill in the blanks with *will, (')ll, would, (')d* or *could,* and practice the conversations.

1. A: .... you like to go to a movie with us tonight?
   B: I'................. like to, but I can't. Thanks for the invitation.
   A: Sure. We'................. try again sometime.

2. A: .... anyone like anything else?
   B: I'................. have some more potatoes, please.

3. A: I'................. help you with that.
   B: Thank you.

4. A: Are you going to be around this weekend?
   B: I probably ....
   A: .... you give me some help with my car on Saturday?
   B: OK. About 2:00?
   A: Fine. I'................. see you then.

2

Pronunciation

In words of three syllables, the stress is usually on the first or second syllable (Sáturday, Novèmber).

Where's the stress in these words? Practice saying them.

anything	restaurant
tomato	customer
probably	celebrate
important	holiday
potatoes	vegetable
together	November

3

4

Event

dinner
a party
a barbecue

Day

Saturday
New Year's Eve
the Fourth of July
Thanksgiving

Time

6:00
8:00
noon
1:00

Reason

visit my parents
be out of town/be away
have out-of-town guests

A, invite your partner to your house.
Choose an event and a day from the
suggestions above. **B,** respond to A's
invitation. If you can't come, give a
reason. **A,** if B can come, set a time.
Have conversations like these:

A: Would you like to come to dinner
   on Saturday?
B: Sure! That would be really nice.
A: Great.
B: What time?
A: Oh, about 6:00.
B: Thanks a lot. I'll see you then.

OR

A: Would you like to come to dinner
   on Saturday?
B: I'd like to, but I'm going to visit
   my parents that day. Thanks for
   the invitation.
A: Sure. We'll try again sometime.

1. bring you some aspirin

2. mail that for you

3. help you pick those up

4. open that for you

5. get those down for you

6. help you with those

● **A,** choose a picture (1, 3 or 5) and act out what's happening.
B, find the picture A is acting out and offer to help. **A,** thank B.

A: (acts out picture #5)
B: I'll get those down for you.
A: Thank you.

● **B,** choose a picture (2, 4 or 6) and act it out. **A,** offer to help.

● **B,** this time, ask your partner to help you. **A,** agree to help. Change *you* to
me, that to *this* and *those* to *these.*

B: (acts out picture #4) Could you open this for me, please?
A: Sure, I'd be glad to.

EXERCISE 3 (role-play, pairs)

Language Focus

making, accepting and refusing invitations

New Words and Expressions

be away, barbecue, Fourth of July, guest, Labor Day, New Year's Eve

Teaching Suggestions

1. Have students look over the choices listed under *Event, Day, Time* and *Reason.*

2. Teach new words and expressions as needed. Thanksgiving is explained in this unit's Culture Capsule. On the Fourth of July, Americans celebrate their independence from Great Britain.

3. Have students study the first conversation. Ask if they can think of holidays in their country or countries. List them on the board. Ask about what kind of meal or party they would have for each holiday. List that information next to the appropriate holiday and the time when the occasion would most likely begin. Then ask them if they can think of other reasons for not accepting an invitation; for example, going to visit relatives or friends, parent's/relatives' going to be here.

4. Have two students model the first conversation. Then have them reverse roles and model the conversation again, but with different information.

5. Next have the class work in pairs and practice the first conversation.

6. For the second conversation, follow the same procedure.

Workbook

You can now assign Exercises A and B.

EXERCISE 4 (role-play, pairs)

Language Focus

offering to help, requesting help and agreeing to help, object pronouns, demonstrative pronouns; review of separable two-word verbs

New Words and Expressions

act out, aspirin, bring, get (something) down, I'd be glad to, those

Teaching Suggestions

1. Have students study the pictures and captions.

2. Teach new words and expressions, as needed.

3. Explain that you are going to act out one of the pictures, and ask students which one you are acting out. Act out any picture except number 5 (the one in the example conversation).

4. Have two students model the first example conversation, in which A acts out number 5. Then have students do the first conversation in pairs.

5. (Optional) You can give students the option of refusing the offer for help by saying, *I think I can manage, thanks.*

6. Have two students model the example conversation in the second part. If necessary, go over the changes of pronouns in each request by asking students what they would say in each case. Otherwise, let them do it on their own.

7. (Optional) Ask students if they can think of other situations in which a person might offer or request help. List the situations on the board, and ask students how they would offer help. Have them work in pairs as in Teaching Suggestions 3 and 4.

Workbook

You can now assign Exercise C.

EXERCISE 5 (pairs)

Language Focus

have to/don't have to; review of *can* for permissibility

New Words and Expressions

accept, credit card, dress up, make a reservation

Names

Buckley's /bákliz/
Caesar's /sízərz/
Manuel's /mænwélz/
Acropolis /əkrápəlıs/
Spiro's /spíroz/

Teaching Suggestions

1. Teach new words and expressions, as needed.

2. This is an information gap exercise. Go over the key to the restaurant guide with the class. Then have two students model an example.

3. The students do the exercise in pairs.

4. Check their answers by asking: *Where do you have to make a reservation? Where do you have to dress up? Where can you pay by credit card?*

EXERCISE 6 (role-play, pairs)

Language Focus

be going to vs. *will*, ordering in a restaurant

New Words and Expressions

appetizer, baked, beef, broiled, chicken, entrée, fruit cup, grilled, lamb chops, lobster, Maine, menu, order, prime rib, salad bar, shrimp cocktail, sirloin steak, soup of the day

Teaching Suggestions

1. Have students study the menu.

2. Teach new words and expressions, as needed.

3. Go over the pronunciation of each item with the students.

4. Have students study the example conversation. On the board write: *I'm going to have the steak. I'll probably have the steak.* Ask: *What's the difference?* Explain: *"Going to" means B is sure or has already decided. "Will probably" means B isn't sure/hasn't decided yet.* Summarize: *If you are sure, you should say, "I'm going to," and if you're not sure, you should say, "I'll probably."*

5. Help two students model the example conversation. Make sure that A answers B's last question: If A only says *Yes*, then make sure B asks, *What're you going to have?* Have students do the exercise in pairs.

6. Ask various students to tell the class what their partners are going to have.

7. (Optional) Ask what foods they would find on a typical menu in their country or countries. Are some things the same as on this menu?

5

You want to go to some of these restaurants. Ask your partner about them.

A: Do I have to make a reservation at .... ?
B: Yes, you do.   OR   No, you don't.
A: Do I have to dress up?
B: Well, men have to wear jackets and ties.
    OR   No, you don't. It's informal.
A: Can I pay by credit card?
B: Yes, you can.
    OR   They don't accept credit cards.

 Reservations are necessary.

 Men must wear jackets and ties.

 The restaurant accepts most credit cards.

 No credit cards. Cash only.

A

1. Ask B about some of these restaurants:

Buckley's   Little Tokyo
Caesar's   Manuel's
Atlantic Sushi

2. Answer B's questions. Use this guide:

	📞	🎀	Credit	$
Buckley's		•		•
Caesar's	•		•	
Atlantic Sushi				•
Little Tokyo			•	
Manuel's	•	•		•

B

1. Answer A's questions. Use this guide:

	📞	🎀	Credit	$
Hunan Palace	•	•		•
The Jade Garden			•	
The Little Chef			•	
The Acropolis			•	
Spiro's		•		•

2. Ask A about some of these restaurants:

The Hunan Palace   The Acropolis
The Jade Garden   Spiro's
The Little Chef

6

A and B, you're having dinner at Buckley's. Look at the menu. Decide what you want to order. Ask your partner about his or her choices.

A: What're you going to have?
B: I'm going to have the sirloin steak.
    OR   I'm not sure. I'll probably have the sirloin steak. What about you?
A: I ....
B: Are you going to have an appetizer?

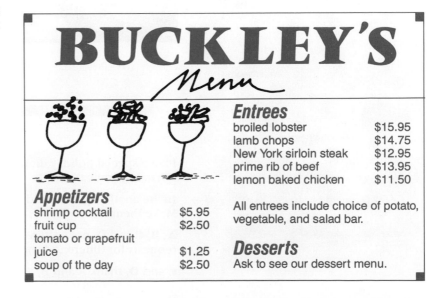

BUCKLEY'S
Menu

Appetizers
shrimp cocktail	$5.95
fruit cup	$2.50
tomato or grapefruit juice	$1.25
soup of the day	$2.50

Entrees
broiled lobster	$15.95
lamb chops	$14.75
New York sirloin steak	$12.95
prime rib of beef	$13.95
lemon baked chicken	$11.50

All entrees include choice of potato, vegetable, and salad bar.

Desserts
Ask to see our dessert menu.

7

A, you're the waiter or waitress. **B** and **C,** you're customers at the restaurant.

A: Are you ready to order?
B: Yes, I'll have the ....
A: How would you like your ....?
   Rare, medium or well done?
B: ...., please.
A: Would you like an appetizer?
B: Yes, I'd like the ....
   OR   No, thank you.
A: What kind of ....
   would you like? We have ....
B: ...., please.
A: Thank you. You can help yourself to the salad bar anytime.

(later) . . .

A: Would you like anything else?
B: Yes, could you bring us your dessert menu? And I'd like some more coffee, please.
C: Certainly.

8
Culture Capsule

Thanksgiving is an important holiday in the United States. It's a special time when friends and family get together and share a meal. The meal usually includes roast turkey, stuffing, cranberry sauce, sweet potatoes, mashed potatoes, squash and other vegetables, and pumpkin and apple pies.

The first Thanksgiving was in 1621. Native Americans and early settlers from Europe shared a meal after a very difficult winter. They gave thanks for food and for life itself.

Americans now celebrate Thanksgiving on the fourth Thursday in November.

What's an important holiday in your country? When is it? How did it begin? Is there a special meal? What is it? Does everyone celebrate this holiday?

9
Put It Together

Plan a special holiday dinner with your partner. Decide: When will it be? What will you eat?

Invite another pair of students to join you. Greet them when they arrive. Make them feel welcome.

A, B, C and **D,** now you're eating dinner. **A** and **B,** offer food. **C** and **D,** make requests for different dishes.

C and **D,** thank A and B, and say good night.

EXERCISE 7 (role-play, threes)

Language Focus

ordering in a restaurant

New Words and Expressions

baked, french fried, help yourself to, how would you like your, mashed, medium, rare, spinach, well done

Teaching Suggestions

1. Have students read the example conversation and the information about the entrées and vegetables.

2. Teach new words and expressions, as needed.

3. (Optional) Point out the special use of *I'll* in ordering food. The customer can say either, *I'll have the* .... , or, *I'd like the* .... (The use of *will* here should be learned as a formula, as it does not easily fit into one of the usual uses of *will.*)

4. Go over the pronunciation of the new words.

5. Have two students model the example conversation for the class; or you play the waiter/waitress's role and have a student play the customer's role. First A orders a main dish. Then B asks about an appetizer, a vegetable, and a potato choice.

6. Have students work in threes, one waiter/waitress and two customers. Then have them switch roles so that the waiter/waitress can be a customer.

7. Ask various students to report what their partners ordered.

8. (Optional) Discussion: Ask students what kind of vegetables and other side dishes would appear on a typical menu in their country or countries.

9. (Optional) Find out if students know how to ask for the check at the end of the meal and whether they know about the custom of tipping in the U.S. Explain if they don't. Customer: *Could I/we have the check, please?,* or *I'd/we'd like the check, please.* Tax is added to the bill. It is customary to leave 15 to 20 percent of the untaxed portion of the bill as a tip. Ask students about the customs in their country or countries.

Workbook

You can now assign Exercises D–F.

EXERCISE 8 Culture Capsule (whole class)

Culture Focus

Thanksgiving in the United States, holidays in your students' country or countries

New Words and Expressions

cranberry sauce, difficult, give thanks for, life itself, Native American, roast (*adj.*), sauce, settler, share (*v.*), squash, stuffing, sweet potato, winter

Teaching Suggestions

1. Have students read the Culture Capsule silently, or read it aloud to them.

2. Teach new words and expressions, as needed.

3. Have students read the Capsule again. Let them ask questions about it.

4. Ask students the questions. Discuss the similarities and differences between the students' holidays and Thanksgiving. If your students are from the same country, ask them to talk about several of their holidays. If your students are from different countries, they can work in pairs and ask and answer the questions. Have them report the information they learned, and discuss the similarities and differences.

5. (Optional) Have students write a brief explanation about a holiday in their country or countries, similar to the one about Thanksgiving. If your students are from different countries, compile an information sheet and distribute it to them.

EXERCISE 9 Put It Together (role-play, pairs, two pairs)

Language Focus

inviting someone, accepting an invitation, welcoming someone, offering (food), making a request (for food), thanking someone, taking leave

New Words and Expressions

request

Teaching Suggestions

1. Have students read the instructions. Explain that there are four parts to the exercise. In the first part, they will plan a special holiday dinner. Ask students to think about their answers to the questions in the Culture Capsule and to use them as a guide in the first part. Have them do the first part in pairs.

2. Elicit the appropriate language for the second part of the exercise, or have the students look at the Checklist to help them remember how to invite someone, accept an invitation, and how to greet someone. Designate the pairs who will invite (A and B), and the pairs who will be invited (C and D).Have them do this part of the exercise.

3. Elicit the appropriate language for the third and fourth parts of the exercise, or have them look at the Opening Conversation and of the Checklist again.

4. Have the students complete the exercise, and have one or two groups perform the role-play, starting with the invitation.

CHECKLIST

Teaching Suggestions

1. See the general suggestions in the Checklist page in Unit 1.

2. (Optional) For additional grammar practice, students make statements or ask questions about themselves, using *will* and *be going to*.

3. (Optional) From time to time, you may wish to have students review the Checklist part by part, and then quiz them orally in class, with books open or closed. For example: T: *You are going to have a New Year's Eve party. How do you invite someone?* and so on.

OPTIONAL WRITING PRACTICE

This is your first year in the United States. An American family invites you to their Thanksgiving dinner. Write a letter home to a member of your family, telling him or her about the invitation, and explaining Thanksgiving.

Dear _____

_____
_____
_____
_____
_____
_____
_____
_____
_____

I know how to . . .

USE THESE FORMS

☐ **Will**

for talking about the future with the verb be
I'll be out of town on Saturday.
Dinner won't be ready for a while.

for promising
We'll try again sometime.

for offering to help
I'll take your coat.

for deciding
I'll have some more meat.

☐ **Will vs. Going To**

When plans are definite, going to *is usually used.*
I'm going to have the steak.
(That's my final decision.)

When there is some uncertainty, will *is usually used with words like* probably *and* maybe.
I'll probably have the steak.
(I probably will, but maybe I won't.)

When the verb is be, *either* will *or* going to *can be used for definite future plans.*
I'll be out of town on Saturday.
I'm going to be out of town on Saturday.

USE ENGLISH TO

☐ **invite someone**
Would you like to come to dinner on
  Thanksgiving?

☐ **accept an invitation**
Sure! That would be really nice.

☐ **decline an invitation**
I'd like to, but I'm going to be out of town.
Thanks for the invitation.

☐ **welcome someone**
Come on in. Make yourself comfortable.

☐ **offer help**
I'll take your coat.

☐ **offer food**
Would you like anything else?

☐ **accept an offer of food**
I'd like some more coffee, please.
I'll have some more meat.

☐ **decline an offer of food**
No, nothing for me, thanks.

☐ **make a request**
Could I have a little of each?
Could you give me some help with my car?

☐ **order in a restaurant**
I'll have/I'd like the steak.
How would you like your. . . . ?
Medium, please.

☐ **talk about these subjects**
holidays   food
dinner at someone's house
restaurants   menus

☐ **UNDERSTAND THESE EXPRESSIONS**

Cash only.
Certainly. (formal)
Come again!
Good night.
Help yourself.
It was nice meeting you.
No credit cards.
Pass (the potatoes), please.
Sure.

be out of town
be around for (the weekend)
dress up
make a reservation
pay by credit card

CHECKLIST

Listening

1

Choose the appropriate response to each speaker you hear. Number the responses 1, 2, 3 or 4 in each part.

Part 1:

___ a. Sure. We'll try again soon.

___ b. Sure! That would be really nice.

___ c. Would you like to come to our house for dinner?

___ d. I probably will.

Part 2:

___ a. Thank you.

___ b. Yes, I'll have the prime rib, please.

___ c. Nothing more for me, thanks.

___ d. Sure. I'd be glad to.

2

Match the speakers and the situations. In each part, number the situations 1, 2, 3 or 4.

Part 1: The speaker is:

___ a. ordering in a restaurant

___ b. asking for help

___ c. agreeing to help

___ d. offering help

Part 2: The speaker is:

___ a. inviting someone

___ b. declining an invitation

___ c. offering food

___ d. refusing food

3

Some of these conversations take place in someone's house. Others take place in a restaurant. Put a check in the correct column.

	House	Restaurant
1.	☐	☐
2.	☐	☐
3.	☐	☐
4.	☐	☐
5.	☐	☐
6.	☐	☐
7.	☐	☐

4

Write appropriate responses.

1. _____ 4. _____

2. _____ 5. _____

3. _____ 6. _____

LISTENING

EXERCISE 1

Language Focus

inviting someone, accepting and declining an invitation, requesting help, offering help, offering food, ordering in a restaurant, asking about plans

Teaching Suggestions

First Part

1. Have students read the responses. Ask them what they might hear on the tape for which the responses would be appropriate.

2. Play the cassette or read the tapescript.

3. Have students listen again and do the first part of the exercise. When they have finished, go over their answers. Ask them if they remember what they heard for each response.

Answers: 1. b   2. a   3. d   4. c

Second Part

1. Tell students that this part is similar to the first part.

2. Play the cassette or read the tapescript.

3. Have students listen again and do the second part of the exercise.

Answers: 1. d   2. c   3. a   4. b

EXERCISE 2

Language Focus

ordering in a restaurant, requesting help, agreeing to help, offering to help, inviting someone, declining an invitation, offering food, declining an offer of food

Teaching Suggestions

First Part

1. Have students read the instructions. Ask them if any of the responses in the first exercise match the categories they see here.

2. Play the cassette or read the tapescript.

3. Have students listen again and do the exercise. When they have finished, go over the answers with them.

Answers: 1. b   2. a   3. d   4. c

Second Part

1. Tell students that this part is similar to the first part.

2. Play the cassette or read the tapescript.

3. Have students listen again and do the exercise.

Answers: 1. b   2. d   3. a   4. c

EXERCISE 3

Language Focus

greetings, leave-takings, ordering in a restaurant, review of introductions

Teaching Suggestions

1. Have students read the directions.

2. Play the first item as an example. Ask students to decide whether it takes place at home or in a restaurant. (Answer: at a home)

3. Play the entire exercise on the cassette, or read the tapescript.

4. Have students listen again and do the exercise.

5. Go over the answers with the students.

Answers: 1. house   2. restaurant   3. house   4. restaurant
5. restaurant   6. house   7. restaurant

EXERCISE 4

Language Focus

invitations, ordering in a restaurant, offering help, review of self introductions, personal questions based on the language taught in this unit

Teaching Suggestions

1. Play the cassette or read the tapescript.

2. Have students listen and respond in writing. Give them enough time to think about and write their answers.

3. When they're finished, play the tape, and pause after each question or statement. Ask various students how they responded.

Answers: Since answers are personal, they will vary with each student.

104

EPISODE 13 The Moon of India

Key Vocabulary

cop, crowd, dock, fall (*v.*), familiar, fight, gangway, get in someone's way, grab, point, souvenirs, tie up someone

Teaching Suggestions

1. Have students retell the last few episodes: After the Costume Ball, Agatha finds the painting on the floor in her room. She knows the thief was there. Lucy comes into her room and tells her she is a police officer. Robert Grant invites Christina for a drink. He is the thief. He thinks Christina has the Moon of India. He learns that she doesn't have it. He calls Agatha and tells her she must bring the Moon of India to his cabin. If she doesn't, he will kill Christina. Christina is his hostage. Agatha says she will do it. Lucy tells Agatha she will help her.

2. Follow steps 1–4 of Episode 1.

3. Students read the episode again.

4. Ask the comprehension questions.

Answers: 1) Because he doesn't want them to leave the cabin. He doesn't want them to tell other people that he is the thief. 2) Interpol agents. 3) No, she doesn't. He grabs her first. 4) Frank does. 5) It falls on a tray of souvenirs on the dock below. 6) Yes, they do.

5. (Optional) Other possible questions. What is Robert's business meeting? Why don't the Interpol agents help Lucy? Do you think Lucy will find the necklace?

6. Have students close their books and summarize the episode. Check their understanding of the story as they tell it. Correct any misunderstandings.

7. (Optional) Role-play. Students can role-play the dialogue between Lucy and Robert, using role cards.

MOON OF INDIA

Episode Thirteen

Agatha knocks at Robert's door. The door opens and Agatha sees Christina tied to a chair. Robert closes the door quickly. "Where is it?" he demands.

Agatha gives him the necklace. He looks at it and puts it in his jacket pocket.

"Thank you, Agatha. Sorry about this." He ties Agatha up next to Christina. Then he makes a telephone call. "Could you get a taxi for me first thing this morning? Yes, it's Grant. Robert Grant. I have a very important business meeting. Thank you." He puts the phone down, puts his jacket on and points the gun at the two women. "And now I have to say goodbye to you two ladies." He laughs, puts the gun in his pocket and leaves the cabin.

The ship is in port at Malaga. Robert is walking along the deck, looking for the taxi. He sees a man following him. He goes up to another deck. He sees a second man watching him. He starts to run, but the men follow him up and down and across the ship. Robert keeps running. Then he hears a familiar voice. "Stop, Robert." He turns around. Lucy is pointing a gun at him. "So you're a cop," he says.

"Give me the necklace," Lucy replies. He pulls out the necklace and starts to give it to her. Suddenly, he knocks her gun to the ground and grabs her.

"C'mon officer, you're going to help me get off this ship."

They walk to the gangway. The two men, who are Interpol agents, come closer.

"Get back or I'll kill her."

"Do as he says. He has a gun."

When they reach the gangway, there is a group of people waiting to go down. Frank is among them.

"Robert, Lucy, this is a surprise. I didn't know you were. . . ."

"Shut up, Frank," says Robert and shows him the gun.

"Go away, Frank," advises Lucy.

"Lucy, let me help you. . . ." And Frank takes a step towards her.

Robert moves toward Frank and Lucy tries to get Robert's gun. There is a fight and the gun falls to the deck below. Robert looks down for

his gun, and the necklace falls out of his pocket. It falls on the tray of a man selling souvenirs on the dock below. The Interpol agents grab Robert.

Lucy runs down the gangway to get the necklace but the crowds leaving the ship get in her way. The man selling souvenirs, with the real Moon of India on his tray, walks away from the ship. Lucy runs after him.

Comprehension Check

1. Why does Robert tie up Christina and Agatha?
2. Two men are following Robert. Who are they?
3. Does Lucy take the necklace from Robert?
4. Who tries to help Lucy?
5. What happens to the necklace?
6. Do the police catch Robert?

UNIT 14

Herb: There aren't any interesting programs on TV tonight. Do you want to play a game?

Judy: Sure. How about "Do You Know?"?

Herb: All right, but you always win.

Judy: I know. That's why I like it.

Herb: "What's the smallest dog?"

Judy: I'm not sure. It can't be the St. Bernard! It might be the Pekingese. I know! It must be the Chihuahua.

Herb: I think you're right. Let me see. Yes, it's the Chihuahua.

Judy: "Is the Earth getting warmer or cooler?"

Herb: I don't know. I'll say *cooler*.

Judy: I think it's getting warmer. Yes, I'm right.

Herb: You're always right . . . . I'm going to get a Coke. Do you want one?

Judy: Sure.

Herb: Whose turn is it?

Judy: It's your turn to ask a question. It's my turn to answer.

Herb: "Who ran the first four-minute mile?"

Judy: Oh, what was his name? He was British, wasn't he? Roger something. Roger Bannister. He did it in the early '50s. 1954?

Herb: "Roger Bannister, in 1954." See? You're never wrong!

Judy: "Where are the next Summer Olympics going to be?"

Herb: Whose Coke is this?

Judy: It must be yours. I finished mine. Are you going to answer your question?

Herb: I will in a minute. I'm thinking, I'm thinking.

UNIT 14

Unit Language Focus

GRAMMAR: *Might* for possibility, *can't* for impossibility, *must* for probability; whose; tag questions and review of tenses: simple present, present continuous, simple past, *going to* future; review of modal *will* for promising, deciding, future possibility; review of adjective comparisons

COMMUNICATIVE AREAS: Formal and informal invitations and offers; accepting and declining invitations and offers; expressing uncertainty; review of personal information (name, age, marital status, likes/dislikes, physical description, occupation, languages); agreeing and disagreeing

OPENING CONVERSATION

New Words and Expressions

Chihuahua, Coke, cool, the Earth, get warmer, might, must, Pekingese, St. Bernard, whose, win

Names

Chihuahua /tʃɪwáwɑ/
Pekingese /píkəniz/
St. Bernard /seɪnt bərnárd/
Herb /hərb/
Judy /dʒúdi/
Roger Bannister /rádʒər bǽnɪstər/

Teaching Suggestions

1. Warm-up. Ask: *Where are the people in the picture?* Ask students to describe the people (what they're wearing, color of hair, and so on). Ask: *What're they doing?* Ask students to tell you as much as they can about the pictures.

2. Personalize: *What do you like to do when you are at home in the evening? Would you rather be at home alone or with a friend, or a member of your family?* The game *Do You Know* is modeled on *Trivial Pursuit*, a game that became popular in the U.S. in the mid 1980s.

3. Play/read the conversation. Students look only at the pictures.

4. Students listen while reading the conversation silently.

5. Teach new words and expressions, as needed.

6. Let students ask questions about grammar, pronunciation and vocabulary.

7. Students read/repeat the conversation.

8. Ask students about the conversation: *Judy says: "That's why I like it." What does she like? Why does she like it? Judy says: "It can't be the St. Bernard." Why can't it be the St. Bernard? Herb asks: "Whose Coke is this?" Which one is he talking about? Why doesn't he know?*

Who's a better player, Judy or Herb? Who will probably win? Why? What does "four-minute mile" mean? Where are the next summer Olympics going to be? When are they going to be?

9. Divide students into pairs and have them practice the conversation.

10. (Optional) Have one or more pairs role-play the conversation for the class.

Additional Information

Grammar

1. *Will* is used for making a decision (*I'll say "cooler"*) and for making a promise (*I will in a minute*).

2. *Be going to* is used for a planned, definite future or a decision already made (*I'm going to get a soda. Where are the Summer Olympics going to be? Are you going to answer your questions?*).

3. *I'm thinking* vs. *I think:* Throughout this text, *think* has been used in the simple present when a general truth is being stated. An example from this conversation is, *I think it's getting warmer.* At the end of the conversation, Herb says, *I'm thinking.* The progressive is used here to show the act of thinking in progress.

4. *Must* is used for inference when logic shows the information to be true, but some objective evidence is missing. In the opening conversation, Judy says, *It must be yours,* because the glasses are close together, so there is a possibility that it might be hers. Logically it's not hers, because the glass in question still has some soda in it, and as she has finished hers, hers must be the empty one. Another example: *If I see you walk in the door with a wet umbrella, I can say, "It must be raining." Although I have not seen the rain itself (the objective evidence), I can guess that it is raining from your wet umbrella.*

Vocabulary and Usage

The whole conversation is very informal because this is a married couple. Formality and informality are contrasted in Exercises 4 and 5.

SPEAKING

EXERCISE 1 (pairs)
Language Focus

expressing certainty and uncertainty, review of
comparatives and superlatives, tenses, *wh-* questions

New Words and Expressions

Halley's Comet, Taj Mahal

Names

Halley's Comet /hǽliz kámət/
Taj Mahal /tɑʒ məhál/

Teaching Suggestions

1. Have students study the questions on both cards.

2. Go over the pronunciation of the new words in the questions.

3. Help two students model the example conversation, showing the three different possible answers and reactions to the same question. (*OR* you might want to take the role of B to provide the three different possibilities.)

4. This is an information gap exercise. Make sure everyone understands the procedure. Students do the exercise in pairs as described. When they've finished, ask who knew the answers to all the questions. Ask which ones were easy and which ones were difficult.

If You Have Time

Have students make up their own *Do You Know* cards and play the game.

Speaking

1

Ask and answer the questions on Herb's and Judy's cards. Have conversations like these:

A: What's the smallest dog?
B: The Chihuahua.
  OR I'm not sure. I think it's the Chihuahua.
A: You're right.

OR

A: What's the smallest dog?
B: I don't know.
A: It's the Chihuahua.

OR

A: What's the smallest dog?
B: Is it the Pekingese?
A: No, it's the Chihuahua.

A

1. Ask B questions 2, 3 and 5 on Herb's card.

DO YOU KNOW?

- **1.** What's the smallest dog?
- **2.** Where do people use yen for money?
- **3.** Are the world's oceans getting bigger or smaller?
- **4.** Who ran the first four-minute mile?
- **5.** When is Halley's Comet going to come again?

Answers: 2. in Japan
         3. bigger
         5. in 2060

2. Try to answer B's questions.

B

1. Try to answer A's questions:

2. Ask A questions 1, 2 and 4 on Judy's card.

DO YOU KNOW?

- **1.** Where's the Taj Mahal?
- **2.** What country has the biggest population?
- **3.** Is the Earth getting warmer or cooler?
- **4.** Who invented the telephone?
- **5.** Where are the next Summer Olympics going to be?

Answers 1. in India
        2. the People's Republic of China
        3. Alexander Graham Bell (Canadian)

2

Pronunciation

Practice saying these sentences with your partner. Match questions with answers.

1. What's the smallest dog?

2. Is the Earth getting warmer or cooler?

3. Whose turn is it?

4. Whose Coke is this?

a. It must be yours. I finished mine.

b. It can't be the St. Bernard. It must be the Pekingese.

c. It's your turn to ask a question. It's my turn to answer.

d. I'll say cooler.

3

Have conversations like this. Use *can't, might* and *must*.

A: (points to women's shoes) Whose are these?
B: They can't be Van's. They might be Alexandra's or Ryuko's.
   (points to biggest belt) Whose is this?
A: It must be Van's.

Alexandra
ballet dancer

Yves
deep sea
diver

Van
musician

Ryuko
artist

4

• You and your partner are good friends. Invite him or her to:

play cards	tonight
go to a movie	
go out for pizza	

A: Do you want to ....?
B: Sure. Sounds good.
   OR   Sorry, I can't. I have to do my homework.

• You and your partner don't know each other very well. Invite him or her to:

play tennis	tomorrow
go jogging	afternoon
have lunch together	

B: Would you like to ....?
A: Thanks. I'd like that.
   OR   I'm sorry, I can't, but thanks for the invitation.

5

• You and your partner are good friends. You're at your house.
Offer A: a Coke
         a piece of cake
         a glass of milk

B: I'm going to get ....
   (Do you) want one?
A: Sure.
   OR   No, thanks.

• You and your partner don't know each other very well. You're at your house.
Offer B: a cup of coffee
         some cookies
         some fruit

A: Would you like ....?
B: Yes, please.
   OR   Nothing for me, thank you.

EXERCISE 2 (whole class, pairs)

Language Focus

intonation and stress patterns in *wh-* and choice questions and answers

Teaching Suggestions

1. Have students practice the four questions first, paying special attention to the sentence stress and rhythm. Then have them practice the answers. Note that in answers a, b and c, the words that are stressed are usually the ones that contrast with each other in some way.

2. Have them work in pairs and ask and answer the questions, first concentrating on the stress and rhythm, and then trying to say them as quickly and fluently as possible.

EXERCISE 3 (whole class, pairs)

Language Focus

inference with *might, can't, must, whose;* review of noun + *'s,* this/these, it/they

New Words and Expressions

artist, ballet dancer, belt, deep-sea diver, musician

Names

Alexandra /ælɛgzǽndrə/
Yves /iv/
Van /væn/
Ryuko /rjúko/

Teaching Suggestions

Note: It is not necessary for the students to know the names of the articles in the illustrations; however, in case they ask: ballet shoes, flippers; a gold chain, an earring, a submersible watch; belts; a drum, paintbrushes, a tutu. Yves is wearing a diving mask and an oxygen tank. Ryuko is wearing a painter's smock.

1. Have students read the instructions. Have two students model the example conversation. Make sure that they point to the appropriate illustration. Ask students: *Why can't the shoes be Van's?* Elicit or answer: *Because they're too small.* Ask: *Why might they be Ryuko's or Alexandra's? Because they're women's shoes.* Ask: *Why must the belt be Van's? Because it's too big for the others.* Explain: *So we say "can't" when it's impossible, we say "might" when it's possible, and we say "must" when we're almost 100 percent sure.*

2. Have students do the exercise in pairs.

3. (Optional) Have each student find something of his or hers to put on a desk at the front of the room. Hold up each item and ask, *Whose is/are this/these?* Students respond using *can't, might, must* where appropriate. Explain that if they are certain, they can say *It's*

.... *'s,* and if they're 80 percent certain, they can say *It's probably* .... *'s.*

EXERCISE 4 (role-play, pairs)

Language Focus

inviting and responding to invitations formally and informally

New Words and Expressions

homework, sounds good

Teaching Suggestions

1. Have students read all the instructions and examples. Ask them, *What's the difference in the language between the first and second parts?* (informal/formal)

2. Ask: *Who would you have the first conversation with?* (family members, friends) *With whom would you have the second conversation?* (someone you don't know well, your boss, your teacher, someone older than you)

First Part

1. Teach new words and expressions, if necessary.

2. Have two students model the first example conversation. Ask students to think of other invitations and times. (Unit 12 could be a source of ideas.) List their ideas on the board. Tell them they can also use those ideas when doing the exercise.

3. Have students do the exercise in pairs. When they've finished, ask various students: *S1, what did S2 invite you to do? S2, are you going to (go to a movie with S1)?* and so on.

Second Part

1. Follow the same procedure as in Teaching Suggestions 2 and 3 above.

2. Have students close their books. Tell them to take turns as A and B and to invite each other formally and informally. Remind B to pay attention to what A says in order to respond appropriately.

EXERCISE 5 (role-play, pairs)

Language Focus

offering something and responding to offers formally and informally, review of countable/uncountable nouns

New Words and Expressions

glass (of) milk

Teaching Suggestions

1. Teach new words and expressions, if necessary.

(*continued*)

2. Have students read the instructions for both parts.

3. Have them think of other things they would usually offer someone in their own homes, and list them on the board.

4. Have students do the first part of the exercise. Tell them to use the items on the board, as well.

5. When they have finished, ask various students: *S1, what did you have at S2's house?*

6. Have students do the second part of the exercise, and follow the same procedure as above.

7. Have students close their books. Tell them to take turns as A and B and to offer things formally or informally. Remind B to pay attention so as to answer appropriately.

Workbook

You can now assign Exercises A and B.

EXERCISE 6 (whole class, pairs)

Language Focus

tag questions with *be, can,* and *will*

New Words and Expressions

presidential election, president

Teaching Suggestions

First Part

1. Have students read the instructions and the first example sentence.

2. Give another example: *The last day of this month is a* (day of the week), *isn't it?* Say: *I think that's right, but I'm not sure. Am I right?* Ss: *Yes/No.* Give examples of facts about which your students can be reasonably, but not 100 percent, sure. For example, if you have a large class, you could say, *There are* .... *people in our class.* Limit your examples to sentences with *be, can,* or *will.*

3. Say: *Herb asks Judy: "What's the smallest dog?" At first Judy is not sure. So she might say: "The Chihuahua is the smallest dog, isn't it?"* or, *"The Pekingese isn't the smallest dog, is it?"* Ask: *What's the answer to the first question?* Ss: *Yes, it's the smallest dog.* T: *The second question?* Ss: *No, it isn't the smallest dog.*

4. Write the two example sentences on the board, and underline the verbs. Ask students how tags are formed. Have students close their books while you write some of the example sentences from the book on the board, leaving off the tags. Have students supply the tags.

5. Have students practice saying the pairs of tag questions with the correct intonation.

Second Part

1. Have students read the second part of the exercise. Explain that the statements are about U.S. geography and U.S. presidents.

2. Teach new words and expressions, as needed.

3. Have two students model the example conversations. Point out that the answer can be the same, even if the question is different.

4. Have students do the exercise in pairs. Circulate to make sure they're using the correct intonation and tags.

5. Go over the questions and answers as a class.

6. (Optional) Have students make a list of statements about the government or geography in their country/ countries and practice a similar exercise.

Third Part

1. Have students think of questions they could ask each other. If necessary, supply a few examples. List their questions on the board.

2. Have them do the exercise in pairs.

6

When you think something is true, but you're not completely sure, you can say it like this:	When you think something is not true, but you're not completely sure, you can say it like this:
affirmative *negative tag* *statement* *question*	*negative* *affirmative* *statement* *tag question*
He was English, wasn't he? ⤴	He wasn't French, was he? ⤴

● Practice saying these sentences. Notice how the tag questions change.

1a. The Chihuaha is the smallest dog, isn't it?
2a. There are five questions on Judy's card, aren't there?
3a. The questions are difficult, aren't they?
4a. Herb was right, wasn't he?
5a. Judy will win the game, won't she?
6a. Four people can play, can't they?

b. The Pekingese isn't the smallest dog, is it?
b. There aren't any good TV programs tonight, are there?
b. The questions aren't easy, are they?
b. Judy wasn't sure, was she?
b. Herb won't win the game, will he?
b. Eight people can't play, can they?

● Are these statements true or false? Have conversations like these:

There are 50 states in the U.S.

A: There are 50 states in the U.S., aren't there?
B: Yes, there are.

OR

A: There aren't 50 states in the U.S., are there?
B: Yes, there are.

Texas is the biggest state.

A: Texas is the biggest state, isn't it?
B: No, it isn't. Alaska is.

OR

A: Texas isn't the biggest state, is it?
B: No, it isn't. Alaska is.

1. There are 50 states in the U.S.
2. Texas is the biggest state.
3. George Washington was the first president of the U.S.
4. There's a presidential election every two years.
5. Women can be president.
6. There will be a presidential election in 1996.
7. There are a lot of Japanese cherry trees in Washington, D.C.
8. Rhode Island is the smallest state.
9. California and Oregon are on the Pacific Coast.
10. John Kennedy was the youngest president.
11. People can be president for more than eight years.
12. There will be a presidential election in 1994.

A

1. Use tag questions to tell B what you think about statements 1–6 above.

2. Listen to B and say if he or she is right or wrong.
   Answers: 7. T 8. T 9. T 10. T 11. F 12. F

B

1. Listen to A and say if he or she is right or wrong.
   Answers: 1. T 2. F (Alaska is) 3. T 4. F 5. T 6. T

2. Use tag questions to tell A what you think about statements 7–12 above.

● **A,** ask B five real questions using question tags. **B,** answer with true information. For example, A: *You're studying Russian, aren't you?* B: *No, I'm not.*

7
Culture Capsule

Chess

Scrabble

Gin

Scrabble is a word game. Each player gets seven letters and has to make words. The letters have different points and the player with the most points wins.

Gin is a card game. Each player gets ten cards and has to match them in groups of three and four.

Chess is a game for two players. Each player has sixteen pieces on a board with sixty-four squares.

Do people in your country play these games? Do you know how to play these games? What (other) games can you play? Which ones do you like the best?

8

Use your own ideas to fill in the information about Mata Kira. Have conversations like this:

A: How old is she?
B: I think she's 25. What do you think?
A: I think so too.

OR

A: How old is she?
A: I think she's 25.
A: Really? I don't think so. I think she's 40.

Name _Mata Kira_
Age_____
Marital status_____
Children_____
Occupation_____

Place of birth_____
Languages_____
Home city_____
Habits _Usually gets up at 6 A.M_
Dislikes_____

9
Guess Who!

What do you know about the other people in your class? Make statements about one person until your partner guesses who it is. Use the ideas below.

A: She's from Tokyo and she likes jazz.
B: Is it Yoko?
A: No, it isn't. She's wearing a white sweater.
B: Is it Sumi?
A: No. She went to California last year.
B: Oh, it must be Kimiko.
A: Right!

Ideas

1. likes/doesn't like tennis, movies, Indian food, sports cars
2. plays the violin, piano, drums
3. has long hair, short hair, curly hair
4. moved/went to .... last week, month, year
5. is going to get married/study computer science next year
6. will probably be a famous .... someday

10
Put It Together

Ask about your partner's ideas for his/her future.

A: What are you going to do after this course/this summer/next year?
B: .... How about you?
A: ....
B: Would you like to .... in the future?
A: .... What about you?
B: ....
A: Will you ever .... ?
B: ....

Some Ideas

take a long vacation
write a book
travel
study (Russian)
be (an astronaut)

EXERCISE 7 Culture Capsule (whole class)

Culture Focus

popular games in the U.S.

New Words and Expressions

chess, gin, Scrabble™

Teaching Suggestions

1. Find out if students know what chess, gin and Scrabble are. Refer them to the illustrations. If students have never heard of these games, they may look them up in a dictionary.

2. Ask students the questions about games. If your students are from different countries, you can have them work in pairs and report similarities and differences to the class.

3. (Optional) A student can explain how to play a popular game from his or her country in a subsequent class. Or you can bring in a Scrabble game, and your students can try their hand at it.

EXERCISE 8 (pairs, whole class)

Language Focus

review of tenses, asking for and giving opinions, agreeing and disagreeing, asking about and giving personal information (name, age, marital status, children, occupation, languages, nationality, habits, dislikes)

New Words and Expressions

marital status

Names

Mata Kira /mɑtɑ kirɑ/

Teaching Suggestions

1. Have students read the instructions.

2. Teach the new expression, if necessary.

3. Give students time to fill in the possible answers. Then have two students model the example conversation, giving their own answers. If S1 has filled in the same information as S2, then you should disagree.

4. Have students do the exercise in pairs. When they've finished, ask the whole class the questions to see the variety of responses.

Workbook

You can now assign Exercises C and D.

EXERCISE 9 Guess Who? (pairs or whole class)

Language Focus

must for inference, review of tenses, talking about likes and dislikes, physical description

New Words and Expressions

drums, get married, piano

Names

Yoko /joko/
Sumi /sumi/
Kimiko /kimiko/

Teaching Suggestions

1. Have students read the instructions, the example conversation and the other ideas. Ask them if they want to add their own ideas. List their ideas on the board.

2. Ask students to take a moment to think of how they would describe different people in the class, based on the ideas.

3. Have two students model the example conversation. If you feel they can, ask them to model an actual example, rather than using the one in the text.

4. Have students do the exercise in pairs, or have different students take turns with the whole class guessing. Alternatively, in a large class, you can have the students play the game in groups of three or more.

5. (Optional) If your class is small, you could have students ask about famous people, or people they all know, in addition to the class members.

EXERCISE 10 Put It Together (pairs)

Language Focus

review of *will/be going to/would like to*

New Words and Expressions

astronaut

Teaching Suggestions

1. Have students read the instructions and example.

2. Teach the new word, if necessary.

3. Give students time to think about the questions they could ask. They can also think back to the questionnaires they wrote in Unit 12. Have them do the exercise in pairs. Circulate, providing help with vocabulary and questions

4. Ask various students to report on their partners. For example: *S2 is going to* .... *after this course. She'd like to* .... *I asked her, "Will you ever* .... *?" She said, "I hope so"* (or, *I hope not*).

5. (Optional) Have students ask you the questions.

CHECKLIST

Teaching Suggestions

1. See the general suggestions in the Checklist page in Unit 1.

2. (Optional) For additional grammar practice with *might, can't,* and *must,* have three students leave the room. Have one student knock on the door. The other students guess who it is. (It *might* be S1, S2 or S3.) Have the student come in. Then have one of the two remaining students knock on the door. Have the class make similar statements: *It can't be S1. It might be S2 or S3.* Have the second student come in. Have the third student knock on the door. *It must be S3.*

3. (Optional) From time to time, you may wish to have students review the Checklist part by part and then quiz them orally in class, with books open or closed. For example:

    T: *You want to invite a good friend to play cards tomorrow night. What would you say?*
    Ss: *Do you want to play cards tomorrow night?*
    T: *How would your friend answer?* and so on.

OPTIONAL WRITING PRACTICE

Write an invitation like the one below on the board, and have students make up similar ones. Explain that *RSVP* means *please respond* (it's actually from the French, *Répondez, s'il vous plaît*). If time permits, you could discuss other kinds of parties (dinner party, cocktail party, open house, New Year's Eve/Day, etc.). Another option is to have students write directions to their homes from school as an enclosure for the invitation.

You are invited to: _____

_____

Time: _____

Place: _____

_____

RSVP

I know how to . . .

USE THESE FORMS

☐ **Might/Can't/Must**

Might *expresses possibility*.
It might be the Pekingese.

Can't *expresses impossibility*.
It can't be the St. Bernard.

Must *expresses probability*.
It must be the Chihuahua.

☐ **Whose**

| Whose | turn | is | it | ? |
| | Coke | | this | |

☐ **Tag Questions**

| *affirmative* | *negative* |
| *statement* | *tag* |

You're studying English, aren't you?
Alaska is the biggest state in the U.S., isn't it?
There are fifty states, aren't there?
Women can be president, can't they?
There will be a presidential election in
1996, won't there?

| *negative* | *affirmative* |
| *statement* | *tag* |

You're not studying Russian, are you?
Texas isn't the biggest state anymore, is it?
There aren't fifty-one states, are there?
People can't be president for more than
eight years, can they?
There won't be an election in 1995, will
there?

USE ENGLISH TO

☐ **invite someone to do something—
informally**
Do you want to play cards tonight?
Sure. Sounds good.
Sorry, I can't. I have to . . . .

☐ **and more formally**
Would you like to play tennis tomorrow?
Thanks. I'd like that.
I'm sorry, I can't, but thanks for the
invitation.

☐ **offer something—informally**
I'm going to get a Coke. (Do you) want
óne?
Sure./No, thanks.

☐ **and more formally**
Would you like some fruit?
Yes, please./Nothing for me, thanks.

☐ **express uncertainty**
I'm not sure.

☐ **talk about these subjects**
games   future plans

☐ **UNDERSTAND THESE EXPRESSIONS**

All right.
I'm not sure.
It's (your) turn.

get something (a soda)
get warmer/cooler
play a game
play cards

CHECKLIST

Listening

1

Part 1: You will hear six people speak. Match each one with the correct picture. Write the number of the speaker in the box.

Part 2: Listen again to the tape. From the list, choose the best response for each item you hear. Write its letter in the blank.

1. __   a. Hello, this is Chuck Wick. Is Marta there?
2. __   b. Hi! Come on in!
3. __   c. How do you do?
4. __   d. I'm sorry, I can't, But thanks for the invitation.
5. __   e. It depends. How much is it?
6. __   f. No, thank you. I'm just looking.
        g. Really?
        h. Same here. Take it easy.
        i. Sure. Here it is.
        j. Yes, some. How much do you need?
        k. You're welcome.
        l. Whose is that?

2

Are these conversations between friends or strangers? Check the correct column.

	Friends	**Strangers**
1.	☐	☐
2.	☐	☐
3.	☐	☐
4.	☐	☐
5.	☐	☐
6.	☐	☐
7.	☐	☐
8.	☐	☐
9.	☐	☐
10.	☐	☐

3

Here are some questions from earlier units. Give true answers.

1. _____
2. _____
3. _____
4. _____
5. _____
6. _____
7. _____
8. _____
9. _____
10. _____

LISTENING

EXERCISE 1
Language Focus
review of asking to borrow something, introductions, phone conversations, shopping, informal good-byes

Teaching Suggestions
First Part

1. Have students listen and match the speakers with the pictures.

2. Go over the answers.

Answers: 1. b 2. f 3. e 4. c 5. a 6. d

Second Part

1. Point out that there are only six speakers, but twelve possible responses. Give students time to study the responses so that they know what they have to choose from.

2. Play the cassette or read the tapescript.

3. Have students listen again and do the exercise.

Answers: 1. i 2. c 3. a 4. f 5. j 6. h

EXERCISE 2
Language Focus
review of the language used in introductions, greetings, making appointments/reservations, shopping, telephone conversations, asking for directions, ordering in a restaurant

Teaching Suggestions
1. Have students read the instructions.

2. Teach the word *strangers,* if necessary.

3. Play the cassette or read the tapescript.

4. Have students listen again and do the exercise. Go over the answers with them, stopping after each conversation, if necessary.

Answers: 1. strangers 2. friends 3. strangers
4. strangers 5. friends 6. strangers 7. friends
8. strangers 9. strangers 10. strangers

EXERCISE 3
Language Focus
review of questions and answers about a variety of topics

Teaching Suggestions
1. Tell students they can give short answers; for example: If they hear the question, *Where are you from?* they can answer with the name of their country or city.

2. Play the cassette or read the tapescript.

3. Have students listen again and do the exercise. Ask them if they remember any of the questions. (In some cases the answer is *yes* or *no,* so it might be difficult to remember the questions.)

Answers: Since answers are personal, they will vary with each student.

EPISODE 14 The Moon of India

Key Vocabulary

buyer, copy, hide, jail, press conference, send a message, similar, street vendor

Teaching Suggestions

1. Have students retell the last few episodes: Robert Grant is the thief. He holds Christina as a hostage. He tells Agatha to bring him the necklace. She does. He also ties up Agatha. But two Interpol agents follow him. Lucy points a gun at him and asks for the necklace. Robert grabs her gun. He puts the gun in her back and they walk to gangway. Frank is near the gangway and tries to help Lucy. Robert drops his gun and the necklace. The Interpol agents get Robert. The necklace falls on a tray of souvenirs on the dock below. Lucy runs off the ship and follows the man with the tray of souvenirs.

2. Follow steps 1–4 of Episode 1.

3. Students read the episode again.

4. Ask the comprehension questions.

Answers: 1) Officer Lucy Cardozo. Because she caught the thief and returned the necklace to the museum. 2) Because somebody searched his room. 3) Because she worked at the City Museum and boarded the *Princess* in Venice. 4) Because Agatha had the necklace. She loved Christina and didn't want Robert to kill her. So she gave him the necklace. 5) Yes, they did. 6) Because his mystery story was so similar to the real story.

5. (Optional) Other possible questions. Do you think Robert Grant is his real name? Do you think Frank will finish his story? Do you think Frank and Christina will see each other after the trip?

6. Have students close their books and summarize the conclusion of the story. Check their understanding of the story as they tell it. Correct any misunderstandings.

7. (Optional) Role-play. Students can role-play the conversation among Agatha, Christina, Lucy and Frank, using role cards.

MOON OF INDIA

Episode Fourteen

At the City Museum in New York, the director of the museum, Alexander Gray, is giving a press conference. Lieutenant Washington is with him. "The Moon of India is back home. The police have done an incredible job. Robert Grant, the man who stole the Moon of India and killed his partner is in jail. I would like to thank the police and one officer in particular, officer Lucy Cardozo. She caught Robert Grant and returned the Moon of India to us. Officer Cardozo is not with us today. But we, the people of this city, and especially the staff of this museum, thank her for a job well done."

At a party on the ship, Lucy, Frank, Christina and Agatha are talking.

"Why did he hide the necklace in our room?" asks Christina.

"He knew the police thought that the Moon of India was on the ship because of Paul Richardson's last words," explains Lucy, "and if they found the necklace in your room, they might think you stole it."

"Of course, I work at the museum, so they might suspect me."

"He planned to sell the necklace to a buyer in Marseilles, but he changed his plans because he was worried. I searched his room the night before. He knew somebody searched his room, but he didn't know who it was. In Barcelona, we followed him. We knew he had to sell the necklace, and we wanted him to take us to his buyer."

"Good thinking," says Agatha.

"You know the rest of the story," Lucy continues. "Agatha found the necklace. Robert came back to get it, and when he found it wasn't there, he used Christina as a hostage. But Agatha and I had a plan, and with the help of two Interpol agents, we caught him."

"When did the Interpol agents get on the ship?" asks Frank.

"We sent a message to Interpol after Robert called Agatha. They came on board the ship as soon as it docked in Malaga."

"And the buyer?" asks Frank.

"We've arrested him, too," says Lucy.

"There is one thing I would like to ask you, Frank," says Christina.

"Sure."

"Did you know that the Moon of India was on the ship?"

"No."

"Did you know that Lucy was a police officer?"

"No."

"I don't understand. The mystery story you're writing is so similar to what really happened."

"I can't explain it. Maybe I should be a detective."

"Take my place," says Lucy. "I need a vacation."

"Moon of India, get your Moon of India necklaces. One for nine dollars, two for fifteen. A steal at the price."

Comprehension Check

1. Who does Alexander Gray thank at the press conference? Why?
2. How did Robert Grant know the police suspected him?
3. Why did Robert Grant think the police would suspect Christina?
4. Why did Robert Grant use Christina as a hostage?
5. Did the police catch the buyer?
6. Why does Lucy think Frank knew about the Moon of India?

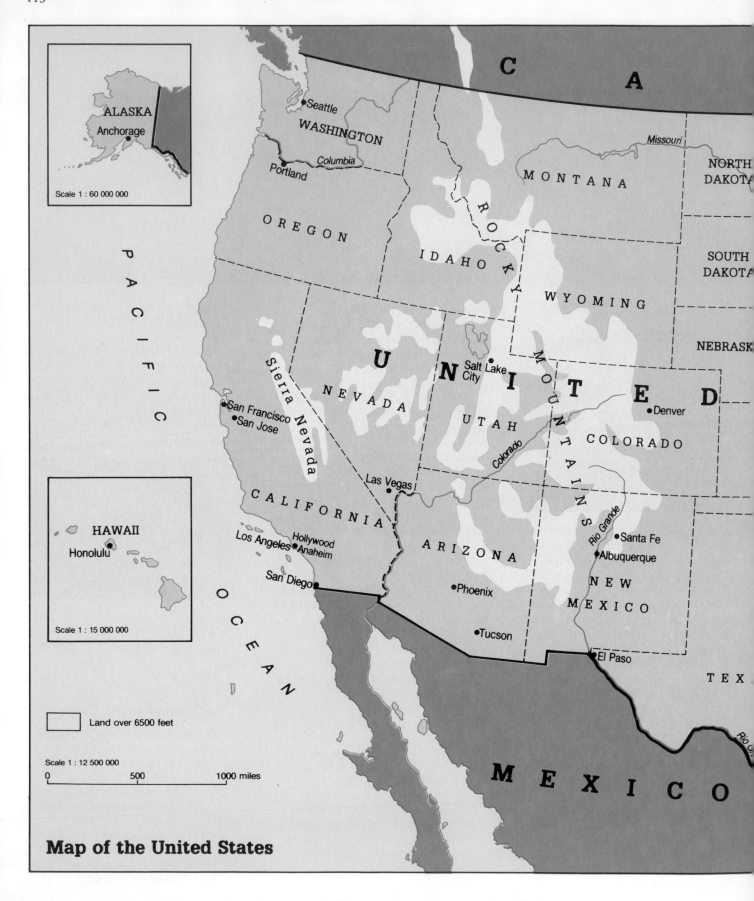

Map of the United States

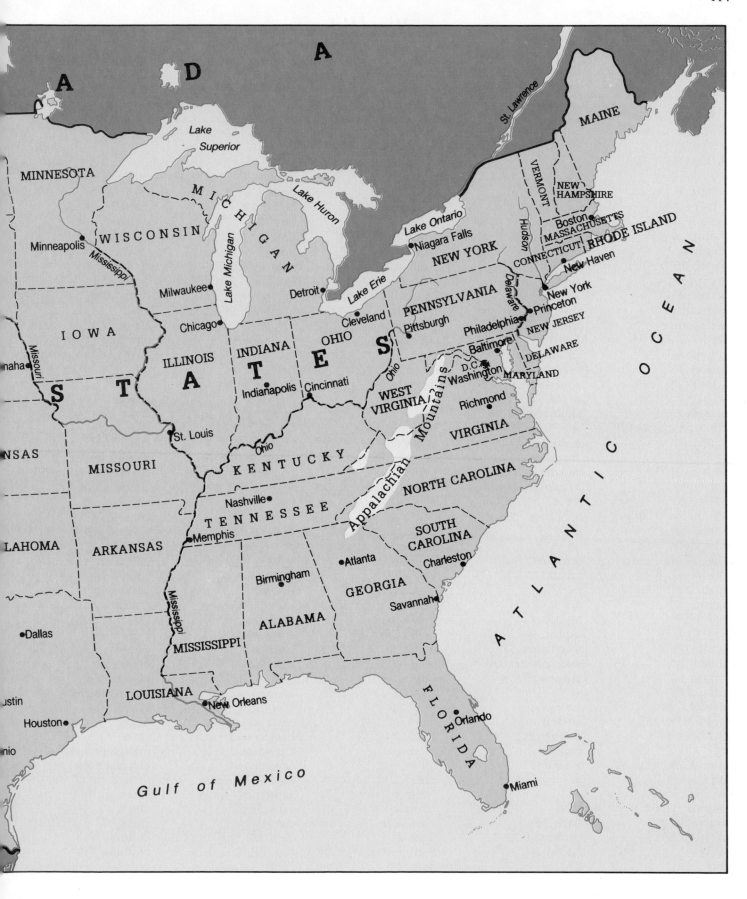

Word List

This word list contains both the active and receptive words on the first seven pages of each unit of the Student Book. The list does not include words which occur only in *The Moon of India* or the names of people and geographical locations. The page numbers next to each word indicate where it occurs for the first time. In cases where the same word is used with two different meanings, the page where each meaning first occurs is given.

A

a *1*
a little *1*
a lot of *13*
a while *97*
ability *30*
about *1*
above *26*
accept *6*
accident *33*
accountant *45*
accounting *45*
across from *9*
act out *99*
action *46*
activity *29*
actor *5*
actress *2*
ad (advertisement) *95*
add *11*
address *9*
adjective *22*
advice *61*
affirmative *108*
afford *81·*
after *100*
after all *81*
afternoon *29*
again *11*
agency *27*
agent *57*
ago *33*
agree *18*
ahead *74*
airport *57*
alike *29*
all right *28*
alone *37*
alphabet *11*
also *17*
always *26*
am ('m) *1*
AM *25*
ambulance *61*
American *2*
amount *52*
an *2*
and *1*

announce *19*
announcer *9*
annual *25*
another *21*
answer *2*
antelope *87*
anthropology *44*
any *2*
anymore *41*
anything *49*
anyway *68*
apartment *9*
apologize *6*
apology *6*
appetizer *100*
apple *51*
appointment *25*
appropriate *95*
April *37*
apron *42*
aquarium *68*
Arabic *3*
are *1*
area code *26*
aren't *9*
arrive *52*
artist *107*
arts *93*
as *52*
ask *2*
ask for *3*
aspirin *99*
asignment *57*
assistant *71*
astronaut *108*
at *3*
attention *6*
attractive *89*
August *25*
aunt *21*
avenue *11*
average *69*

B

back *10*
backward *28*
bacon *29*
bad *25*

bag *52*
baked *101*
baked goods *53*
bakery *27*
ballet dancer *107*
banana *51*
bank *46*
barbeque *99*
baseball *29*
basketball *31*
bathing suit *43*
bathroom *13*
be *6*
be around *97*
be away *99*
beach *18*
beans *52*
beautiful *84*
because *47*
become *75*
bed *9*
bedroom *9*
beef *100*
begin *30*
be in charge of *17*
be in good shape *25*
below *15*
belt *107*
best *83*
better *17*
between *10*
be up *26*
big *81*
bike *61*
billion *83*
biology *44*
birth *39*
black *12*
block *74*
blond *36*
blouse *42*
blue *12*
book *3*
bookcase *9*
bookstore *75*
boot *43*
boring *89*
born *33*

borrow *1*
both *17*
bottle *52*
bow *5*
box *7*
boy *41*
boyfriend *75*
Brazilian *5*
bread *49*
breakfast *26*
bring *99*
British *105*
broiled *100*
brother *18*
brother-in-law *23*
brown *9*
bucket *59*
building *9*
bus *5*
business trip *71*
businesswoman (man) *4*
but *9*
butcher *53*
butter *29*
buy (bought) *53*
by *1*
by the way *4*
bye *60*

C

cable *93*
call *27*
camp *26*
campus *23*
can (n) *42*
Can I help you? *49*
can't *28*
can('t) make it *25*
Canadian *106*
capacity *81*
capital *3* (place)
capital *11* (letter)
capsule *5*
car *19*
card *25*
carefully *2*
carrot *53*

cartoons *91*
cash *78*
casually *43*
cat *81*
celebrate *98*
celebrity *39*
cent *49*
cereal *26*
certainly *17*
chair *9*
chalk *11*
change (n) *49*
change one's mind *17*
channel *93*
charge *17*
chart *26*
cheap *81*
check *12*
check into *57*
check-out counter *53*
check out of *62*
checkup *25*
cheese *53*
cheetah *81*
chemist *17*
chemistry *44*
cherry *51*
chess *108*
chicken *100*
child *20*
children *18*
Chinese *5*
choice *20*
choose *5*
cinnamon *53*
circle *7*
city *3*
class *7*
classical music *91*
classmate *45*
classroom *11*
clean up *63*
clock *66*
close *4*
clothes *43*
clothing *75*
coat *97*

Irregular Verbs: Past Tense

be	was, were	lose	lost
begin	began	make	made
bring	brought	mean	meant
buy	bought	meet	met
catch	caught	put	put
choose	chose	read	read
come	came	ring	rang
cost	cost	run	ran
do	did	say	said
drive	drove	see	saw
eat	ate	sell	sold
fall	fell	shake	shook
feel	felt	sing	sang
find	found	sit	sat
fly	flew	speak	spoke
forget	forgot	spend	spent
get	got	steal	stole
give	gave	swim	swam
go	went	take	took
grow	grew	teach	taught
have	had	tell	told
hear	heard	think	thought
hide	hid	understand	understood
hold	held	wear	wore
know	knew	write	wrote
leave	left		

TAPESCRIPT

UNIT 1   Page 7

Exercise 1 *If you are reading the tapescript, pause 5 seconds after each item.*

Complete these conversations: Circle *a* or *b*.

1. MAN 1: Excuse me, do you speak English?
2. MAN 2: Yes, I do, a little.
   MAN 1: Great! Could I borrow your pen?
3. MAN 2: Sure. Here it is.
4. MAN 1: Thank you. Where are you from?
   MAN 2: I'm from Japan. What about you?
5. MAN 1: I'm Mexican, from Cuernavaca. What are you doing in the United States? Are you here on vacation?
6. MAN 2: No, I'm studying English.
7. MAN 1: Really? What do you do?
8. MAN 2: I'm a teacher.
   MAN 1: Well, it's a small world! I'm a teacher, too! By the way, my name's Jose Montoya.
   MAN 2: How do you do? I'm Koji Asaba.

Exercise 2 *If you are reading the tapescript, pause 5 seconds after each item.*

Listen to each question and answer about the famous people in this unit. Mark the answers *T* (true) or *F* (false).

1. A: Is Brooke Shields American?
   B: No, she isn't.

2. A: What does Pierre Cardin do?
   B: He's a fashion designer.

3. A: Where's Yosuhiro Nakasone from?
   B: He's from Italy.

4. A: Is Hanae Mori a Japanese fashion designer?
   B: Yes, she is.

5. A: What does Gloria Vanderbilt do?
   B: She's a businesswoman.

6. A: Is Diahann Carroll French?
   B: Yes, she is.

7. A: Is Jesse Jackson from the United States?
   B: Yes, he is.

8. A: Where's Catherine Deneuve from?
   B: She's American.

Exercise 3 Margaret Winters is an English teacher. She and a friend are looking at this picture of Margaret's class. Fill in the countries and the occupations, using the information below.

FRIEND: What's that picture? Could I look at it?
MARGARET: Sure. Here it is. It's my English class.
FRIEND: Are they all from different countries?

MARGARET: Uh-huh, almost. Two are from Japan.
FRIEND: Is this woman Japanese?
MARGARET: Yes, that's Akiko. She's a writer. She writes for a newspaper in Osaka.
FRIEND: Hmmm. And this guy next to her? Where's he from?
MARGARET: That's Christophe. He's from Canada. Montreal.
FRIEND: So he speaks French, then.
MARGARET: Right. In fact, he's a French teacher. He teaches in a high school. Next to Christophe is Sami. He's from Brazil.
FRIEND: What does he do in Brazil?
MARGARET: He's an actor on television. Good-looking, isn't he?
FRIEND: I guess so. He looks like an actor, anyway. . . . Who's this on the right?
MARGARET: Maria, from Italy. She's a singer.
FRIEND: Hmmm. Do you have any other pictures of her?

Exercise 4 *If you are reading the tapescript, pause 10 seconds after each item.*

Give true answers.

1. Do you speak English?
2. Where are you from?
3. What do you do?
4. Are you French?
5. Are you an actor?
6. Where's Washington, D.C.?

UNIT 2   Page 15

Exercise 1 *If you are reading the tapescript, pause 5 seconds after each item.*

Anne is taking people's names and addresses.

Part 1: Listen for the spelling of each person's name. Circle the correct letter.

1. ANNE: What's your name, please?
   MAN 1: Frank Gilmore.
   ANNE: How do you spell your last name, Mr. Gilmore?
   MAN 1: G-I-L-M-O-R-E.
   ANNE: And what's your address?
   MAN 1: 55 Harris Avenue.
   ANNE: Thank you. Next?

2. ANNE: What's your name, please?
   MAN 2: Ray Braun.
   ANNE: How do you spell your last name, Mr. Braun?
   MAN 2: B-R-A-U-N.
   ANNE: B-R-A-U-N?
   MAN 2: That's right.
   ANNE: And what's your address?
   MAN 2: 80 Green Street.
   ANNE: 18 or 80?
   MAN 2: 80.
   ANNE: Thank you, Mr. Braun. Next?

3. ANNE: Your name, please?
   WOMAN 1: Ingrid Andersen.
   ANNE: How do you spell that?
   WOMAN 1: My last name? A-N-D-E-R-S-*E*-N.

ANNE: Andersen with an E. Your address?
WOMAN 1: 1276 Hill Road.
ANNE: 1276. . . . Thank you.

4. ANNE: Could I have your name, please?
   MAN 3: Rich Reid.
   ANNE: How do you spell Reid?
   MAN 3: R-E-I-D.
   ANNE: Your address, Mr. Reid?
   MAN 3: 500 Belmont Avenue.
   ANNE: Pardon?
   MAN 3: 500 Belmont Avenue.

5. ANNE: May I have your name?
   WOMAN 2: Pat McCloud.
   ANNE: How do you spell your last name?
   WOMAN 2: M-C, capital C-L-O-U-D.
   ANNE: Could you repeat that, please?
   WOMAN 2: M-C, capital C-L-O-U-D.
   ANNE: What's your address, Ms. McCloud?
   WOMAN 2: 905 Williams Road.
   ANNE: 905 Williams Road. Thank you. Next?

6. ANNE: Name, please?
   WOMAN 3: Doris Waitt. With two T's. W-A-I-T-T.
   ANNE: Address?
   WOMAN 3: 50 High Street.
   ANNE: 15?
   WOMAN 3: No, 50. Five-oh.
   ANNE: Thank you. Next? Oh. That's all.

Part 2: Listen again to the conversations and fill in the street number for eacy person's address.

Exercise 2 *If you are reading the tapescript, pause 5 seconds after each item.*

Gail and Manuel are playing *What's My Word?* Fill in the correct letters as you hear them.

GAIL: How many letters are there in your word?
MANUEL: Umm . . . Ten.
GAIL: Good. Long words are easy. Are there any O's?
MANUEL: No, there aren't. Not so easy, huh?
GAIL: OK, are there any E's?
MANUEL: Yes, there are two. The fifth letter is an E. The tenth letter is an E, too.
GAIL: The fifth and the tenth. Is there an I?
MANUEL: There are two I's. The first letter and the seventh.
GAIL: The first is an I, and the seventh is an I. How about R's? Are there any?
MANUEL: Uh-huh. The fourth letter's an R. You're getting better!
GAIL: Thanks. OK, number 4 is an R. N. Is there an N?
MANUEL: There's one of those, too! Number 2.
GAIL: The second letter is an N. is there a D?
MANUEL: Yes! The sixth letter is a D.
GAIL: H? Are there any H's?
MANUEL: No. No H's.
GAIL: Is there a C?
MANUEL: Yes. The third letter is C.
GAIL: Good. The third letter is C. Any L's?
MANUEL: There's one L. It's the ninth letter.

GAIL: I think I know. Is there a B? The eighth letter?
MANUEL: You're right. The eighth letter is a B.
GAIL: The word is "incredible."
MANUEL: Right! Incredible!
GAIL: Thank you.

Exercise 3 *If you are reading the tapescript, pause 10 seconds after each item.*

Sandy wants to take a picture of some people in her office. Find the people in the picture. Write their numbers below their names.

SANDY: OK, everybody. Are you ready? Janice? Janice! On the left. Howard, you sit next to Janice. That's next to Janice, Howard. Doug, you're tall. Stand in back of Howard. Diane, next to Howard. Next to Howard, Diane! Allen, you go on the right. On the right, Allen. Rosa, you're between Diane and Allen. Kristin, in back of Rosa—in back of Rosa, please. I'll go between Doug and Kristin, in back of Diane. OK, everybody? Smile!

Exercise 4 *If you are reading the tapescript, pause 10 seconds after each item.*

Give true answers.

1. Are there any As in your last name?
2. Is there a three in your address?
3. What's your name?
4. What's your address?

UNIT 3   Page 23

Exercise 1 *If you are reading the tapescript, pause 10 seconds after each item.*

A man is showing a friend pictures of his family. Fill in each person's relation to the man. Use the words from the box.

EDWARD: Now, on the left, that's my brother Charles, with my sister-in-law, Diana.
FRIEND: Your sister-in-law is very pretty.
EDWARD: Yes, she certainly is. . . . Next is my other brother, Andrew, with his wife, Sarah. People usually call her Fergy.
FRIEND: He's good-looking. You look like him, you know.
EDWARD: That's what people say.
FRIEND: Are those your parents?
EDWARD: Yes, that's my mother and father. . . . Next to them is my mother's sister, my Aunt Margaret.
FRIEND: Does she have any children?
EDWARD: Yes, two. My cousins, David and Sarah.
FRIEND: Oh, who's that? He's really cute!
EDWARD: My nephew Harry. He's Charles and Diana's boy.
FRIEND: Is that your grandmother on the right?
EDWARD: Yes, it is. My mother's mother.
FRIEND: Do you have any other brothers and sisters?
EDWARD: One sister, Anne. But we don't have a picture of her here.

Exercise 2 *If you are reading the tapescript, pause 5 seconds after each item.*

Jeanne is asking Marie about Marie's family. Mark the statements *T* (true) or *F* (false).

JEANNE: What's your husband's name, Marie?
MARIE: Mark. Mark Joseph Ornato, Junior.
JEANNE: Whew! Do you and Mark have any children?
MARIE: Yes, we have a son and a daughter.
JEANNE: How old are they?
MARIE: Terry's 20. She's a dancer, in New York.
JEANNE: Does she have her own apartment?
MARIE: No, she's only 20. She lives with my brother and sister-in-law.
JEANNE: And your son? What does he do?
MARIE: Bob's a student at Connecticut College. He's 19.
JEANNE: Does he have an apartment?
MARIE: No, he lives in a room in my sister's house near the college.
JEANNE: So, you have a brother in New York and a sister in Connecticut. Do you have any other brothers or sisters?
MARIE: No, there are just the three of us. But that's enough about me. Tell me about your family, Jeanne. You have three children, right?
JEANNE: That's right. Rachel is 22. She's. . . .

Exercise 3 *If you are reading the tapescript, pause 5 seconds after each item.*

Marina Polis is the fifth international visitor to MHI. Listen to this interview and answer the questions about her. Circle the letter of the correct answer.

INTERVIEWER: Where do you work, Mrs. Polis?
MARINA: At a hospital in Athens.
INTERVIEWER: Oh, and what exactly do you do there?
MARINA: I'm in charge of supplies.
INTERVIEWER: Do you live in Athens, too?
MARINA: Yes, I do. I have a small apartment in the city.
INTERVIEWER: Do you have a family?
MARINA: My husband and I have one daughter. She's in school here, in the United States.
INTERVIEWER: Really? Where?
MARINA: At the University of Michigan.

Exercise 4 *If you are reading the tapescript, pause 10 seconds after each item.*

Give true answers.

1. Where do you come from?
2. Where do you work?
3. Where do you live?
4. Do you live in an apartment?
5. Does your family have a television?
6. Are you married or single?
7. Do you have any brothers or sisters?
8. Do you have any children?

UNIT 4   Page 31

Exercise 1 *If you are reading the tapescript, pause 10 seconds after each item.*

Write the phone numbers as you hear them.

1. A: What's your number at home?
   B: 387-5950.

2. A: What's your number at work?
   B: 357-4875.

3. A: What's your number at home?
   B: 740-9651.

4. A: What's your home phone number?
   B: 661-6600.

5. A: Do you have a phone at work?
   B: Yes, the number's 924-3434, extension 512.

6. A: Could I have your number at work?
   B: Uh-huh, it's 668-2732.

Exercise 2 *If you are reading the tapescript, pause 10 seconds after each item.*

Listen to the telephone conversations, and answer the questions.

1. A: Good morning, Public Library.
   B: What time do you open today?
   A: At nine o'clock.
   B: Thank you.
   A: You're welcome.

2. A: House of Pizza.
   B: When do you close tonight?
   A: At ten-thirty.
   B: OK, thanks.

3. A: Hello.
   B: Is this the Photo Factory?
   A: Yes, it is.
   B: When do you open today?
   A: In ten minutes, at eight-thirty.
   B: And what time do you close?
   A: Four forty-five.

4. A: Good afternoon, West Side Market.
   B: Could you tell me when you're open?
   A: Ten to ten, Monday through Saturday.
   B: Are you ever open on Sundays?
   A: No, we aren't.

5. A: Steak Out Restaurant.
   B: I wondered whether you were open today.
   A: Yes, we are, until eleven-fifteen tonight.
   B: Are you open on Sundays?
   A: From noon to nine. We're closed Tuesdays.
   B: Thanks a lot.
   A: You're welcome. 'Bye.

Exercise 3 *If you are reading the tapescript, pause 5 seconds after each item.*

Do you hear *can* or *can't?* Circle the correct one.

1. FRIEND: Mary, do you like to dance the tango?
   MARY: I can't dance the tango, but I can dance the samba.

2. FRIEND: Joseph, you speak Portuguese and Spanish, don't you?
   JOSEPH: No. I can't speak Portuguese, but I can speak Spanish.

3. TERRY: I'll never be a secretary. I can't type and I can't take shorthand.

4. BOB: When should I meet you?
   WIFE: How about at three o'clock?
   BOB: I can't make it at three. Can I meet you at four?
   WIFE: OK.

Exercise 4

Gus Tate plays on the Globals basketball team. Howard Shortell is asking him about his life. Mark the statements *T* (true) or *F* (false).

Part 1:

HOWARD: This is Howard Shortell. I'm here talking to Gus Tate. Great game, Gus.
GUS: Thanks, Howard.
HOWARD: Tell me, Gus . . . You play basketball six months a year. Is that difficult?
GUS: It isn't easy, Howard. I'm away from home almost every night. I usually eat in restaurants and sleep in hotels. After a game, I go back to the hotel and go to bed. Sometimes I get up early, but I usually sleep until nine or ten. Then I eat a big breakfast. We exercise for two hours and we play for three hours every day. It's not that easy, Howard.

Part 2:

HOWARD: Tell us about your family life, Gus. What do you do at home?
GUS: My wife and I talk, read, watch TV, play with the kids.
HOWARD: Do you and your wife ever go out at night?
GUS: No, we're usually at home.
HOWARD: Do you usually sleep late?
GUS: Oh, no. I always get up early. I go to work every day. I have my own business, you know.
HOWARD: Do you ever play any basketball?
GUS: Are you kidding? My sons and I play every day! I love basketball!

Exercise 5 *If you are reading the tapescript, pause 10 seconds after each item.*

Give true answers.

1. When do you usually get up?
2. Do you ever have cereal for breakfast?
3. Where do you usually eat breakfast?
4. What do you do after class?
5. Do you ever watch TV in the morning?

UNIT 5   Page 39

Exercise 1 *If you are reading the tapescript, pause 5 seconds after each item.*

You'll hear eight questions. Some are in the present tense. Some are in the past tense. Check the correct column.

1. Do you speak English?
2. What do you do?
3. What did you say?
4. What's your address?
5. What did you do last night?
6. How do you like your English class?
7. When were you born?
8. Were you in school in 1950?

Exercise 2 *If you are reading the tapescript, pause 5 seconds after each item.*

Complete the conversations. Choose *a* or *b.*

1. A: Did you see *Butch Cassidy and the Sundance Kid?*
   B: Yes, I did.
   A: Were Paul Newman and Robert Redford in it?

2. A: Was Marlon Brando in *The African Queen?* I can't remember.

3. A: I saw Ginny Call yesterday.
   B: Who?
   A: Ginny Call. She was in our class in high school.

4. A: Who invented the telephone?

5. A: In what month was your son born?

6. A: What was Alfred Hitchcock famous for?

Exercise 3 *If you are reading the tapescript, pause 5 seconds after each item.*

Match the celebrity with his or her date of birth.

A: Hmm, this is really interesting. It's a list of famous people, and it tells when and where they were born.
B: Oh yeah? We can find out how old people are! Is Clint Eastwood in there?
A: Uh-huh. He was born in San Francisco, California, on May 31, 1930.
B: 1930? He doesn't look that old. How about Mick Jagger?
A: Dartford, England. July 26, 1943.

B: Jane Fonda? She's in good shape, too.
A: She was born in New York. December 21, 1937. She *is* in good shape for her age.
B: What about B.B. King? I really like his records.
A: 1925! September 16, 1925. Listen to this. He was born in Itta Bena, Mississippi. That's a strange name. I wonder about Woody Allen. I love his movies.
B: I think he was born in New York.
A: I do, too. Yes, New York, December 1, 1935.
B: Is Whitney Houston in there? Speaking of good shape . . .
A: Just a minute. August 9, 1964. You know who's my favorite? Speaking of good shape . . . Mikhail Baryshnikov . . . Latvia. July 26, 1943.

Exercise 4 *If you are reading the tapescript, pause 10 seconds after each item.*

Give true answers.

1. When's your birthday?
2. Where were you born?
3. Did you grow up there?
4. Where did you begin school?
5. Did you like school?
6. Who was your favorite teacher?

UNIT 6   Page 47

Exercise 1

Alice is a stranger. She doesn't know the people at the party. Dennis knows some of the people at the party. Listen to the conversation between Alice and Dennis. Match the people in the picture with the names below.

ALICE: Which one is Joan?
DENNIS: She's wearing blue jeans and a white shirt and she's talking to Fred.
ALICE: Which one is Fred?
DENNIS: He's sitting on the sofa talking to Joan. He's wearing brown pants.
ALICE: And Joan's sitting on the sofa, too?
DENNIS: Right.
ALICE: Which one is Sue?
DENNIS: She's wearing a skirt and a yellow blouse. She's standing next to the stereo.
ALICE: OK. I see her. And who is she talking to?
DENNIS: She's talking to Melanie.
ALICE: Melanie's wearing gray pants and a blue sweater.
DENNIS: That's right. And that's Joe. He's playing the guitar.
ALICE: And who's standing next to Joe?
DENNIS: That's Monica. She's wearing a blue dress.
ALICE: And who's opening the soda?
DENNIS: That's Mark.
ALICE: There's a woman next to Mark. She's wearing blue jeans and a white shirt.
DENNIS: That's Mark's girlfriend.
ALICE: What's her name?
DENNIS: Jessica.

Exercise 2 *If you are reading the tapescript, pause 5 seconds after each item.*

Complete the conversations. Choose *a* or *b*.

1. A: Hey, Joe. How's your boy, Nicky? Is he still living in England?

2. A: I'm taking a course in computers at the Adult Ed Center.
   B: Really? My wife's taking an accounting course there.
   A: An accounting course? Why?

3. A: My daughter has a new job. She works in a law office now.
   B: How does she like it?

4. A: What courses are you taking?
   B: Biology, English and algebra.
   A: Do you like your biology course?

5. A: Who usually teaches biology?
   B: Professor Jones.
   A: Is he teaching it this year?

6. A: Do you like your English course?
   B: Yes, I do.
   A: When does it meet?

7. A: Where's Mary?
   B: At home.
   A: What's she doing?

8. A: What're you doing?
   B: I'm packing for my trip to Hawaii.
   A: Do you need this heavy jacket?

Exercise 3 *If you are reading the tapescript, pause 10 seconds after each item.*

Give true answers.

1. Where are you studying English?
2. When does your English class meet?
3. Are you taking any other courses?
4. Do you want to travel in the United States?

UNIT 7   Page 55

Exercise 1

Maggie and John are making a shopping list. Listen to their conversation, and complete the list.

MAGGIE: Let's see. We need cheese and milk. Do we have any vegetables?
JOHN: Not very many. Let's get carrots and string beans.
MAGGIE: OK. How about eggs?
JOHN: We need eggs. Let's get a dozen.
MAGGIE: Do we have any bread?
JOHN: No. We need bread. We need butter, too.
MAGGIE: Do we have any jam?
JOHN: Yes, a lot.
MAGGIE: How about fruit?
JOHN: We have a lot of bananas, but we don't have any oranges.

MAGGIE: Then why don't we get some oranges? Should we get some peaches?
JOHN: No. They're too expensive.

Exercise 2

Fill in the missing prices.

A: Attention shoppers! Attention shoppers! We'd like to tell you about this week's specials. In the dairy department we have eggs at $1.25 a dozen. That's right. $1.25 for a dozen eggs. Our American cheese is on sale for $2.99 a pound. Butter is on special at a low $2.75 a pound. That's $2.75 for a pound of butter. In the produce department, Red Delicious apples are on sale for 65 cents a pound and string beans are only 78 cents a pound. We also have a special on strawberry jam. A one-pound jar of strawberry jam is $2.25. We hope you'll take advantage of these super savings.
B: What did he say? How much are the apples?
C: 65 cents a pound.
B: Thank you.

Exercise 3

What did Mr. Harriman buy?

MR. HARRIMAN: Hello, dear. I'm home. Can you help me put away the groceries?
MRS. HARRIMAN: Sure. What did you buy? You have six bags of groceries!
MR. HARRIMAN: Well, cheese was on sale, so I bought three pounds.
MRS. HARRIMAN: Here it is. Three pounds of cheese. What're these?
MR. HARRIMAN: Ten cans of soup.
MRS. HARRIMAN: Ten cans of soup! That's a lot.
MR. HARRIMAN: The soup was on sale. A real bargain.
MRS. HARRIMAN: Oh, and a dozen eggs.
MR. HARRIMAN: No, there are three dozen.
MRS. HARRIMAN: Three dozen! Oh. On sale.
MR. HARRIMAN: And six loaves of bread.
MRS. HARRIMAN: On sale. And apples. How many pounds of apples?
MR. HARRIMAN: Five pounds. And four pounds of bananas. They were a real bargain.
MRS. HARRIMAN: And beans. Good grief! How many pounds of string beans did you buy?
MR. HARRIMAN: Only eight.
MRS. HARRIMAN: Eight pounds! And four, five, six, seven jars of jam?
MR. AND MRS. HARRIMAN: On sale!

Exercise 4 *If you are reading the tapescript, pause 10 seconds after each item.*

Give true answers.

1. Do you have any change on you?
2. How often do you go grocery shopping?
3. Do you ever shop at a supermarket?
4. Do you like bread?
5. What's one of your favorite foods?

UNIT 8   Page 63

Exercise 1 *If you are reading the tapescript, pause 5 seconds after each item.*

Listen to each dialogue. Check the correct box.

1. A: Are you going to go grocery shopping tomorrow?
   B: No, I went grocery shopping yesterday.

2. A: Are you going to wash the car on Saturday?
   B: No, I'm going to wash it on Sunday.

3. A: Are you going to clean up the house this afternoon?
   B: No, John cleaned it up last Saturday.

4. A: Are you going to vacuum the living room this weekend?
   B: No, I vacuumed it last weekend.

5. A: Are you going to pick the children up later?
   B: No, my husband's going to pick them up.

Exercise 2 *If you are reading the tapescript, pause 5 seconds after each item.*

You're going to hear six conversations. Listen and decide which suggestion completes each conversation.

1. A: It's dark in here.
   B: Where's the light?
   A: Over there.

2. A: It's cold in here.
   B: Do you have a sweater?
   A: Yes.

3. A: Look at this room!

4. A: The stereo's too loud.

5. A: I don't know these words.
   B: Do you have a dictionary?
   A: Yes.

6. A: It's hot in here.
   B: You're wearing a sweater, aren't you?
   A: Yes.

Exercise 3 *If you are reading the tapescript, pause 8 seconds after each item.*

These people are going to stay at the Park Hotel in Amsterdam this week: Elizabeth Taylor, Jane Fonda, Sean Penn and Paul McCartney. Which nights are they going to stay there? Write their names in the reservation book at the correct dates.

A: Are we going to have any famous people with us this week?
B: Yes indeed. It's going to be an interesting week.
A: Really! Who's going to be here?

125

B: Well. Sean Penn is here now. He arrived on Monday the 25th.
A: That was yesterday.
B: Right. He arrived yesterday, the 25th. He's going to leave on the 30th.
A: And who else?
B: Elizabeth Taylor is going to arrive this evening.
A: How long is she going to stay?
B: Two days.
A: Oh, you mean until the 28th?
B: Yes. And then Paul McCartney is going to arrive on the 29th. He's only going to stay for one night.
A: Anyone else?
B: Yes. Jane Fonda is going to be here for the weekend.
A: Which nights is she going to stay?
B: Friday and Saturday.

Exercise 4 *If you are reading the tapescript, pause 5 seconds after each item.*

Part 1: You are going to hear five phone conversations. Some have messages, some don't. Check the correct box.

1. A: Hello.
   B: Hello, this is Terry Anderson. May I please speak to Mrs. Kister?
   A: I'm sorry, she's not here right now. Can I take a message?
   B: Yes. Please tell her that I called.
   A: What was your name again?
   B: Terry Anderson.
   A: Thanks.
   B: Good-bye.
   A: Good-bye.

2. A: Hello.
   B: Hello, this is Sarah McCormack. Is Terry there?
   A: Yes, he is. Just a minute, please.

3. A: Hello, this is Terry Anderson. Is Kathy there?
   B: No, she isn't. Can I take a message?
   A: Yes. Please tell her I called, and ask her to call me at this number: 355-2951.
   B: 355-2951?
   A: That's right.
   B: Good-bye.
   A: Good-bye.

4. A: Hello.
   B: Hello. Is Terry Anderson there? This is Kathy.
   A: I'm sorry. You have the wrong number.
   B: Oh, sorry.

5. A: Hello.
   B: Hello. Is Terry Anderson there?
   A: This is Terry.
   B: Oh, hi, Terry. This is Kathy.

Part 2: *If you are reading the tapescript, pause 10 seconds after each item.*

Now listen again and write down the messages. These are the names you're going

to hear: Terry Anderson, Mrs. Kister, Kathy, Sarah McCormack.

Exercise 5 *If you are reading the tapescript, pause 10 seconds after each item.*

Give true answers.

1. What are you going to do tonight?
2. Are you going to have dinner at home?
3. What are you going to do this weekend?
4. Who are you going to see?

UNIT 9   Page 71

Exercise 1

Sue Thompson is going to take a business trip to Nashville. Her assistant, Max Martin, makes two phone calls for her. He's new, and he makes a lot of mistakes. Correct Max's memos.

Part 1: Max calls the bus station.

CLERK: Central Bus Station. Can I help you?
MAX: Yes, thanks. When are there buses to Nashville?
CLERK: There are three every day except Sundays. When do you want to get there?
MAX: Could you tell me about all three of them?
CLERK: You can leave here at 9:17 AM, 1:18 PM and 7:01 PM. You arrive in Nashville at 11:36, 3:41 and 9:28.
MAX: I'm sorry, could you repeat that, please? More slowly?
CLERK: Leave here at 9:17 AM. Get to Nashville at 11:36 AM. Leave here at 1:18 PM. Get to Nashville at 3:41 PM. Leave here at 7:01 PM. Get to Nashville at 9:28 PM.
MAX: Thank you. Do you have to change buses?
CLERK: You do on the 1:18, but you don't on the others. There's a 15-minute wait between buses.
MAX: How much does it cost?
CLERK: One-way fare is $16.36. Round-trip is $29.
MAX: Are there any trains? Or do you have to go by bus?
CLERK: This is the bus station, sir. But I know that there aren't any trains. Yes, you do have to go by bus.
MAX: I see. Thank you very much.
CLERK: You're welcome.

Part 2: Max calls a travel agent.

TRAVEL AGENT: Good morning, Valley Travel Agency.
MAX: Good morning. This is Max Martin, calling for Sue Thompson. Can you suggest a good hotel in Nashville?
TRAVEL AGENT: You could try the Hotel Magee. It's very nice, and it's right downtown.
MAX: How much is it for one person?
TRAVEL AGENT: $85. Can I make a reservation for you?
MAX: I'll call back. Thank you.
TRAVEL AGENT: You're welcome. Good-bye.

Exercise 2 *If you are reading the tapescript, pause 5 seconds after each item.*

Complete the conversations. Choose a or b.

1. A: How can I get downtown from here?

2. A: How can I get downtown from here?
   B: You can take a taxi, a bus, or a local train.
   A: How often do the buses run?

3. A: How often do the buses run?
   B: Every two hours, between 10 AM and 5 PM.
   A: How long does it take?

4. A: How long does it take?
   B: About 45 minutes.
   A: How much does it cost?

5. A: How much does it cost?
   B: Four-fifty.
   A: Is that one-way or round-trip?

6. A: Is that one-way or round-trip?
   B: One-way.
   A: Do I have to change buses?

7. A: Do I have to change buses?
   B: No, you don't.
   A: When's the next bus?

8. A: When's the next bus?
   B: At 2:47.
   A: It's 2:45 now! When's the next one after that?

Exercise 3

Wilfred Klutz gets on a bus at Colesville. Listen and decide which picture describes his trip.

DRIVER: Good morning. This is the 9 o'clock express, Colesville-Hinkston.
WILFRED: Did he say Hinkston or Pinkston?
WOMAN: Hinkston.
WILFRED: I have to get off the bus. I'm on the wrong one. I have to get off. I'm on the wrong bus.
DRIVER: I can't stop. This is an express.
WILFRED: But I have to get to Pinkston.
DRIVER: Sorry. You'll have to go all the way to Hinkston. Hinkston! Hinkston!

WILFRED: How can I get to Pinkston from here?
WOMAN: This is Hinkston.
WILFRED: Not Hinkston, Pinkston.
WOMAN: Hmm. You can take a bus to Newton and change to a train there.
WILFRED: Isn't there another way?
WOMAN: You can take a taxi. But it's expensive.
WILFRED: I'll take the bus to Newton.

TICKET AGENT: May I help you?
WILFRED: Yes. I'd like a ticket to Pinkston on the next train. When is the next train?
TICKET AGENT: At 2:35.
WILFRED: Do I have to change trains?

WILFRED: And what time does it get into Pinkston?

TICKET AGENT: 3:40. Do you want one-way or round-trip?

WILFRED: One-way, please. Oh, please.

Exercise 4 *If you are reading the tapescript, pause 10 seconds after each item.*

Give true answers.

1. How do you usually get to your English class?
2. Do you have a car?
3. Do you drive to work?
4. Is public transportation in your country good?

UNIT 10   Page 79

Exercise 1 *If you are reading the tapescript, pause 5 seconds after each item.*

Look at the picture and listen to the information. Is the information true or false? Write *T* or *F*.

1. A: Can I walk to the post office from here?
   B: Yes, you can. It isn't far. It's at the corner of Bolton Street and Gamble Street, next to City Hall.

2. A: Is the Hollywood Hotel very far? Can I walk to it from here?
   B: No, it isn't very far. You can walk. It's on the corner of Gamble Street and Bolton Street, across from the post office.

3. A: I have to buy some shoes. Where can I go?
   B: Why don't you go to the shoe store on Ellsworth Street? It's right on the corner, next to a Japanese restaurant.

4. A: Could you tell me where the Grand Supermarket is?
   B: Sure. It's on Gamble Street, at the corner of Bolton.

5. A: Is there a Mexican restaurant near here?
   B: Yes, there is. It's on Gamble Street, next to the supermarket.

6. A: I have to buy some clothes for the kids.
   B: Why don't you go to the new store on Bolton Street? It's between the Museum of Natural History and the Japanese restaurant.

Exercise 2 *If you are reading the tapescript, pause 5 seconds after each item.*

This is a map of Greenwich Village. You're going to hear three people ask for directions. Follow the directions to each place and write the number of the conversation in the circle. Each person begins at 5th Avenue, between 8th and 9th Street.

1. A: Walk up to 9th Street. Turn left on 9th. Go one block to 6th Avenue. It's on your right.

2. Begin again at 5th Avenue, between 8th and 9th Street.
   A: Walk down to 8th Street. Go one long block to 6th Avenue.
   B: Right on 8th, one long block to 6th.
   A: At 6th Avenue walk across the street to Greenwich Avenue. Go 4½ blocks on Greenwich Avenue to 7th Avenue.
   B: 4½ blocks on Greenwich to 7th Avenue.
   A: Turn left onto 7th Avenue. It's on your right, across the street.
   B: Left on 7th and it's across the street. Thanks a lot.

3. Begin again at 5th Avenue, between 8th and 9th Street.
   A: Walk down 5th Avenue to Washington Square Park.
   B: Down to the park.
   A: Go through the park to Washington Square South.
   B: Uh-huh.
   A: Make a left and go about half a block.
   B: I go left and it's about half a block. Thanks.
   A: You're welcome.

Exercise 3 *If you are reading the tapescript, pause 5 seconds after each item.*

Listen to the five short conversations. Number the traffic signs in the correct order, 1–5.

1. A: Right! Turn right! You can't turn left here. You have to turn right.

2. A: Uh, how fast are you going?
   B: Oh, about 50.
   A: Well, you'd better slow down. The speed limit here is 30.

3. B: How fast are you going?
   A: Oh, about 30.
   B: Why don't you go a little faster? This is the interstate, you know. You can go 65. In fact, you'd *better* go 65.

4. A: Can I park over there? Do you know?
   B: I don't know. But you can park right here.
   A: Oh, I can't see the sign . . . For how long?
   B: Twenty minutes.

5. A: Straight! Go straight ahead! You can't turn here. You have to go straight!

Exercise 4 *If you are reading the tapescript, pause 10 seconds after each item.*

Give true answers.

1. Is there an American restaurant near your home?
2. Are there any grocery stores in your neighborhood?
3. From your home, how many blocks do you have to walk to a bus or train station?
4. Do people in your country drive on the left or on the right?

UNIT 11   Page 87

Exercise 1 *If you are reading the tapescript, pause 5 seconds after each item.*

Listen to the conversation and check the correct answer.

A: Here's an interesting quiz in this morning's newspaper. Want to try it?
B: Sure. Go ahead.
A: "What's the world's smallest country?"
B: There are a lot of small countries. There's Andorra, there's Monaco, there's San Marino, there are ˜ome Caribbean islands. . . . I think it's San Marino.
A: Really? I don't think so. Do you want to hear the answers now? Or do you want to wait?
B: Let's hear them now.
A: OK. . . . Monaco is less than one square mile: .73. It is small! San Marino is next. Twenty-four square miles.
B: Don't look at the next answer.
A: OK. Next question. "What's the fastest animal in the world?"
B: I think it's the cheetah.
A: I think so too. . . . We're right. The cheetah is the fastest. It can run 65 miles per hour. Hmm. Antelope are almost as fast. They can run 60 miles an hour. OK. Next question. "What's the world's tallest building?"
B: It was the Empire State Building, but I don't think it is now. The World Trade Center?
A: I think the Sears Tower in Chicago is taller. . . . I'm right. The Sears Tower is 1,454 feet tall. The World Trade Center is 1,350 feet. Next question. "What's the biggest city, in population?"
B: Mexico City is going to be the biggest, they say, but I don't think it is yet. I think it's Tokyo.
A: I think it's Shanghai. . . . No, you're right. Tokyo. 11,695,000 people. Shanghai has 11,320,000. "What's the heaviest animal?"
B: That's easy. Elephants are the heaviest.
A: I agree with you. . . . "Elephants can weigh 8 tons." That's 16,000 pounds! "A hippopotamus can weigh 10,000 pounds." Not even close.
B: Interesting. Are there any more questions?
A: That's it. There'll be another quiz tomorrow, though.
B: Good. That was fun.
A: I think so, too.

127

Exercise 2 *If you are reading the tapescript, pause 5 seconds after each item.*

Which picture is correct, according to the conversation? Circle *a* or *b*.

1. A: What's the matter?
   B: I can't wear this sweater. It's too big— or I'm too small.

2. B: Is that bed going to be long enough for you?
   A: No, it isn't. I'm too tall.
   B: Maybe we can get another room.
   A: No, it's OK. I always have this problem in hotel rooms. The beds are never long enough for me.

3. A: Are you old enough to drive?

4. A: What do you think of that painting?
   B: Not much. Too big, too expensive, too modern and very ugly.
   A: I agree with you. We're just too old-fashioned, aren't we?

Exercise 3 *If you are reading the tapescript, pause 10 seconds after each item.*

Give true answers.

1. I like modern houses. Do you agree with me?
2. Do you like bigger cars or smaller cars?
3. What's more important, an interesting job or a good salary?
4. Which is more enjoyable for you, a vacation at the ocean or a vacation in the mountains?

UNIT 12   Page 95

Exercise 1 *If you are reading the tapescript, pause 5 seconds after each item.*

Listen to the questions. There are two correct answers for each question. Choose the one that gives your true opinion.

You will hear. "1. Do you like Walt Disney movies?" The correct answer can be *a* or *b*.

1. Do you like Walt Disney movies?
2. Do you like to eat out at foreign restaurants?
3. Would you rather watch TV or go out in the evening?
4. Would you rather go to a movie than a basketball game?
5. Will your life probably change a lot in five years?
6. Would you like to go to Antarctica for your next vacation?
7. Will we have another world war someday?
8. Do you think people will live on the moon someday?

Exercise 2 *If you are reading the tapescript, pause 5 seconds after each item.*

This is part of a questionnaire that someone filled out. Listen to the radio ads. Would she like to attend the events they advertise? Check *Probably* or *Probably Not*.

1. ANNOUNCER 1: This Friday evening at 8 o'clock, there will be a great musical event at the Jorgenson Auditorium. The Geneva Symphony Orchestra will be making its first American appearance, in a program of Vivaldi, Beethoven and Rachmaninoff. Tickets are still available. Call 525-8054.

2. ANNOUNCER 2: The Waaaay Outs! They're new! They're hot! Don't miss 'em! At the Village Gate! Saturday! 9 to 12! BE there!

3. MALE VOICE: Did you know there's a new Brazilian restaurant in town?
   FEMALE VOICE: No, really?
   MALE VOICE: It isn't open yet. It's opening this weekend. Would you like to go?
   FEMALE VOICE: Sure. I'd like to try it.
   ANNOUNCER 3: If you're looking for a taste of Brazil, you'll like Cafe Brazil, at 53rd and 3rd. Opening for dinner this Saturday, at 5 PM. You'll be most welcome.

4. ANNOUNCER 4: It's going to be the game of the season! Both teams are headed for the World Series! See the Connecticut Yankees and the Delaware Blues— Friday, 7:30, Blues Stadium! Get your tickets now!

5. NEWSCASTER: "One Giant Step for Mankind. . . . " Neil Armstrong will be at the Little Theater this Friday evening at 8:30 to talk about his journey to the moon. Tickets are $7.50 and $10.00. Part of the proceeds will go to the National Aeronautics and Space Administration. Hear Neil Armstrong this Friday at 8:30, at the Little Theater.

Exercise 3 *If you are reading the tapescript, pause 5 seconds after each item.*

You will hear people talk about their likes and dislikes. Choose the appropriate response for each.

1. My favorite color is red.
2. I like James Bond movies.
3. My favorite sport is basketball.
4. I like to listen to music.
5. I'd rather go to movies than play sports.
6. I don't especially like jazz.
7. For my next vacation, I'd like to go to an exciting place.

Exercise 4 *If you are reading the tapescript, pause 10 seconds after each item.*

Give true answers.

1. Do you like classical music?
2. What's your favorite movie?
3. Would you rather listen to music or watch TV?
4. Do you like to play sports?
5. Would you like to go to Antarctica someday?
6. Will your life be different in five years?

UNIT 13   Page 103

Exercise 1 *If you are reading the tapescript, pause 8 seconds after each item.*

Choose the appropriate response to each speaker you hear. Number the responses 1, 2, 3 or 4 in each part.

Part 1:
1. Would you like to come to dinner Thursday?
2. I'd like to, but I'm going to have an out-of-town guest. Thanks anyway.
3. Are you going to be around for New Year's Eve?
4. I probably will. I don't have any plans.

Part 2:
1. Could you bring me some aspirin, please?
2. Would anyone like anything else? More vegetables? More potatoes?
3. I'll open that for you.
4. Are you ready to order?

Exercise 2 *If you are reading the tapescript, pause 8 seconds after each item.*

Match the speakers and the situations. In each part, number the situations 1, 2, 3 or 4.

Part 1:
1. Could you help me with this, please?
2. I'll have the broiled lobster, please.
3. I'll pick those up for you.
4. Sure. I'd be glad to.

Part 2:
1. I'd like to, but I'm going to visit my parents. Thanks for the invitation.
2. Nothing for me, thank you.
3. Would you like to come to a New Year's Eve party at our house?
4. Would you like some dessert?

Exercise 3 *If you are reading the tapescript, pause 5 seconds after each item.*

Some of these conversations take place in someone's house. Others take place in a restaurant. Put a check in the correct column.

1. A: Come on in. Here, I'll take your coat.
   B: Thanks.

2. A: What're you going to have?
   B: I'm going to have the lamb chops.

3. A: Make yourself comfortable. Dinner won't be ready for a while.

4. A: Are you ready to order?
   B: Yes, I'll have the baked chicken.

5. A: I'll have the baked potato and the string beans, please.
   B: Thank you. You can help yourself to the salad bar anytime.

6. A1: Thanks a lot. It was a wonderful dinner. Good night.
   B and A2: Good night! Come again!

7. A: Could you bring me some more coffee?
   B: Certainly. Would you like anything else?
   A: Yes, I'd like to see your dessert menu, please.

Exercise 4 *If you are reading the tapescript, pause 12 seconds after each item.*

Write appropriate responses.

1. How would you like your steak?
2. What kind of potatoes would you like? We have french fried, mashed and baked.
3. Would you like to come to dinner at our house this Saturday?
4. Hi. I'm Cathy and Don's niece, Liz.
5. I'll help you with those.
6. Good night!

UNIT 14   Page 111

Exercise 1 *If you are reading the tapescript, pause 8 seconds after each item.*

Part 1: You will hear 6 people speak. Match each one with the correct picture. Write the number of the speaker in the box.

1. Excuse me, could I borrow your newspaper?
2. I'd like you to meet Ms. Ryan.
3. Hello?
4. Can I help you?
5. I need some change. Do you have any?
6. So long, it was really good seeing you.

Part 2: Listen again to the tape. From the list, choose the best response for each item you hear. Write its letter in the blank.

Exercise 2 *If you are reading the tapescript, pause 5 seconds after each item.*

Are these conversations between friends or strangers? Check the correct column.

1. A: Dr. Hellman, I'd like you to meet Roy Cousins, our sales manager. Dr. Hellman is from our San Francisco office, Roy.
   B: How do you do, Mr. Cousins?

2. A: Hi, Betty. How's it going?
   B: OK, Bill. How are things with you?
   A: Great!

3. A: Good morning, Dr. Crino's office.
   B: Hello, this is Tom Putney. I'd like to make an appointment for a checkup.

4. A: Good evening, Barnaby's Restaurant. May I help you?
   B: Yes, I'd like to make a reservation for two for dinner on Friday.

5. A: Carol! How are you?
   B: Fran, it's good to see you! You look great! How's your family?

6. A: Can I help you?
   B: No, thank you. We're just looking.

7. A: Pat! Do you have any change?
   B: How much do you need?
   A: Not much. Just some nickels and dimes.

8. A: Hello.
   B: Hello, this is Bonnie Hawkins. May I please speak to Mrs. Hahn?
   A: She's not here right now. Can I take a message?
   B: Could you tell her I called, please?

9. A: Excuse me, could you tell me where the Holly Inn is?
   B: Certainly. It's at Fifth and Main. Go straight ahead two blocks. Turn left. It's on the next corner, on your right.
   A: Thank you very much.

10. A: Are you ready to order, sir?
    B: Yes, I'll have the lamb chops, please.

Exercise 3 *If you are reading the tapescript, pause 10 seconds after each item.*

Here are some questions from earlier units. Give true answers.

1. What's your name?
2. Where do you live?
3. Do you have brown eyes?
4. Do you like classical music?
5. Are you wearing black shoes?
6. Where are you sitting right now?
7. Where were you born?
8. What did you do last night?
9. What are you going to do tomorrow?
10. Are you going to take another English course?

STUDENT BOOK ANSWER KEY

UNIT 1

Exercise 1
1. Where are Laura and Andrew Scott from?
   h. They're from the United States.
2. Is Kenichi Nakano in Paris on vacation?
   e. No, he isn't.
3. Are Andrew and Laura Americans?
   b. Yes, they are.
4. Where are Laura, Andrew and Kenichi?
   g. They're in Paris.
5. Is Laura an actress?
   a. No, she isn't.
6. Where's Kenichi from?
   c. He's Japanese.
7. Are Andrew and Laura from France?
   f. No, they aren't.
8. Is Kenichi a fashion designer?
   d. Yes, he is.

Exercise 2
see Exercise 1 in the Student Book (SB)

Exercise 3
1. A: Do you speak English?
   B: Yes, I do, a little.
2. A: Could we borrow your map?
   B: Sure. Here it is.
3. A: Where are you from?
   B: I'm Japanese, from Osaka.
4. A: Are you in Paris on vacation?
   B: No, I'm studying French.
5. A: What do you do?
   B: I'm a fashion designer.

Exercise 4
A: Excuse me, could I borrow your pen/pencil?
B: Sure. Here it is.
A: Thank you.
B: You're welcome.
A: Excuse me, could I borrow your dictionary/English book?
B: I need it right now. I'm sorry.
A: That's OK.

Exercise 5 (Pronunciation)

Capital cities	Countries
Brasilia	Brazil
Cairo	Egypt
Moscow	The Soviet Union
Ottawa	Canada
Paris	France
Rome	Italy
Tokyo	Japan
Washington, D.C.	The United States

Exercise 6
see example in SB

Exercise 7
see Exercise 6 in SB

Exercise 8
see Exercise 6 in SB

Exercise 9
Possible Conversation:
A: Where are you from?
B: I'm American. What about you?
A: I'm Japanese.
OR I'm American, too!
B: What do you do?
A: I'm a fashion designer. What about you?
B: I'm a writer. By the way, I'm Harold Robbins.
OR I'm a fashion designer, too! By the way, I'm Calvin Klein.
A: My name's Hanae Mori. How do you do?

Exercise 10 (Culture Capsule)
open conversation

Exercise 11
see Exercise 9 in SB

Exercise 12
Possible Answer:
I'm Jeanne Rabenda. I'm a writer. I'm from the United States. This is Gail Cooper. She's a photographer. She's from the United States, too.

Exercise 13 (Put It Together)
open conversation

UNIT 2

Exercise 1
1. a mirror
2. some curtains
3. some pictures
4. an end table
5. a telephone
6. a table lamp
7. a floor lamp
8. a bed
9. a coffee table
10. some books
11. an easy chair
12. a dresser

Exercise 2
Possible Answers:
One/A . . .
lamp/telephone on the end table
mirror between the windows
end table to the right of the sofa
floor lamp to the left of the sofa
brown sofa in front of the windows
coffee table in front of the sofa
easy chair across from the sofa

Some/Any . . .
curtains on the window
books on the coffee table
pictures between the windows

Exercise 3
First Part
1 first (1st)
2 second (2nd)
3 third (3rd)
4 fourth (4th)
5 fifth (5th)
6 sixth (6th)
7 seventh (7th)
8 eighth (8th)
9 ninth (9th)
10 tenth (10th)
11 eleventh (11th)
12 twelfth (12th)
13 thirteenth (13th)
14 fourteenth (14th)
15 fifteenth (15th)

Second Part
The first/eighth letter is an R.
The second/fourth/seventh/ninth letter is an E.
The third/fifth letter is an M.
The sixth letter is a B.
The tenth letter is a D.

Exercise 4
see example in SB

Exercise 5 (Pronunciation)
Two hundred Woodland Street
Four oh nine Fuller Avenue
Seven ninety nine Eleventh Street
Seventeen twelve Park Avenue
Five fifty five Highland Avenue
Nineteen eighty seven East Road
Two oh six Green Street

Exercise 6
see example in SB

Exercise 7 (Pronunciation)
Possible Answers:

/s/	/z/	/əz/
apartments	beds	addresses
streets	numbers	actresses

Exercise 8 (Information Gap)
see SB

Exercise 9 (Culture Capsule)
open conversation

Exercise 10 (Put It Together)
see example in SB

UNIT 3

Exercise 1
1. does   Switzerland.
2. do   MHI.
3. is   Miami, Florida.
4. does   Medical supplies.
5. are   Twelve and seventeen.
6. does   A small town near the city.

Exercise 2
1. Does   Yes, he does.
2. Does   No, he doesn't.
3. Does   Yes, she does.
4. Do   No, they don't.
5. Do   Yes, they do.
6. Does   Yes, he does.

Exercise 3

First Part
Possible Questions and Answers:
A: Where do Carole and Jim Richards come from?
B: Sydney, Australia.
A: Do they have any children?
B: No, they don't.
B: Where does Felicidad Diaz teach?
A: At ABC Hospital.
B: Does she live with her parents?
A: Yes, she does.

Second Part
see example in SB

Exercise 4
see opening conversation in SB

Exercise 5 (Information Gap)
see SB

Exercise 6 (Pronunciation)
see SB

Exercise 7 (Information Gap)
Possible Conversation:
A: Do Dr. and Mrs. Martin Adams live on Guilford Street or Guilford Avenue?
B: They live on Guilford Street.

A: Does Mr. David Albright live at 9 Belmont Avenue or 12 Belmont Avenue?
B: He lives at 9 Belmont Avenue.

Exercise 8

First Part
Possible Conversation:
A: Where do you live?
B: At 54 East Wacker Drive./On East Wacker Drive./In Chicago./In Illinois.
A: Where do you work?
B: I work at SES Industries.
A: What exactly do you do?
B: I'm in charge of the art department.

Second Part
see SB

Exercise 9

First and Second Parts
open conversations

Exercise 10

First Part
wife's—her
husband's—his
my wife's and my—our
son's—his
sons'—their
daughter's—her
daughters'—their

Second Part
see example in SB

Third and Fourth Parts
open conversations

Exercise 11 (Put It Together)
open conversation

UNIT 4

Exercise 1
1. How much sleep do you usually get? When do you usually get up?
   a. I always get eight hours of sleep. I usually get up at 7:00.
   b. It depends. Sometimes I'm up at noon. Sometimes I sleep until 3:00 or 3:30.
2. Do you usually eat a good breakfast? What do you usually have?
   a. I have juice, eggs, toast, cereal and coffee every day.
   b. I never eat breakfast.

3. What do you do in the evening? Do you ever go out?
   a. I go out five or six times a week.
   b. Sometimes I read or watch TV. I never go out during the week. I go out on weekends about twice a month.
4. Do you take a vacation every year?
   a. Yes, I go camping in Alaska for two weeks every year.
   b. A vacation from what? I never work. I'm always on vacation.

Exercise 2
A: What's your phone number?
B: Seven two four//three oh//four five area code six two three//eight five six//nine five//six eight
A: What's your number at work?
B: area code four two five//nine two six//seven six//five two//eight nine six//two two//one one//extension one two//seven one

Exercise 3

First Part
7:30   seven-thirty
8:00   eight/eight o'clock
9:00   nine/nine o'cloc'
9:45   nine forty-five
12:00 (twelve) noon
3:00   three/three o'clock
4:30   four-thirty
5:15   five-fifteen
6:05   six oh five
10:20 ten-twenty
12:00 (twelve) midnight

Second Part
(Information Gap)
see SB

Exercise 4 (Information Gap)
see SB

Exercise 5 (Pronunciation)
see SB

Exercise 6

First Part
see SB

Second and Third Parts
see examples in SB

Exercise 7 (Culture Capsule)
open conversation

Exercise 8
see example in SB

Exercise 9

Possible Conversation:
A: When does Lannie usually get up?
B: At 11:00.
A: What does she usually do on weekends?
B: She visits friends and she goes shopping. Sometimes she goes dancing.
A: Does she ever take a vacation?
B: Yes, she usually takes a vacation twice a year.

Exercise 10 (Put It Together)

open conversation

UNIT 5

Exercise 1

First Part

1. Who were James Dean's parents?
   Mildred and Winton Dean.
2. Where was he born?
   In Marion, Indiana.
3. Were times good in 1931?
   No, they weren't.
4. Did his parents have much money?
   No, they didn't.
5. When did they move to California?
   In 1935.
6. Did James Dean grow up in Fairmount, Indiana?
   Yes, he did.

Second Part

Possible Questions and Answers:
A: Did Jimmy like school very much?
B: No, he didn't.
A: Was he good-looking?
B: No, he wasn't.
A: Where did he go to high school?
B: Fairmount High.

Exercise 2

Possible Conversation:
A: Where were you born?
B: In Merrick, New York.
A: Did you grow up there?
B: Yes, I did.
OR No, I didn't. I grew up in Tempe, Arizona.
A: Where did you go to high school?
B: John F. Kennedy High School in Tempe.
OR I'm still in high school.
A: Did you like school?
OR Do you like school?
B: Yes, I did./No, I didn't.
OR Yes, I do./No, I don't.
A: Did you like sports?
OR Do you like sports?
B: Yes, I did./No, I didn't.
OR Yes, I do./No, I don't.

A: Were you good at them?
OR Are you good at them?
B: Yes, I was./No, I wasn't.
OR Yes, I am./No, I'm not.

Exercise 3 (Information Gap)

see SB

Exercise 4

1. No, she isn't.
2. No, he doesn't.
3. Yes, he does.
4. No, she doesn't.
5. No, he doesn't.
6. Yes, he is.

Exercise 5

First Part

I—me
you—you
she—her
he—him
we—us
they—them

Second Part

Nancy: short, blond hair
Ginny: tall, black hair, thin, glasses
Larry: tall, blond hair, glasses
Ken: average height, red hair

Exercise 6 (Pronunciation)

Possible Answers:

/t/	/d/	/əd/
crossed	died	landed
reached	opened	invented

Exercise 7

A: What happened on April sixth, nineteen oh-nine?
B: Peary reached the North Pole.

A: . . . in eighteen seventy-six?
B: Bell invented the telephone.

A: . . . on May twenty-first, nineteen twenty-seven?
B: Lindbergh crossed the Atlantic alone.

A: . . . on November twenty-second, nineteen sixty-three?
B: John F. Kennedy died.

A: . . . July twentieth, nineteen sixty-nine?
B: Men landed on the moon.

A: . . . September, nineteen eighty-eight?
B: The Olympics opened in Seoul.

Exercise 8

see example in SB

Exercise 9 (Put It Together)

open conversation

UNIT 6

Exercise 1

1. What's Danny doing?
   Putting cans on the shelf.
2. What's the customer doing?
   Shopping.
3. What's Michael doing?
   Taking a walk.
4. What's Paula doing?
   Writing a report.
5. What's Harry's wife doing?
   Waiting for Harry.

Exercise 2

1. What's Tom wearing?
   A brown jacket, a white shirt, white sneakers and tan pants.
2. What's Harry's wife wearing?
   A purple dress and black high-heeled shoes.
3. What's Paula wearing?
   A blue suit and a red and white blouse.
4. What's Michael wearing?
   A red shirt, blue jeans, brown boots, a yellow jacket and a gray hat.
5. What's Danny wearing?
   A blue shirt, gray pants, gray sneakers and a green apron.
6. What's the customer wearing?
   A brown skirt, a white blouse, an orange sweater and brown shoes.
7. What's Harry wearing?
   A white jacket, a green shirt, a blue and white tie, black shoes and gray pants.

Exercise 3

B: What's Annie wearing?
A: A sun hat, a jacket, a bathing suit, gloves and boots.

A: What's James wearing?
B: A wool hat, sunglasses, a T-shirt, pants and sandals.

Exercise 4

First Part

Alaska: A jacket, gloves, boots, a wool hat and pants.
Hawaii: A sun hat, a bathing suit, sunglasses, a T-shirt and sandals.

Second Part

I need to take a jacket, gloves, boots, a wool hat and pants to Alaska.
I need to take a sun hat, a bathing suit, sunglasses, a T-shirt and sandals to Hawaii.

Exercise 5 (Culture Capsule)

open conversation

Exercise 6
see example in SB

Exercise 7
Possible Conversation:
A: What courses are you taking?
B: I'm taking European History, Biology and Intro to Anthropology.
A: How do you like your history course?
B: A lot./It's OK./Not very much.
A: Who's teaching it?
B: Professor Stern.
A: How do you like your biology course?
B: It's OK.

Exercise 8
see example in SB

Exercise 9
A: Is . . . still studying Spanish?
B: . . . 's studying Japanese.
   . . . wants to travel to Japan.
A: Is . . . still living in New York?
B: . . . 's living in Mexico.
   . . . wants to learn Spanish.
A: Is . . . still working as a waiter?/ working at the grocery store?
B: . . . 's studying accounting.
   . . . wants to be an accountant./
   . . . 's looking for another job.
   . . . wants to make more money.

Exercise 10 (Pronunciation)
see example in SB

Exercise 11 (Put It Together)
open conversation

UNIT 7

Exercise 1
Possible Questions and Answers:
A: How many pennies are there in a dollar?
B: A hundred. How many nickels are there in a quarter?
A: Five. How many dimes are there in a dollar?
B: Ten. How many quarters are there in a dollar?
A: Four

Exercise 2
see example in SB

Exercise 3 (Information Gap)
Possible Conversations:
1. A: The rye bread/apple pie looks good. Should we get some?
   OR The lemon cookies/whole wheat rolls look good. Should we get some?
   B: It depends. How much is it?
   OR It depends. How much are they?
   A: Two dollars a loaf./Ninety-five cents a piece.
   OR Forty-five cents each./Three dollars a dozen.
   B: That's not bad. Let's get some
   OR That's kind of expensive. I don't think we need any.

2. A: Do we have any jam/honey?
   OR Do we have any cherries/ bananas?
   B: Not much.
   OR Not many.
   A: Let's get some.
   OR Why don't we get some?
   B: How much is it?
   OR How much are they?
   A: Three dollars a jar./Two dollars a jar.
   B: That's a good price. How much should we get?
   OR
   A: Two dollars a pound./Forty-five cents a pound.
   B: That's a good price. How many should we get?
   A: Two jars/pounds.

Exercise 4 (Pronunciation)
First and Second Parts
see SB

Exercise 5
$1.75 a dollar and seventy-five cents/ a dollar seventy-five
$1.99 a dollar and ninety-nine cents/ a dollar ninety-nine
$7.05 seven dollars and five cents/ seven oh five
$3.09 three dollars and nine cents/ three oh nine
$2.19 two dollars and nineteen cents/two nineteen
$19.39 nineteen dollars and thirty-nine cents/nineteen thirty-nine

Exercise 6
How much is the . . . ?
cheese
butter
jam
honey

How much are the . . . ?
peaches
apples
bananas
string beans
carrots
tomatoes
eggs

Exercise 7
First and Second Parts
see SB

Exercise 8
First and Second Parts
see examples in SB

Exercise 9 (Culture Capsule)
open conversation

Exercise 10 (Put It Together)
see SB

UNIT 8

Exercise 1
1. A: At 6:30, is 001 going to pick up a package at the airport or drop it off?
   B: He's going to drop it off.
2. A: At 7:05, is 001 going to get on Y's plane or get off it?
   B: He's going to get on it.
3. A: In Amsterdam, is 001 going to get on Y's plane or get off it?
   B: He's going to get off it.
4. A: At 8:30, is 002 going to pick up Agent 001 or drop him off at the airport?
   B: He's going to pick him up.
5. A: Is 003 going to check into Y's hotel or check out of it?
   B: She's going to check into it.
6. A: At Y's hotel, is 003 going to put on her disguise or take it off?
   B: She's going to put it on.
7. A: At 10:00, is 003 going to turn on the power or turn it off?
   B: She's going to turn it off.

Exercise 2
see opening conversation

Exercise 3

A: In picture one, what did the husband say?
B: "Pick me up at 6:30."
A: What did the wife do?
B: She picked him up.
A: In picture two, what did the mother say?
B: "Clean up your room."
A: What did the daughter do?
B: She cleaned it up.
A: In picture three, what did the father say?
B: "Turn off the stereo."
A: What did the son do?
B: He turned it off.
A: In picture four, what did the mother say?
B: "Take off your boots."
A: What did the children do?
B: They took them off.
A: In picture five, what did the teacher say?
B: "Look up these words in the dictionary."
A: What did the students do?
B: They looked them up.
A: In picture six, what did the teacher say?
B: "Get on the bus."
A: What did the students do?
B: They got on it.

Exercise 4

First Part
see SB

Second Part
A: Who's making a shopping list?
B: 001.
A: What's he going to do?
B: He's going to go food shopping.
A: Who's turning on the TV?
B: 002.
A: What's he going to do?
B: He's going to watch TV.
A: Who's holding a bucket?
B: 003.
A: What's she going to do?
B: She's going to wash the floor.
A: Who's holding a vacuum cleaner?
B: Agent X.
A: What's he going to do?
B: He's going to vacuum the bedroom.
A: Who's putting clothes in a laundry bag?
B: Agent Y.
A: What's she going to do?
B: She's going to do the laundry.

Third Part
see example in SB

Exercise 5 (Pronunciation)

A: Who's going to watch TV?
B: 002. Who's going to go grocery shopping?
A: 001. Who's going to make dinner?
B: Control. Who's going to do the laundry?
A: Agent Y. Who's going to vacuum the living room?
B: Agent X. Who's going to wash the car?
A: 003.

Exercise 6

First and Second Parts
see SB

Exercise 7 (Information Gap)
see examples in SB

Exercise 8 (Culture Capsule)
open conversation

Exercise 9 (Put It Together)
open conversation

UNIT 9

Exercise 1
Possible Conversation:
A: How often do the trains run? Do you know?
B: Yes, before midnight every forty-five minutes, and after midnight every two hours.
A: How long does it take?
B: Thirty-five minutes.

Exercise 2

First Part
Possible Conversation:
B: When's the next train?
A: There's one in fifteen minutes, at 3:00.
B: Do I have to change for Cambridgeport?
A: No.
B: How much does it cost?
A: One-way is $7.00. Round-trip is $13.00.

Second Part
B: There's one in an hour and a half, at 6:00.
A: Do I have to change for Milton?
B: No.

Third Part
A: There's one in forty minutes.
B: Do I have to change for Naperville?
A: Yes. Change at the downtown station.

Exercise 3 (Pronunciation)

First Part
see SB

Second and Third Parts
A: How can I get to Fifth Avenue from here?
B: You can take a bus, a taxi or a subway.
A: When do trains run to Summit in the morning?
B: There's one at 5:28, one at 8:11 and one at 10:13.
B: Are there any good hotels near here?
A: There's the Grand, the Woodvale and the Linden.
B: Do I have to change trains at the downtown station?
A: Change for Westfield, Livingston and Morristown.

Exercise 4 (Information Gap)
Possible Conversations:
1. A: Excuse me, how often do the trains run to Greenville from here?
   B: You have to take the bus. There aren't any trains.
   A: When do the buses run?
   B: At 3:31 AM, 6:16 AM and 2:27 PM.
   A: How long does it take?
   B: About four hours.
   A: How much does it cost?
   B: One-way is $12.25. Round-trip is $24.50.
   A: Do I have to change on the 3:31?
   B: Yes. (Change at Unionville.)

2. B: Excuse me, how often do the buses run to Libertyville from here?
   A: You have to take the train. There aren't any buses.
   A: When do the trains run?
   B: At 9:06 AM, 11:17 AM and 7:48 PM.
   A: How long does it take?
   B: About three hours.
   A: How much does it cost?
   B: One-way is $8.50. Round-trip is $15.50.
   A: Do I have to change on the 11:17?
   B: Yes. (Change at Balesville.)

Exercise 5
open conversation

Exercise 6

First Part
see SB

Second Part
Possible Conversations:
A: Excuse me, how can I get to Government Center?
B: Take the Orange Line to State. Then change to the Blue Line and go toward Bowdoin. Get off at Government Center.
A: . . . Copley Square?
B: Take the Orange Line to State. Then change to the Blue Line and go toward Bowdoin. Get off at Government Center. Then change to the Green Line and go toward Cleveland Circle. Get off at Copley.
A: Thank you very much.

B: Excuse me, how can I get to Harvard University?
A: Take the Orange Line to Downtown Crossing. Then change to the Red Line and go toward Alewife. Get off at Harvard.
B: . . . Symphony Hall?
A: Take the Orange Line to Downtown Crossing. Then change to the Red Line and go toward Alewife. Get off at Park Street. Then change to the Green Line and go toward Boston College/Cleveland Circle/Riverside Reservoir/Arborway. Get off at Symphony.
B: Thank you very much.

Exercise 7 (Information Gap)
see SB

Exercise 8 (Culture Capsule)
open conversation

Exercise 9 (Put It Together)
open conversation

UNIT 10

Exercise 1
1. Don't park here.
2. Don't turn here.
3. Don't pass here.
4. Don't turn right here.

Exercise 2
Possible Answer:
Turn left on(to) High street. Go five blocks. Turn left (at the light) on Sixth Street. Go two blocks. It's on your left.

Exercise 3
Possible Conversation:
A: Go straight ahead to the next light. Turn right on Main Street. Go two blocks to Third Street. Turn left. Go one and a half blocks. It's in the middle of the block on your right.
B: It's the hardware store.

Exercise 4 (Information Gap)
see SB

Exercise 5 (Pronunciation)

First Part

còffee shop	fùrniture store
pòst office	clòthing store
tràvel agency	bòokstore
shòe store	hàrdware store
drùgstore	

Second Part
A: Where can you buy shoes?
B: At a shoe store.

A: Where can you buy stamps?
B: At a post office.

A: Where can you buy paint?
B: At a hardware store.

A: Where can you buy chairs?
B: At a furniture store.

A: Where can you buy books?
B: At a bookstore.

A: Where can you buy plane tickets?
B: At a travel agency.

A: Where can you buy toothpaste and shampoo?
B: At a drugstore.

Exercise 6 (Information Gap)
1. chairs—Emerson's Furniture. It's on Michigan Avenue next to Valley Travel Agency. (1)
2. shoes—Miller's Shoe Store. It's on the corner of Drew Road and Michigan Avenue across from Valley Travel Agency. (5)
3. stamps—the post office. It's on Drew Road between the movie theater and Valley Travel Agency. (2)
4. vegetables—P&A Grocery. It's on Michigan Avenue next to Miller's Shoe Store. (6)
5. traveler's checks—Third National Bank. It's on Drew Road across from the post office. (4)
1. paint and paintbrushes—Robert's Hardware. It's on Barnard Street next to Valley Travel Agency. (5)
2. toothpaste and shampoo—Lucas Drugstore. It's on the corner of Yale Street and Barnard Street. (4)

3. bread and rolls—Betty's Bakery. It's on the corner of Montclair Avenue and Barnard Street. (2)
4. flowers—Ellen's Flowers. It's on Barnard Street across from Valley Travel Agency. (3)
5. clothes—Michael's Men's Clothing. It's on Montclair Avenue next to Betty's Bakery. (1)
OR Diane's Clothing for Women. It's on the corner of Barnard Street and Montclair Avenue next to City Hall. (6)

Exercise 7 (Pronunciation)
see SB

Exercise 8 (Information Gap)

First and Second Parts
see SB

Exercise 9 (Put It Together)
open conversation

UNIT 11

Exercise 1

First Part
Possible Questions and Answers:
A: Which is heavier, the two-door or the four-door?
B: The four-door. Which one is more expensive?
A: The four-door. Which one is cheaper, the two-door or the sports car?
B: The two-door. Which one is lighter?
A: The two-door. Which one is faster, the four-door or the sports car?
B: The sports car. Which one is bigger?
A: The four-door. Which one is slower?
B: The four-door. Which one is smaller?
A: The sports car.

Second Part
Possible Questions and Answers:
A: Which one is the fastest?
B: The sports car. Which one is the heaviest?
A: The four-door. Which one is the most expensive?
B: The sports car. Which one is the cheapest?
A: The two-door. Which one is the lightest?
B: The two-door. Which one is the biggest?
A: The four-door. Which one is the slowest?

B: The four-door. Which one is the smallest?

A: The sports car.

Exercise 2

Possible Conversation:

A: I think small cars are better. They're more economical than big cars.

B: I agree. Big cars are too expensive.

OR I don't agree. Small cars aren't powerful enough./Big cars are more comfortable than small cars.

A: I think big cars are better. They're more comfortable than small cars.

B: I agree. Small cars are too uncomfortable.

OR I don't agree. Big cars aren't economical enough./Small cars are cheaper than big cars.

Exercise 3 (Information Gap)

see SB

Exercise 4

First Part

1. A: What's the matter?
   B: This pizza is too hot. I can't eat it.
2. A: What's wrong?
   B: This sofa is too heavy. I can't move it.
3. A: What's the matter?
   B: These gloves are too expensive. I can't afford them.

Second Part

1. A: What's wrong?
   B: I can't see that movie. I'm not old enough.
2. A: What's the matter?
   B: I can't reach those cookies. I'm not tall enough.
3. A: What's wrong?
   B: I can't figure out that problem. I'm not smart enough.

Exercise 5

First Part

see SB

Second Part

Possible Questions:

Which is healthier, ice cream or fruit?

Which is smaller, New York City or Tokyo?

Which is more interesting, a good book or a good movie?

Exercise 6

1. What's the fastest car?
2. What's the most popular song in your country right now?
3. Who's the most famous man/woman from your country?
4. Who's the most powerful person in the world?

Exercise 7 (Culture Capsule)

open conversation

Exercise 8 (Put It Together)

First Part

Possible Conversations:

A: Which house do you like best?

B: The modern/expensive one.

OR The one in the middle.

C: What do you like about it?

B: It's modern./I like modern houses.

A: Why do you like it better than the others?

B: It's more interesting and more attractive.

OR The other ones are boring. Which house do *you* like best?

C: The smallest one.

B: What do you like about it?

C: It's old-fashioned.

A: Why do you like it better than the others?

C: I think it's more attractive.

OR It's good for us because it's the smallest and cheapest.

Second Part

open conversations

UNIT 12

Exercise 1

see opening conversation in SB

Exercise 2

First and Second Parts

see examples in SB

Third Part

my—mine
your—yours
his—his
her—hers
our—ours
their—theirs

Exercise 3

First and Second Parts

see examples in SB

Exercise 4 (Pronunciation)

see SB

Exercise 5

First and Second Parts

see SB

Exercise 6

B3 is yours.
C2 is his.
C1 is hers.
B2 and B3 are ours.
D1 and D2 are theirs.

Exercise 7 (Pronunciation)

deprèssed   ràther
different   hèllo
ticket   màybe
fòreign   èvening
sòmeday

Exercise 8

First Part

1. Will you visit Antarctica someday?
2. Will there be peace in the world someday?
3. Will we have another world war someday?
4. Will people live to be 150 someday?
5. Will you be famous someday?
6. Will I be very rich someday?

Second Part

1. Do you think you'll drive across the U.S. someday?
2. Do you think people will live on the moon someday?
3. Do you think you'll go to the moon someday?
4. Do you think our English will be perfect someday?
5. Do you think I'll be a movie star someday?

Exercise 9 (Culture Capsule)

open conversation

Exercise 10 (Put It Together)

First Part

Possible Questionnaire Questions:

What's your favorite food?

Do you like to play sports?

Would you rather watch TV or a movie?

Would you like to take a vacation around the world someday?

Second Part

open conversation

UNIT 13

Exercise 1

1. A: Would you like to go to a movie with us tonight?
   B: I'd like to, but I can't. Thanks for the invitation.
   A: Sure. We'll try again sometime.
2. A: Would anyone like anything else?
   B: I'll have some more potatoes, please.
3. A: I'll help you with that.
   B: Thank you.
4. A: Are you going to be around this weekend?
   B: I probably will.
   A: Could you give me some help with my car on Saturday?
   B: OK. About 2:00?
   A: Fine. I'll see you then.

Exercise 2 (Pronunciation)

ánything	réstaurant
tomáto	cústomer
próbably	célebrate
impórtant	hóliday
potátoes	végetable
togéther	Novémber

Exercise 3
see example in SB

Exercise 4

First, Second and Third Parts
see examples in SB

Exercise 5 (Information Gap)
see SB

Exercise 6
see example in SB

Exercise 7
see SB

Exercise 8 (Culture Capsule)
open conversation

Exercise 9 (Put It Together)
open conversation

UNIT 14

Exercise 1 (Information Gap)
see SB

Exercise 2 (Pronunciation)
see opening conversation

Exercise 3
Possible Answers:
The ballet shoes must be Alexandra's. They can't be Yves' or Van's.
The women's shoes might be Alexandra's or Ryuko's.
The flippers must be Yves'.
The earring might be Van's, Yves', Alexandra's or Ryuko's.
The watch must be Yves'.
The 24-inch belt might be Alexandra's or Ryuko's. It can't be Yves' or Van's.
The 32-inch belt must be Yves'.
The 38-inch belt must be Van's.
The drum must be Van's.
The paintbrushes must be Ryuko's.
The tutu must be Alexandra's.

Exercise 4
see SB

Exercise 5
see SB

Exercise 6

First Part
see example in SB

Second Part
Possible Questions and Answers:
1. A: There are 50 states in the U.S., aren't there?
   B: Yes, there are.
2. A: Texas is the biggest state, isn't it?
   B: No, it isn't. Alaska is.
3. A: George Washington wasn't the first president of the U.S., was he?
   B: Yes, he was.
4. A: There isn't a presidential election every two years, is there?
   B: No, there isn't. There's one every four years.
5. A: Women can be president, can't they?
   B: Yes, they can.
6. A: There won't be a presidential election in 1996, will there?
   B: Yes, there will.
7. A: There are a lot of Japanese cherry trees in Washington, D.C., aren't there?
   B: Yes, there are.
8. A: Rhode Island isn't the smallest state, is it?
   B: Yes, it is.
9. A: California and Oregon are on the Pacific Coast, aren't they?
   B: Yes, they are.
10. A: John Kennedy wasn't the youngest president, was he?
    B: Yes, he was.
11. A: People can't be president for more than eight years, can they?
    B: No, they can't.
12. A: There will be a presidential election in 1994, won't there?
    B: No, there won't.

Exercise 7 (Culture Capsule)
open conversation

Exercise 8
open conversation

Exercise 9
see example in SB

Exercise 10 (Put It Together)
Possible Conversation:
A: What are you going to do after this course?
B: I'm not sure. How about you?
A: I'm going to travel.
B: Would you like to take another course in the future?
A: I don't think so. What about you?
B: I don't know.
A: Will you ever get married?

WORKBOOK ANSWER KEY

UNIT 1

Exercise A
1. is/she's
2. are/they're
3. is/it's
4. are/you're
5. are/we're
6. is/he's
7. am/I'm

Exercise B
1. she's not/she isn't
2. they're not/they aren't
3. it's not/it isn't
4. you're not/you aren't
5. we're not/we aren't
6. he's not/he isn't
7. I'm not

Exercise C
1. are
2. are
3. is
4. isn't
5. am
6. is not
7. are
8. is

Exercise D
1. i
2. g
3. e
4. d
5. b
6. a
7. f
8. h
9. c

Exercise E
1. She's an actress.
2. Is she from France?
3. Where's she from?
4. She's Italian, from Rome.
5. I'm from Italy, too.
6. Is she on vacation?
7. No, she isn't.

Exercise F

Conversation 1
A: Is she an actress?
B: No, she isn't. She's a singer.
A: Where's she from?
B: She's from France.

Conversation 2
A: Is he a writer?
B: No, he isn't.
A: Is he from the United States?
B: Yes, he is.

Conversation 3
A: Are they American?
B: No, they're not. They're Italian.
A: Are they teachers?
B: Yes, they are.

Conversation 4
Students answer according to their own experience.

Exercise G
1. Brigitte Rameau is French. She comes from France. She speaks French. She is a teacher.
2. Mark Thane is American. He comes from the United States. He speaks English. He is a writer.
3. Gina and Carlo Menotti are Italian. They come from Italy. They speak Italian. They are teachers.
4. Students answer according to their own experience.

Exercise H
1. Brazilian/Portuguese
2. Egypt/Egyptian
3. France/French
4. Japanese/Japanese
5. Russian/Russian
6. American/English

Exercise I
1. Excuse me,
2. Yes, I do.
3. Sure. Here it is.
4. Are you American?
5. we are.
6. Where are you from?
7. Are you
8. I am.
9. What do you do?
10. I'm a writer, too!
11. How do you do?

UNIT 2

Exercise A
1. a
2. an
3. an
4. an
5. a
6. a
7. an
8. a
9. an
10. a

Exercise B
1. Is
2. there
3. one
4. front
5. any
6. some
7. room
8. an
9. isn't
10. Is
11. there
12. next
13. to
14. Where
15. is
16. on

Exercise C
Possible Answers:
1. The books are in the bookcase.
2. The lamp is next to the bookcase.
3. The plant is on the coffee table.
4. The bookcase is across from the coffee table.
5. The easy chair is behind the lamp.
6. The window is in back of the coffee table.

Exercise D
/s/ checks, maps, notebooks, states, students
/z/ movies, names, pencils, questions, writers
/əz/ addresses, boxes, houses, paintbrushes, places

Exercise E
1. The first letter is a d.
2. The second letter is an i.
3. The third letter is a c.
4. The fourth letter is a t.
5. The fifth letter is an i.
6. The sixth letter is an o.
7. The seventh letter is an n.
8. The eighth letter is an a.
9. The ninth letter is an r.
10. The tenth letter is a y.
The word is dictionary.

Exercise F
1. a
2. a
3. the
4. an
5. a
6. the
7. a
8. the
9. the
10. the
11. an
12. the
13. any
14. any
15. some
16. some
17. the
18. the
19. some
20. the
21. the
22. the
23. the
24. some
25. any
26. the
27. some
28. some
29. the
30. the
31. the
32. some
33. some
34. the
35. a
36. the
37. the
38. an
39. the
40. a
41. the
42. the

Exercise G
1. Is there
2. there's
3. Is there
4. there's
5. Are there
6. there are
7. Are there
8. there are
9. Is there
10. There's
11. there isn't

Exercise H
1. Sixty-nine
2. three-oh-eight
3. five-eleven
4. one-hundred
5. twelve-seventy-six

Exercise I
Possible Answers:
1. What's your name, please?
2. How do you spell your last name?
3. And what's your address?

Exercise J

Students answer according to their own experience.

UNIT 3

Exercise A

1. do	9. s
2. do	10. does
3. are	11. s
4. Is	12. s
5. is	13. Does
6. Do	14. doesn't
7. don't	15. s
8. does	

Exercise B

1. Alice	7. Bob
2. Bob	8. Bob
3. Alice	9. Bob
4. Alice	10. Alice
5. Alice	11. Alice
6. Bob	12. Alice

Exercise C

1. does she/She lives in an apartment.
2. Is she/No, she isn't.
3. is she/She's 18.
4. Is she/Yes, she is.
5. does she have/She has one brother.
6. does he/He teaches chemistry.
7. Does he live/No, he lives in an apartment.
8. Is he/No, he's 44.
9. Is he/Yes, he is.
10. Does he have/Yes, he has two sisters.

Exercise D

1. Bill: Hi, Jan. How's it going?
   Jan: OK, thanks, Bill.
2. Jan: Grandfather, I'd like you to meet Bill Hall. Bill, this is my grandfather, James Guest.
   Mr. Guest: How do you do, Bill?
   Bill: Hello, Mr. Guest. It's nice to meet you.
3. Bill: Well, I'd better get back to work. Good-bye for now. See you later, Jan.

Exercise E

/s/ makes, speaks, takes, works, writes
/z/ agrees, comes, designs, drives, lives, sells
/əz/ changes, manages, practices, teaches

Exercise F

1. in	4. in
2. in	5. On
3. at	6. at

Exercise G

1. My brother's name is Bill.
2. Her sister's name is Cindy.
3. Our children's names are Carrie and Dean.
4. Their nephews' names are Danny and David.
5. His daughters' names are Janet, Sharon and Laurie.

Exercise H

Students answer according to their own experience.

UNIT 4

Exercise A

1. Hello,	12. every day
2. this	13. What's
3. 'd like to	14. at
4. for	15. in
5. Can	16. ever
6. in	17. never
7. at	18. How often
8. can.	19. usually
9. at	20. Can
10. from	21. in
11. to	22. can't

Exercise B

Possible Answers:
1. I have a checkup once a year.
2. I work from 9 to 5.
3. I'm usually home in the evening.
4. I always go to bed at 11:30.
5. I eat breakfast at 7:30 every day.
6. Sometimes I watch TV.
7. I go swimming twice a week.
8. I go jogging every night.

Exercise C

1. It's six-thirty AM.
2. It's seven-fifteen AM.
3. It's ten AM.
4. It's one-ten PM.
5. It's three-forty-five PM.
6. It's eight-fifty PM.

Exercise D

Possible Answers:
1. Is this Emerson's Furniture?
2. Could you tell me when you're open?
3. Are you open on Saturdays?
4. When do you open?
5. You open at 8?
6. Are you open on Sundays?

Exercise E

1. Luis can speak Spanish, and he can read English.
2. Luis can type, but he can't use a computer.
3. Luis can't play the guitar, and he can't read music.
4. Luis can't ride a bike, but he can drive a car.

Exercise F

Possible Answers:
When do you usually get up? What kind of classes are you taking? What do you usually do on weekends? Do you ever go out?

Exercise G

Students answer according to their own experience.

UNIT 5

Exercise A

Possible Answer:
She was born on June 1, 1926, in Los Angeles, California. Her parents called her Norma Jean. She lived near Los Angeles, but she didn't live with her family, and she wasn't a happy child. She went to high school, but she didn't graduate. She moved to Hollywood and changed her name to Marilyn Monroe. She married a baseball player, Joe DiMaggio, but their marriage ended. She didn't have any children. She made 21 movies and died on August 4, 1962.

Exercise B

1. was	8. Did
2. was	9. Did
3. did	10. did
4. Did	11. Did
5. Did	12. did
6. Was	13. did
7. Did	

Exercise C

1. me	6. him
2. you	7. me
3. them	8. you
4. us	9. her
5. it	10. her

Exercise D

1. A: Ruth Field? I remember her. She was short, and she wore glasses.
   B: That's right. Well, she lives in Florida now.
2. A: Ted Holmes? I remember him. He was tall and had blond hair.
   B: That's right. Well, he works in New York now.
3. A: Peter Yates? I remember him. He was good-looking, and he was good at sports.
   B: That's right. Well, he's a doctor now.
4. A: Alice Cartwright? I remember her. She wore glasses and had black hair.
   B: That's right. Well, she has red hair now.

Exercise E

/t/ asked, finished, liked, practiced, watched, worked
/d/ called, closed, happened, listened, moved, remembered
/əd/ completed, ended, graduated, lifted, needed, wanted

Exercise F

1. January first
2. February second
3. March thirty-first
4. June twenty-sixth
5. July third
6. August fourth
7. October eleventh
8. December twenty-fifth

Exercise G

1. in
2. in
3. on
4. on
5. in
6. in

Exercise H

Students answer according to their own experience.

Exercise I

Students answer according to their own experience.

UNIT 6

Exercise A

1. Pat: Beth! Is that you?
   Beth: Pat, you look great. How's it going?
   Pat: Not bad. It's good to see you. How's your family?
   Beth: They're fine.
2. Pat: I'd better go. My husband's probably waiting for me right now.
   Beth: OK. It was really good seeing you.
   Pat: Same here. Take it easy.

Exercise B

1. these days
2. still
3. anymore
4. last month
5. now
6. usually
7. this year
8. ever
9. once a month
10. every week
11. right now

Exercise C

1. Victor sleeps from 11 PM to 7 AM. Victoria sleeps from noon to 8 PM.
2. Victor rides the bus to work from 8 to 8:15 AM.
   Victoria rides the bus to work from 10:30 to 10:45 PM.
3. Victor works from 8:30 AM to 5 PM. Victoria works from 11 PM to 7 AM.
4. Victor eats dinner from 6 to 6:30 PM. Victoria eats dinner from 8 to 8:30 AM.
5. Victor watches TV from 7 to 11 PM. Victoria watches TV from 8:30 to 11:30 AM.

Exercise D

1. He's working./She's watching TV.
2. He's sleeping./She's working.
3. He's eating./She's sleeping.
4. He's watching TV./She's riding the bus to work.
5. He's riding the bus to work./She's eating.

Exercise E

Possible Answers:
Victor works in an office. He usually wears a tie, a suit and shoes to work./ Now it's the weekend. He's wearing pants, a sweater, sneakers and a shirt./ Victoria's a police officer. She usually wears a uniform to work./Now she's on vacation. She's wearing jeans, a blouse, a jacket and boots.

Exercise F

Students answer according to their own experience.

Exercise G

Possible Answers:
Victoria's a happy person. She likes her life. She has a lot of friends and is never lonely. She likes her work and doesn't want to change jobs. She doesn't need to make more money.

Victor isn't a happy person. He doesn't like his life. He doesn't have a lot of friends, and he's usually lonely. He doesn't like his work. He wants to change jobs, and he needs to make more money.

Exercise H

Students answer according to their own experience.

UNIT 7

Exercise A

1. 25
2. 4
3. 10
4. 20
5. 5
6. 5

Exercise B

1. d
2. a
3. e
4. c
5. f
6. b

Exercise C

1. I have 65¢. I don't have any pennies. I need 35¢.
2. I have 49¢. I don't have any nickels. I need 51¢.
3. I have 36¢. I don't have any dimes. I need 64¢.
4. I have 31¢. I don't have any dimes. I need 69¢.

Exercise D

1. any/some
2. some/some
3. any/some/some/some
4. any/any/some/some/any

Exercise E

1. many/many
2. much/much
3. much/much/much
4. many/many

Exercise F

1. How much are/a pound
2. How much are/a dozen
3. How much is/a pound
4. How much is/a pound
5. How much are/a dozen
6. How much is/a pound

Exercise G

yes apple/box of cookies/can of soup/dress/egg/oven/vegetable/watch

no bacon/biology/chemistry/information/jewelry/juice/milk/toast

Exercise H
Possible answers:
1. People eat bacon, cookies, eggs and vegetables.
2. They drink juice and milk.
3. They wear dresses, jewelry and watches.
4. They study biology and chemistry.

Exercise I
1. e
2. d
3. a
4. b
5. c, a

UNIT 8

Exercise A
1. Pick up
2. Clean up
3. Turn off
4. Drop off
5. Pick up
6. Look up
7. Clean up

Exercise B
1. No, he isn't. He's going to pick them up.
2. Yes, he is.
3. No, he isn't. He's going to turn them off.
4. No, he isn't. He's going to drop them off.
5. No, he isn't. He's going to pick them up.
6. Yes, he is.
7. Yes, he is.

Exercise C
Possible Answer:
Mr. Yung is going to leave Chicago at 5:21 PM Friday on Superflight Airlines flight 227. He is going to arrive in New York at 7:15 PM. He is going to change planes and leave New York at 8:36 PM on SF flight 957. He is going to arrive in Mexico City at 1:18 AM Saturday.

Exercise D
Students answer according to their own experience.

Exercise E
1. Chicago
2. Could I please have
3. Carl Yung
4. Y-U-N-G
5. 555-3211

Exercise F
1. Hello
2. Hi
3. this is (student's name)
4. Is Anita there
5. she isn't
6. Can I take
7. just tell her I called
8. OK
9. Thanks
10. 'Bye
11. Hello.
12. Hello. This is (student's name). May I please speak to Mrs. Madsen?
13. She's not here right now. Can I take a message?
14. Could you tell her (student's name) called, please?
15. All right.
16. Thank you.
17. Good-bye.

UNIT 9

Exercise A
Possible Order:
1. Is there a bus or train to Thunder Bay?
2. There's a bus. There aren't any trains.
3. When do the buses run?
4. There's one every day, at 7 in the morning.
5. How long does it take?
6. It gets to Thunder Bay at 11:55 PM.
7. Do I have to change buses?
8. No, you don't.
9. How much does it cost?
10. $38.80 one way.

Exercise B
1. Can I get to
2. 's the next bus
3. does it take
4. does it cost
5. do they run

Exercise C
a. 2
b. 3
c. 1
d. 5
e. 4

Exercise D
1. I have to change at New Haven.
2. She has to change at New Haven.
3. He doesn't have to change at New Haven.
4. They have to change at New Haven.
5. I don't have to change at New Haven.
6. They don't have to change at New Haven.
7. You don't have to change at New Haven.
8. She has to change at New Haven.

Exercise E
Possible Answers:
1. A: How can I get from Jackson to Memphis?
   B: You can go by bus.
   A: How long does it take?
   B: It takes 3 hours and 48 minutes.
2. A: How can I get from Birmingham to New Orleans?
   B: You can go by train.
   A: How long does it take?
   B: It takes five hours and one minute.

Exercise F
Possible Answers:
1. A: How can I get to Carnegie Hall?
   B: Take the B/D/N/R train. Get off at 57th Street. You can walk to Carnegie Hall from there. It's at 7th Avenue and 57th Street.
2. A: How can I get to the United Nations?
   B: Take the number 7 train. Get off at Grand Central. You can walk to the United Nations from there. It's at 1st Avenue and 45th Street.

Exercise G
1. Can you suggest
2. You could try
3. How much is it for two people
4. That's kind of expensive.
5. you could try
6. That's not bad.
7. Can you suggest

UNIT 10

Exercise A
1. Turn left or turn right. Don't go straight ahead.
2. Go straight ahead. Don't turn left, and don't turn right.
3. Don't turn right. Turn left or go straight ahead.
4. Don't turn left. Turn right or go straight ahead.

Exercise B

1. A: Mrs. Granados looks happy.
   B: What happened?
   A: She just heard some good news.
   B: That's great!
2. A: Mr. Sung looks happy.
   B: What happened?
   A: He just became a father.
   B: That's great!
3. A: Mr. Burke looks upset.
   B: What happened?
   A: He just ate a terrible dinner.
   B: That's too bad.

Exercise C

1. You can get stamps at a post office.
2. You can get books at a bookstore.
3. You can get paint at a hardware store.
4. You can get bananas at a grocery store.
5. You can get pants at a clothing store.
6. You can get shoes at a shoe store.

Exercise D

1. drugstore
2. on Main Street between Dunning Avenue and Curtice Park
3. Go straight ahead to the next light. Turn right on Main Street. The drugstore's on the next corner, on the right.
4. grocery store
5. on North Avenue
6. Go straight ahead to the next light. Turn left on Main Street. Go straight ahead to the next light. Turn right on North Avenue. The grocery store is on the left between the bookstore and the laundromat.
7. bakery
8. on Elm Street between Lapham Park and Dunning Avenue
9. Go straight ahead for one block. Turn left on Elm Street. The bakery is on your left.

Exercise E

1. have to buy
2. can I get
3. don't you go
4. I walk there
5. you can
6. isn't far
7. have to buy
8. can I get
9. the travel agency
10. I walk there
11. you can't
12. pretty far

Exercise F

1. A: Are there any British bookstores in town?
   B: Yes, there are two. There's one on 15th Street and another on 24th Street.
2. A: Are there any French bookstores in town?
   B: Yes, there are two. There's one on 63rd Street and another on 52nd Street.
3. A: Are there any German bookstores in town?
   B: Yes, there are two. There's one on 71st Street and one on 10th Street.
4. A: Are there any Spanish and Portuguese bookstores in town?
   B: Yes, there are two. There's one on 8th Street and another on 87th Street.

Exercise G

1. No, you can't. You have to take the bus.
2. Yes, you do.
3. Yes, you can.
4. No, you can't. You have to take the bus.
5. No, you don't. You can take the bus.

UNIT 11

Exercise A

1. b
2. e
3. d
4. a
5. c

Exercise B

1. $15,995
2. 4,150
3. miles
4. per
5. hour
6. seconds
7. 17
8. 8

Exercise C

1. kilometers
2. hectares
3. gallon
4. seconds
5. hour
6. kilograms
7. liters
8. meters
9. mile
10. pound
11. foot
12. grams

Exercise D

1. worse/worst/good
2. bigger/biggest/small
3. earlier/earliest/late
4. cheaper/cheapest/expensive
5. colder/coldest/hot
6. fewer/fewest/most

7. more comfortable/most comfortable/uncomfortable
8. faster/fastest/slow
9. taller/tallest/short
10. heavier/heaviest/light
11. younger/youngest/old
12. better/best/bad
13. more expensive/most expensive/cheap
14. hotter/hottest/cold
15. later/latest/early
16. lighter/lightest/dark
17. older/oldest/young
18. slower/slowest/fast
19. shorter/shortest/tall
20. smaller/smallest/big
21. more/most/least
22. more uncomfortable/most uncomfortable/comfortable

Exercise E

1. Which is bigger, Canada or Brazil?
2. What's the biggest country in the world?
3. Canada is bigger than Brazil.
4. The USSR is the biggest country in the world.
5. Which is higher, Glass Falls or Yosemite Falls?
6. What's the highest waterfall in the world?
7. Yosemite Falls is higher than Glass Falls.
8. Angel Falls is the highest waterfall in the world.
9. Which is more expensive, the Ferrari Mondial or the Rolls Royce Corniche?
10. What's the most expensive car in the world?
11. The Rolls Royce Corniche is more expensive than the Ferrari Mondial.
12. The Aston Martin Lagonda is the most expensive car in the world.

Exercise F

1. too expensive
2. good enough
3. fast enough
4. too small
5. too hot
6. too high/too old/powerful enough

Exercise G

1. better
2. better
3. agree
4. What's
5. money
6. most
7. disagree
8. the most beautiful

9. I think
10. think so, too
11. which
12. colder
13. disagree

Exercise H
Students answer according to their own experience.

UNIT 12

Exercise A
1. I don't like
2. I'd like to
3. I don't like
4. I won't
5. I'll
6. I'd like to
7. I like
8. I like to
9. I'd rather
10. I don't like to
11. I'd rather

Exercise B
1. yours	5. theirs
2. mine	6. ours
3. hers	7. mine
4. yours	8. his

Exercise C
1. Would Jim rather work or sleep? He'd rather sleep.
2. Would Shirley rather eat or shop? She'd rather eat.
3. Would Jim rather eat or shop? He'd rather shop.
4. Would Shirley rather work or sleep? She'd rather work.

Exercise D
1. He's mine, too.
2. It's mine, too.
3. I'd rather, too.
4. I do, too.
5. I don't, either.
6. I don't like red.
7. I'd rather work than eat.
8. Really? I don't.
9. Really? I do.

Exercise E
Students answer according to their own experience.

Exercise F
Possible Answers:
1. I hope so.
2. I already do.
3. I hope so.
4. I hope so.
5. I hope not.

ude _____ ling to their
own exp_____ence.

UNIT 13

Exercise A
1. We'll try again sometime.
2. Could you please pass the turkey?
3. Would you like to come to a party on New Year's Eve?
4. Dinner won't be ready for a while.
5. Are you going to be around for the Fourth of July?
6. What kind of dessert would you like?
7. I'd like to, but I'm going to be out of town.

Exercise B
1. I'd like to, but I'm going to be out of town.
2. Are you going to be around for the Fourth of July?
3. Dinner won't be ready for a while.
4. Could you please pass the turkey?
5. What kind of dessert would you like?

Exercise C
1. Could you help me take these off, please?
2. Could you help me get this down, please?
3. Could you please help me clean this up?
4. I'll drop that off for you.
5. I'll turn that on for you.
6. I'll help you pick those up.

Exercise D
1. New Year's Eve Thanksgiving ~~spinach~~ Fourth of July
2. ~~pumpkin~~ salad appetizer dessert
3. steak ~~mashed~~ prime rib lamb chops
4. ~~Fourth of July~~ French fried baked mashed
5. thanks you're welcome ~~lamb chops~~ please
6. lunch breakfast ~~well done~~ dinner
7. carrots ~~dessert~~ green beans spinach
8. apple peach ~~dinner~~ pumpkin
9. ~~please~~ medium rare well done

Exercise E
1. What are you going to have?
2. I'll probably have
3. Are you going to have
4. Are you ready
5. I'll have
6. I'm going to have
7. How would you like your prime rib
8. Would you like
9. I'd like
10. thank you
11. What kind of potatoes would you like
12. Would you like
13. I'd like some more
14. could you bring us
15. Certainly.

Exercise F
Students answer according to their own choices.

UNIT 14

Exercise A
1. A: Dr. Hummel, I'd like you to meet Jonathan Wilkins.
   B: How do you do, Mr. Wilkins?
2. A: Hi, Steve. I'm Cathy and Don's niece, Liz.
   B: Hi, Liz.
3. A: Would you like some cookies?
   B: Yes, please.
4. A: I'm going to get a Coke. Do you want one?
   B: Sure.
5. A: Would you like to play tennis tomorrow afternoon?
   B: I'm sorry, I can't, but thanks for the invitation.
6. A: Do you want to go to a movie tonight?
   B: Sorry, I can't. I have to do my homework.
7. A: Hello, this is Jean Benson. May I please speak to Mr. Addison?
   B: He isn't here right now. Can I take a message?
   A: Could you tell him I called, please?
8. A: Hi, this is Alex. Is Bob there?
   B: No, he isn't. Can I take a message?
   A: Yes, just tell him I called.

Exercise B

1. They can't be Brian's. They might
   be Jeff's. They might be Laura's.
2. It can't be Charlie's. It can't be
   Rita's. It must be Ron's.
3. It can't be Elaine's. It might be
   Virginia's. It might be Gary's.
4. It might be Rick and Lynn's. It
   might be Norma and Billy's. It can't
   be Esther and Roger's.

Exercise C

1. What's your name?
2. What's your address?
3. Do you live in an apartment?
4. Do you have a telephone?
5. What do you do?
6. Do you have brothers and sisters?
7. How often do you exercise?
8. When do you eat breakfast?
9. Can you drive a car?
10. Where were you born?
11. Did you grow up there?
12. What are you doing these days?
13. What do you usually wear to
    school?
14. What time do you get to school?
15. What courses are you taking?
16. What did you do last night?
17. What will you do tomorrow?
18. Who is your favorite actor?
19. What kind of music do you like?
20. Do you think you'll go to
    Antarctica someday?

Exercise D

Students answer according to their
own experience.